Veggie & Organic London

Russell Rose

Photography by Natalie Pecht

Veggie & Organic London

Written by Russell Rose

Photography by Natalie Pecht
Edited by Andrew Kershman
Maps by Lesley Gilmour
Design by Susi Koch & Lesley Gilmour

Published in 2009 by
Metro Publications
PO Box 6336
London
N1 6PY

Printed and bound in India
© 2009 Russell Rose

British Library Cataloguing in Publication Data.
A catalogue record for this book is available from the British Library.

ISBN   978-1-902910-32-1

Dedicated to the memory of my parents
Lily and Sydney Rose

Acknowledgements

Special thanks to my wife, Tracy Rose, a quintessential dining partner, who enthusiastically encouraged and supported me in writing this Second Edition.

I must also thank publisher Andrew Kershman at Metro Publications Ltd for recognising the need for this book and his editing, Susi Koch and Lesley Gilmour for making the book look so appetising and Lesley Gilmour for her delicious maps. I'm also very grateful to Natalie Pecht for her wonderful photography.

Thanks are also due to the Vegetarian Society, the Vegan Society and the Soil Association for their useful information and Frances Schwartz at East London Organic Gardeners for her help in putting me in touch with various organisations.

About the Author

Russell Rose has been eating his way through London as a restaurant reviewer since 1998 and was a contributor for Metro Crushguide 2002, Sainsbury's Carlton Taste Restaurant Reviews 2003 and restaurant correspondent for Health Eating Magazine and Mondo. He has written on health, food, nutrition and lifestyle for Now Magazine, Daily Express, The Daily Mail, BBC Good Food, Olive and has written for Organic Living and Allergy Free. He has co-written and presented a specialist exercise and diet video, Curvenetics and been a guest food critic on Channel 5 television and London Tonight Channel 3. In 2009, Russell Rose co-authored the fashion guidebook Fashion Fabulous London, reviewing London's TOP 200 fashion shops, boutiques and stores.

Contents

Rootmaster Bustaurant

The London Vegetarian Scene

Vegetarian food

Ding! Ding! It's all aboard a red double decker bus for gourmet veggie at Rootmaster, pick up a free map to guide you around the biggest natural and organic food store in the world (Whole Foods Market Kensington), or just relax at the laid back café with the smallest veggie menu on the planet – The FleaPit. You can even enjoy a canal view or two at Inspiral in Camden or Water House in Shoreditch – London's first truly eco-friendly restaurant. Whatever your choice, London will amaze with the quality of its vegetarian restaurants.

The range of choice, quality and creativity is simply mind boggling. At the top end of the spectrum are first class restaurants run by some of the most innovative chefs in the UK. Amongst the latest are Vanilla Black in Holborn with its sensational vegetarian haute cuisine and Saf in Shoreditch producing brilliantly presented raw-style vegan and organic dishes. At Nahm in the fabulously chic Halkin Hotel, David Thompson is creating miraculous Thai vegetarian food and has been awarded a Michelin Star for his efforts. In Pimlico, Alexis Gauthier at Roussillon offers a spectacular vegetarian multi-course tasting menu, only equalled by Morgan Meuniere at Morgan M in Highbury and Chef Nick Bell's Italian at Apsley's in the elegant Lanesborough Hotel.

Raw food menus are one of the major trends on the London vegetarian scene. The leading exponent in the world is Chad Sarno at Saf, who presents it with haute cuisine panache. Raw Food, sometimes known as Living Food, uses an array of techniques to create delicious uncooked recipes or dishes below 48 degrees centigrade that help lock in flavour and nutrition. Other front runners in this genre and very affordable are VitaOrganic in Soho, Raw Fairies at Bonnington Café and Whole Foods Market in Stoke Newington.

Vegetarian tasting menus are as popular as ever. They really let great chefs rip with their virtuosity and experimentation and the diner will often be memorable. Even the super-celebrity TV chefs, Jamie Oliver at Fifteen and Gordon Ramsay at Claridges, include vegetarian tasting menus in their repertoire. Everyone should try at least one of these gastronomic journeys during their lifetime!

Another major advance on the London scene is the advent of the 'Vegetarian Diner' as exemplified by Eat and Two Veg in Marylebone. Here, mock carnivore dishes reach their zenith. The burger and fries is

1

on a par with Hard Rock and Planet Hollywood and traditional British fare such as Vegetarian Shepherds Pie is nothing less than remarkable. Peking Palace, a superb Chinese eaterie in Archway, is a leading exponent of mock fish Chinese dishes and is constantly developing new recipes. Good Earth in Knightsbridge and Mill Hill are also cooking great mock Chinese cuisine.

Indian vegetarian food continues getting better and better. At one of the swankiest new Indian restaurants to hit the London circuit, Zaika in Kensington, Chef Sanjay Dwivedi is combining Asian herbs and spices that give completely new twists on Indian classics. Further afield the big shift is towards full scale Indian buffets of which perhaps the best is Rani in Finchley, where the standards of presentation and quality are supreme. The great thing about vegetarian buffets is the opportunity to taste so many different dishes and if you don't like one, there's another sixty from which to choose. The restaurants of Drummond Street in Euston – Diwana, Ravi Shanka, and Chutney – have put their prices down, making quality vegetarian banquets affordable to everyone. Further afield in Hendon there's Rajens Thali and Rose Vegetarian and further still is Jay's in Kingsbury.

A gift for vegetarian customers is the fantastic proliferation of the Thai/Chinese £3.00 meal box, £5.50 eat-as-much-as-you-like outlets under such names as Wai and Tai Buffet. These are popping up all over the place. The food is good and my recommendation if you are looking for a cheap eat.

Mediterranean vegetarian food has always been marvellous from a health standpoint and Futures!, near Eastcheap, continues to make flavoursome classics for hungry veggie City workers. On the London falafel scene, Maoz and Just Falafs in Soho and Taboon in Golders Green are just three outfits specialising in this delicious veggie snack. Very delectable too, but more pricey, are the branches of Escas, Nouras and Ottolenghi that offer some of the best mediterranean influenced vegetarian food you'll ever try.

Italian vegetarian grub remains ever popular with pastas and pizzas available on just about every shopping parade in London. Independents such as Story Deli, off Brick Lane, and the two Eco's in Clapham and Chiswick are making a very strong showing. Apsley's at the Lanesborough offer perhaps the best freshly made pasta in London, but at a high price.

The quality of organic restaurant food has remained high with the organic burgers and Lancashire Hot Pot at Eat and Two Veg still one of the highlights. The Natural Kitchen is also a welcome arrival on the London food scene. On the pub circuit, The Duke of Cambridge in Islington follows a classic gastro pub format and offers a good selection of organic beers and wines to accompany the meal.

Many vegetarian restaurateurs I spoke to would love to use organic completely but, because of difficulties in supply and greater expense are holding back, adopting a 'use-organic-where-possible' stance.

As organic food becomes more accessible more restaurants will adopt it. Organic supermarkets such as Planet Organic and Whole Foods Market already run 100% organic canteen eateries and all the main supermarkets have a commitment to increasing their organic range.

Where beauty and cosmetics products are concerned, huge strides have been made in product development with 2006 seeing a 30% increase in the number licensed by the Soil Association. Stella McCartney now has her own range, whilst good inroads continue to be made by Green People, Jurlique and Dr Hauschka. Of note is the Organic Pharmacy on the King's Road, dedicated to all things organic pertaining to wellness and beauty – it now has four branches in London. Retailers such as Space NK, Planet Organic and Whole Foods Market are offering more organic care products than ever.

Talking to people about their decision to become vegetarian, it seems that health comes out top. People are certainly becoming more aware of the benefits of antioxidants and vitamins in fruit and veg. Hardly a week goes by without a report appearing about a particular fruit or vegetable containing a beneficial antioxidant. Whilst supplement manufacturers have been keen to offer solutions in a pill, there is research that whole foods with naturally beneficial antioxidants are better than food supplements.

For London vegetarians and the eco-aware there are many contact organisations for keeping people up to date on the latest issues and research. The most important national ones are The Vegetarian Society, The Vegan Society and the Soil Association. The major and minor ones are listed on page 239.

London also has many vegetarian caterers and the number has been growing in recent years. Organic and vegetarian caterers of note include Flavour, Green & Beans and Passion Organic. At the leading edge of raw/ live food catering are Saf and Raw Fairies. For a full listing see page 290.

Organic Londoners

London has an increasing number of very stylish organic bars serving organic wines, beers and first class cocktails. With a greater array of marvellous organic restaurants, juice bars, cafés, shops, Londoners have more choice than ever when it comes to buying organic.

There has been a marked increase in the take up of organic box schemes and mail order. The green fingered have also shown considerable interest in growing their own organic fruit veg, herbs and plants and there are a number of contact organisations featured in this book that can give advice and even provide an opportunity to participate in a communal garden. A list of organic contact organisations is given on pages 294.

On my travels around London I found amongst organic food enthusiasts a real interest and concern for the environment and for personal health. Many expressed fears about chemicals such as pesticides, herbicides and fungicides, while others just thought the food tasted better. Among mothers there are many that prefer to feed their children organic produce, believing it to better for growing bodies.

In conversation with passionate organic Londoners the topic will soon turn to carbon footprints, provenance, GM foods, superbugs, fair trade, biodynamic farming, damage to the countryside and a sustainable future. They are people that really care about the environment. In 2006, organic food sales in the UK nudged a staggering £2bn. By 2010 sales are estimated to reach a whopping £2.7bn. The recession will affect some of this growth, but with new branches of Planet Organic and the establishment of the vast Whole Foods Market Kensington there are grounds for continued optimism.

How to use this book

Explanation of café/restaurant ratings

People are always asking me 'what's your favourite restaurant? what's the best meal you've ever had?' These are always difficult questions to answer because there are always so many considerations. Taste, choice, price, nationality and how do you compare a meal with modern dishes against a classic one? In an attempt to give an assessment I've included a star rating system to supplement my comments in the reviews based on impressions gained during my visit to the venue. In addition, at the end of the book the Veggie and Organic London Hot List gives a quick guide to help you pick the type of restaurant you want.

Vegetarian choice
★★★★★ – complete vegetarian menu with good vegan choices
★★★★ – over 50% of menu is vegetarian or has a Vegetarian Tasting Menu
★★★ – at least three vegetarian choice of main dishes on menu
★★ – less than three vegetarian choices
★ – don't worry the chef will throw a green salad together for you!

Organic choice
★★★★★ – complete organic menu
★★★★ – over 50% of menu is organic
★★★ – at least 3 organic choices on menu or many organic ingredients
★★ – less than three organic choices
★ – we used to do organic – I'll go and see if the chef has got anything

Taste
★★★★★ – Exceptional
★★★★ – Very Good
★★★ – Good
★★ – Okay
★ – Poor

Price (Including main course & one other course, without drinks)
£   under £10
££   £10-15
£££   £15-20
££££   £20-25
£££££   £25+

Name

Chapter header

Cuisine or shop type

Sub heading

Ratings tab

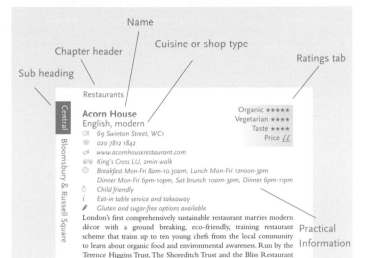

Restaurants

Acorn House
English, modern

Organic ★★★★★
Vegetarian ★★★★
Taste ★★★★
Price ££

⌂ 69 Swinton Street, WC1
☎ 020 7812 1842
🖰 www.acornhouserestaurant.com
🚇 King's Cross LU, 2min walk
🕙 Breakfast Mon–Fri 8am–10.30am, Lunch Mon–Fri 12noon–3pm
Dinner Mon–Fri 6pm–10pm, Sat brunch 10am–3pm, Dinner 6pm–11pm
♙ Child friendly
𝑖 Eat-in table service and takeaway
🍴 Gluten and sugar-free options available

Practical
Information

London's first comprehensively sustainable restaurant marries modern décor with a ground breaking, eco-friendly, training restaurant scheme that trains up to ten young chefs from the local community to learn about organic food and environmental awareness. Run by the Terence Higgins Trust, The Shoreditch Trust and the Bliss Restaurant Consultancy, Acorn House has proved a great success.

At front of house a welcoming reception area with a snazzy counter, serves a glorious array of breakfasts, freshly squeezed vegetable and fruit juices, power shakes, smoothies, pastries, muffins and bagels. Lunchtimes attract local workers and tourists opting for good salads such as *Roast Sweet Pumpkin, seeds and sprouts* or *Grilled Field Mushrooms, fresh herbs and vinegar*. Organic is used where economically possible and currently comprises around 80% of the ingredients.

Acorn House wears it's environmental badge proudly. Food is derived from sustainable sources, local farmers and it serves purified tap water – minimising glass and plastic usage. Takeaway packaging is biodegradable and all kitchen waste is recycled or composted and carbon miles kept to a minimum.

Where Acorn House really scores is on the relaxed atmosphere in the evening when the lights are down and cool fusion music is played. At the far end is a bustling open kitchen while displays are made of the organic drinks available and there are wicker baskets of organic bread and fruit and carefully arranged large vases in the window. The effect is clearly popular because at 10pm it's still buzzing.

The short evening menu changes monthly. *Celeriac, Mascarpone and Horseradish soup* is substantial with a good wholesome flavouring and arrives with a chunk of bread. Acorn House will convert dishes to vegetarian – so do ask what they can do for you. Mozzarella di Buffala, grilled Polenta and black olive sauce was converted by having balsamic

12

Review

Restaurants

Central London

Bloomsbury & Russell Square

Bloomsbury and Russell Square are central, smart and have some charming unspoilt streets and shops. Below are reviews for a wide range of vegetarian restaurants in the area including a branch of the ultra stylish Wagamama, the inexpensive Italian eaterie Mary Ward and London's trailblazing first sustainable restaurant – Acorn House.

Restaurants

1) Acorn House p.12
2) Alara Wholefoods p.13
3) Carluccios p.14
4) Mary Ward Vegetarian Café p.15
5) Planet Organic p.16
6) Tai Buffet p.17
7) Veg p.17
8) The Vegetarian's Paradise p.18
9) Wagamama p.18

Shops

a) Alara Wholefoods p.242
b) Planet Organic p.243

Acorn House
English, modern

Organic	★★★★★
Vegetarian	★★★★
Taste	★★★★
Price	££

🖃 *69 Swinton Street, WC1*

☎ *020 7812 1842*

🖉 *www.acornhouserestaurant.com*

🚌 *King's Cross LU, 2min walk*

🕐 *Breakfast Mon-Fri 8am-10.30am, Lunch Mon-Fri 12noon-3pm*
   Dinner Mon-Fri 6pm-10pm, Sat brunch 10am-3pm, Dinner 6pm-11pm

🌶 *Gluten and sugar-free options available*

🍼 *Child friendly*

i *Eat-in table service and takeaway*

London's first comprehensively sustainable restaurant marries modern décor with a ground breaking, eco-friendly, training restaurant scheme that trains up to ten young chefs from the local community about organic food and environmental awareness. Run by the Terence Higgins Trust, The Shoreditch Trust and the Bliss Restaurant Consultancy, Acorn House has proved a great success.

At front of house a welcoming reception area with a snazzy counter, serves a glorious array of breakfasts, freshly squeezed vegetable and fruit juices, power shakes, smoothies, pastries, muffins and bagels. Lunchtimes attract local workers and tourists opting for good salads such as Roast Sweet Pumpkin, seeds and sprouts or Grilled Field Mushrooms, fresh herbs and vinegar. Organic is used where economically possible and currently comprises around 80% of the ingredients.

Acorn House wears it's environmental badge proudly. Food is derived from sustainable sources and local farmers and it serves purified tap water – minimising glass and plastic usage. Takeaway packaging is biodegradable and all kitchen waste is recycled and carbon miles kept to a minimum.

Where Acorn House really scores is on the relaxed atmosphere in the evening when the lights are down and cool fusion music is played. At the far end is a bustling open kitchen, displays are made of the organic drinks available and there are wicker baskets of organic bread and fruit and carefully arranged large vases in the window. The effect is clearly popular because at 10pm it's still buzzing.

The short evening menu changes monthly. The Celeriac, Mascarpone and Horseradish soup was substantial with a good wholesome flavouring and arrived with a chunk of bread. Acorn House will convert dishes to vegetarian – so do ask what they can do for you. Mozzarella di Buffala, grilled Polenta and black olive sauce was converted by having balsamic vinegar in the sauce instead of anchovy and the result was good.

Mains come up large and the Stilton, Walnut and Treviso risotto was no exception with good texture and appreciable flavour that paired well with a glass of Casa de la Ermita Joven red organic wine. One interesting feature of Acorn House is that you can order different portion sizes to avoid wastage and suit your appetite. One of the chef's grandma's recipes called Nana's traditional style Saag Paneer was very yummy and came with a quality handmade roti. Sloshed down with a glass of Chilean chardonnay organic white, the evening was very enjoyable.

Dessert of Baked Bramley apple filled with raisins was well presented and came with ginger ice cream. A scoop of Caramel Ice Cream slides down well too. For a place that couples organic, environmental awareness with a high level of style, Acorn House is to be commended.

Acorn House's sister restaurant is Water House, see page 97.

Alara Wholefoods
International, buffet, classic

58-60 Marchmont Street, WC1	Organic ★★★★★
020 7837 1172	Vegetarian ★★★★★
www.alara.co.uk	Taste ★★★
Russell Square LU, 1 min walk	Price £
Lunch served Mon-Sat 11am-4.30pm	
Vegan options	
Outside seating	
i Counter service, Eat-in & Takeaway	

You might be forgiven for avoiding cafés with outdoor-seating-only when the clouds are looming. As the raindrops start falling into your hot buffet, swiftly dive inside Alara and the cashier will rapidly roll down an impressive canopy and switch the warming outdoor heaters on. This large neighbourhood vegetarian, health food and alternative remedy shop offers a bargain priced organic hot and cold, help-yourself buffet, with a varied selection of juices, smoothies and hot drinks which is worth braving the elements to enjoy.

It's all a bit of squeeze at lunchtime being jostled at the various serving stations but people are friendly and with a bit of luck you won't get somebody's elbow in your carton, which you fill up as you like and pay by weight (89p/100g) at one of the cashier points. Our two cartons of hot food totalled £8.72, possibly the cheapest veggie organic lunch to be had in London.

The tables look onto busy Marchmont Street and the Vegetarian Paradise opposite (see below). Alara is an established hang out for students and lecturers and also attracts some shirt and tie clad businessmen and a fair few vegetarian tourists staying at the hotels around Russell Square.

The salad station is quite appealing and don't miss the choice of organic balsamic vinegar or Tomari organic soya sauce to enhance the enjoyment of your meal. Food here changes every day but hummous, Greek salad and cottage cheese remain long standing regulars. There are also some organic bread choices for hungry souls at 30p.

From the hot station, the vegan Moroccan Bean Stew of pumpkin, peppers, beans, chickpeas, cous cous and spices tasted satisfyingly enjoyable and is to be recommended whilst the vegan Chickpea Curry with coconut milk, cream and sea salt had good flavour. Vegetable Lasagne – one of the house specials – has definitely improved and the Steamed Mixed Vegetables of carrots, baby corns, brocolli and bell red peppers were of high quality. Coffees here are inexpensive and the delicious sweets include vegan Pear & Nut Cake, Spiced Date and Walnut cake as well as a tempting selection of ice-creams. Alara Wholefoods buy in stock for their shop in large quantities enabling them to sell the organic buffet at a very competitive price. Which just goes to show satisfying organic meals can be offered at bargain prices.

For Alara's Organic Shop see page 242.

Carluccio's Caffé
Italian, classic

▢ *One the Brunswick, WC1*	Vegetarian ★★★★
☏ *020 7833 4100*	Taste ★★★★
✎ *www.carluccios.com*	Price ££
⛁ *Russell Square LU, 1 min walk*	
☺ *Mon-Fri 8am-11pm, Sat 9-11pm, Sun 9am-10.30pm*	
✦ *Vegan options*	
☖ *Child friendly, high chairs*	
☀ *Outside seating*	

Set in the heart of the modern Brunswick shopping centre in Bloomsbury, this moderate sized Carluccio's Caffé is extremely popular at weekends. *For meal review see Carluccio's Caffé, St Christopher's Place (page 35).*

Mary Ward Vegetarian Café
International, classic

Vegetarian ★★★★★
Taste ★★★
Price £

🖼 *42 Queen Square, WC1*

☎ *020 7831 7711*

🚇 *Russell Square or Holborn LU, (5 min walk)*

🕐 *Mon-Thur 9.30am-8.50pm, Fri 9.30am-8.30pm, Sat 9.30am-4pm,*

🥕 *Vegan options*

i *Counter service*

Bargain Italian and Portuguese vegetarian food forms the menu at this adult education centre canteen that's open to the public. Opened in 1998, the café itself is privately owned by Luciano and Daniella who devise this 100% vegetarian selection.

Evening or lunchtime, the café is a hive of activity with enough seats for 48. At 7.30pm the place was positively buzzing with studious people from the evening classes. At midday the dining room is flooded with natural light and lots of busy people. Apart from students it's popular with nurses, doctors and staff from the hospitals on Queen Square and also attracts people of all ages and often strict dietary requirements. Paintings are exhibited around the walls and the best tables are by the window boxes that overlook Queen's Square.

The blackboard menu list changes daily and on the evening I visited included light snacks like spinach and nutmeg vegan soup served with bread as well as a selection of baguettes and sandwiches. For those with more of an appetite, mains included Penne Pasta with veg and Stuffed Tortilla and a mega slice of Spanish Omelette. The Rice Strudel is quite substantial and consists of a warm square pie of spinach, squash, lentil, chickpea and rice with a rather good cheddar cheese topping and a salad of coleslaw, red cabbage, lettuce and mung beans and balsamic oil dressing. The Vegan Coconut Curry had some quite good mild curry flavours and included carrots, potato, courgettes, peas and rice, but was luke warm. Some savvy diners ask for the mains to be warmed up more in the microwave and the serving staff are happy to oblige. Despite the minor quibbles the food is great value with all main courses for under a fiver. One of the thing's I really liked was that no matter how busy she was, Daniella always had time to serve customers with a smile.

Breakfast is until 11.45am and is a basic toast, butter and jam affair although they do bake their own bread and a rather good peanut butter biscuit. Virtually all the food is made on the premises and the cakes and sweet treats are well worth a try. A good inexpensive veggie eaterie.

Planet Organic
Organic Vegetarian, International

	22 Torrington Place, WC1
☎	020 7436 1929
✎	www.planetorganic.com
🚌	Goode Street LU (5 min walk)
⏱	Mon-Fri 8am-9pm, Sat 10am-7pm
	(food served from 12noon – 1 hour before closure), Sun 12noon-6pm
✦	Vegan options..
○	Child friendly
i	Counter Service and takeaway
☀	Outside tables available

Vegetarian ★★★★★
Organic ★★★★★
Taste ★★★
Price £

Finding an empty table at lunchtime on the weekend might prove difficult at this extremely well run Planet Organic, that gets packed out with seminar attendees from nearby London University. Luckily, we found a table and shared with a couple of young students who were discussing politics and the vegetarian stir fry with tofu that they were enjoying. So popular is this completely organic vegetarian café/restaurant that you could find yourself queuing behind as many as 30 people. There was a queue when we visited but the mood was friendly and we were served within just five minutes. The efficiency of the operation is partly due to the large number of serving staff on hand and the simple meal-deal-in-a-box offer of small, medium and large boxes for £2.80, £4.50 and £5.50 respectively. At the weekend there's usually eight hot specials, a soup and seeded roll deal for £2.14 and five special salads that are increased to twelve during weekdays when things are a little more relaxed.

Shepherds Pie of puy lentils with mashed potato flavoured with cumin and paprika is very reasonable but best of all is the roasted potatoes that can be wholeheartedly recommended. Served in a disposable container with wooden knife and fork, a medium size portion seemed perfectly adequate for most. The Penne Pasta comes with mushrooms and a deep taste of cheese, olive, basil and tomato but, as with buffet style pasta, it does have a tendency to clump. The Lasagne is an established feature of the menu, made with spinach, cabbage and tomato sauce with a good amount of flavoursome cheddar cheese.

After 2pm on Sundays the atmosphere is more relaxed with local Fitzrovians and shoppers from nearby Tottenham Court Road enjoying coffee and cakes at the street tables and watching the world go by. Cakes come up as large wedges and the vegan chocolate cake is good and a carrot cake even better, whilst their fresh croissants made by Seven Seeds are reputed to be amongst the best in London. One evening I visited when the place was like a student's common room with just a few non-academics among the crowd and the place buzzing with talk of books and other student concerns. For organic vegetarian fast food made on the premises this is a place to return to again and again.

For the store review see page 267.

Tai Buffet
Thai/Chinese

Vegetarian ★★★
Taste ★★★
Price ££

- 🖼 *53 Warren Street, W1*
- 🚇 *Warren St LU, 2 min walk*
- 🕐 *Mon-Thurs 12noon-10pm, Fri-Sat 12noon-11pm, Sun 12.30pm-10pm*
- 🥕 *Vegan Menu*
- 🍼 *Child friendly*
- i *Eat in (buffet service) and Takeaway*

For food review see Wai, Goodge St (page 67).

Veg
Thai/Chinese

Vegetarian ★★★★★
Price £

- 🖼 *4-6 Theobalds Road, WC1*
- 🚇 *Chancery Lane LU, (10 min walk)*
- 🕐 *Mon-Thurs 12noon-10pm, Fri-Sat 12noon-11pm, Sun 12.30pm-10pm*
- 🥕 *Vegan Menu*
- 🍼 *Child friendly*
- i *Eat in (buffet service) and Takeaway*

For food review see Wai, Goodge Street (page 67).

The Vegetarians Paradise Bhel Poori House
Indian, classic

Vegetarian ★★★★★
Price £

⌨ 59 Marchmont Street, WC1

☎ 020 7278 6881

🚇 Russell Square LU(1 min walk)

🕐 7 days per week, Lunch 12noon-3pm, Dinner 5pm-11pm

🥕 Vegan options

i Table service, Takeaway service

A good value lunchtime destination with an eat-as-much-as-you-like buffet for £4.50. Situated opposite Alara Wholefoods, the chocolate coloured exterior is hardly a fitting entrance to 'paradise'. Still, for some bargain hunting vegetarians the £2.50 buffet take-out box makes up for any deficiency in the décor.

The help-yourself buffet consists of twelve choices, with a classic selection of Indian chutneys. The buffet changes daily and may include a chickpea and potato curry, a mixed vegetable curry with herbs and spices, wholemeal puri bread, naan and basmati rice.

The evening menu has all the Western and Southern Indian faves with a three course deluxe thali for just £7.95. The food here is of reasonable quality and offers excellent value for those trying to find a decent Indian veggie meal on a budget.

Wagamama
Japanese

Vegetarian ★★★
Taste ★★★★
Price £

⌨ 4 Streatham Street, WC1

☎ 020 7323 9223

🖱 www.wagamama.com

🚇 Tottenham Court Road LU, 10 min walk

🕐 Mon-Sat 12noon-11pm, Sun 12noon-10pm

Another branch of this popular noodle chain which manages to combine good fresh food at a budget price.
See Wagamama, *Wigmore Street for a full review (page 48).*
There is also a branch in Camden (page 132).

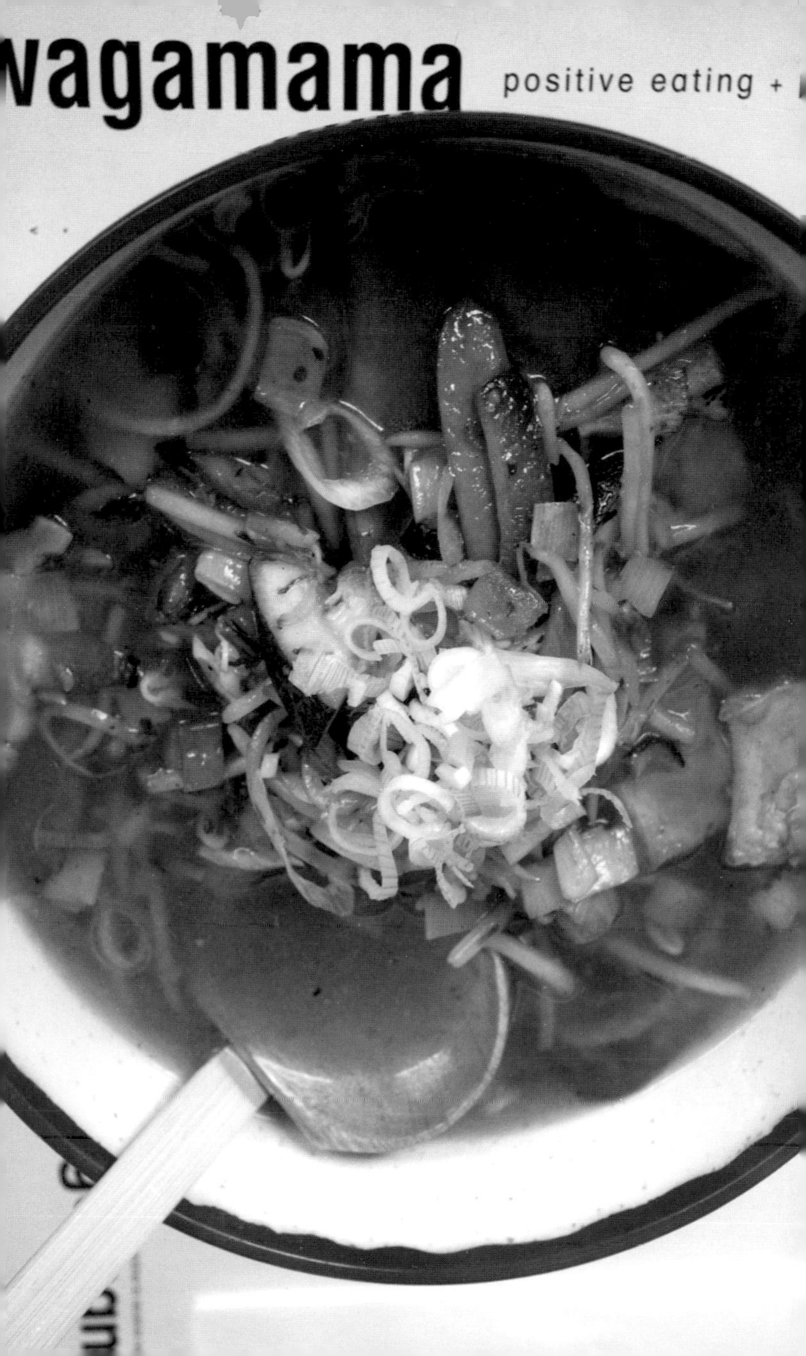
wagamama
positive eating +

Restaurants

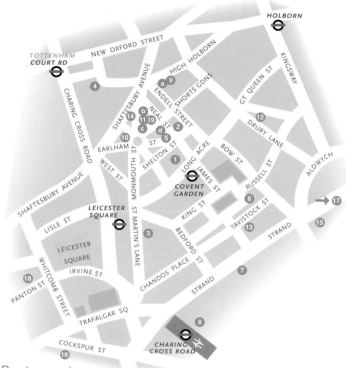

Restaurants

1) Café Pacifico p.21
2) Carluccio's Caffé p.22
3) Chi p.23
4) First Out p.23
5) Food For Thought p.24
6) Just Falafs p.25
7) Leon The Strand p.25
8) Leon Villiers St p.25
9) Le Pain Quotidien
   Aveda Institute p.25
10) Mela p.26
11) Neal's Yard Salad Bar p.27
12) Sarastro p.28
13) Sofra Covent Garden p.29
14) Thai Square Covent
   Garden p.30

15) Thai Square
   The Strand p.30
16) Thai Square
   Trafalgar Square p.31
17) Thai Square
   at the Wig & Pen p.32
18) Woodlands p.32
19) World Food Café p.33

Shops

a) Aveda Institute p.243
b) Monmouth Coffee
   Company p.244
c) Neal's Yard Remedies p.244
d) The Organic Pharmacy p.244

Covent Garden, Leicester Square & The Strand

In vibrant Covent Garden there's inventive country-style Indian food at Mela, vivacious Mexican party atmosphere at Café Pacifico and an opera-themed restaurant at Sarastro. For stylish food in a stylish environment, Le Pain Quotidien at Aveda Institute is a great choice. Around the famous Neal's Yard, vegetarians are spoilt for choice with Neal's Yard Salad Bar, The World Food Café, bargain meals at Food for Thought or, fine Italian dining at Carluccio's flagship restaurant on Garrick Street. For great Turkish food with plenty of veggie choices try Sofra in Covent Garden or for a cheap quick veggie snack, Just Falafs on the Piazza. If you are thinking of Thai food then there are several outlets from which to choose and for great Indian vegetarian food a branch of Woodlands. Nearby too, serving excellent organic coffee, is the Monmouth Street Coffee Company and First Out – a meeting point for gay vegetarians.

Café Pacifico
Mexican, classic

Vegetarian ★★★
Taste ★★★★
Price £££

- 5 Langley Street, WC2
- 020 7379 7728
- www.cafepacifico-laperla.com
- Covent Garden LU (1 min walk)
- Mon-Sat 12noon-11.45pm, Sun 12noon-10.45pm, Bookings only Sun-Fri
- Vegan options
- Child friendly

A famously joyous eaterie that has several good veggie choices on its omnivore menu. Opened in 1982, Café Pacifico is drenched in Mexican atmosphere. The place has a strong vegetarian following and makes a great party venue with a well stocked bar.

Veggie options are marked on the menu. Nachos Rancheros is superb with corn chips covered with beans, melted cheese, ranchera sauce, tomato, lettuce and onion, masses of heavenly sour cream and guacamole. The Spicy Vegetarian Tostada main course consists of two tortillas laden with artichoke hearts, balsamic onions, avocado slices, soft cheeses and salad and is great fun food. Fajita fans can opt for the Vegetarian Special of broccoli cactus, courgette, thai asparagus with baby sweetcorn, onions and peppers. Desserts? Forget them. This is really a starter and main place. Order more side plates and party-on!

Carluccio's Caffè
Italian, classic

Vegetarian ★★★
Taste ★★★★
Price ££

🏠 *2A Garrick Street, London WC2*
☎ *020 7836 0990*
🖥 *www.carluccios.com*
🚇 *Covent Garden or Leicester Square LU (5 min walk)*
🕐 *Mon-Fri 8am-11.30pm, Sat 9am-11.30pm, Sun 9am-10.30pm*
🥕 *Vegan options*
🍼 *Child friendly, high chairs*
i   Booking advised in evenings

The flagship and the biggest of the Carluccio's Caffés extends over two floors in a beautifully designed building situated close to Covent Garden's famous Piazza. There's an excellent private dining room on the first floor that can be booked for parties.

For review see Carluccio's Caffè, *St Christopher's Place (page 35).*

Carluccio's Caffè

Chi Buffet
Thai, Chinese, classic

🖃 *55 St Martin's Lane, WC2*

☎ *020 7836 3434*

🚌 *Leicester Square LU 5min walk*

🕒 *Daily 12noon-11pm*

Vegetarian ★★★★★
Taste ★★★
Price £

Bargain £5 all-you-can-eat vegan Thai/Chinese cuisine.
For food review see Wai, Goodge Street (page 67).

First Out
International, vegetarian

🖃 *52 St Giles High Street, WC2*

☎ *020 7240 8042*

🚌 *Tottenham Court Rd LU, 1 min walk*

🕒 *Mon-Sat 10am-11pm, Sun 11am-10.30pm*

☀ *Outside seating*

i *Eat in & Takeaway service, Counter service*

Vegetarian ★★★★★
Taste ★★★
Price £

Opposite Centrepoint, this all-vegetarian, gay and lesbian café is a popular meeting/pickup place that's been running since 1986. It's friendly, but also cool with a lot of solitary grazers reading the free pamphlets and mags. Pre-and post theatre goers queue at the tempting serving-counter for salads, cold pastas, mezzes and a choice of five quiches. Mains are all under £7 which represent good value and there's also Mexican Nachos and bean burgers, seven jacket potatoes, pre-packaged rolls and on Sunday's they offer a veggie brunch of veggie sausage, garlic and mushrooms. Quiches here are delicious, home-made, doorstop-sized and served with a choice of three mixed salads from the salad bar. The coffee is good and the homemade cakes are highly inviting and enough for two.

Decked out in biscuit, vanilla and a petrol-grey, around the walls are paintings or drawings from established and upcoming artists some of which are for sale for as little as £50. The specials change daily and the blackboard menu changes seasonally. Downstairs is a cosy basement bar with a good range of cocktails, beers and wines and a live DJ every Friday and Saturday night from 7-11pm that's free entry.

Food For Thought
International, Classic

🖳 *31 Neal Street, WC2*
☎ *020 7836 9072*
🚌 *Covent Garden LU (5 min walk)*
🕐 *Mon-Sat 12noon-8.30pm, Sunday 12noon-5pm*
🥕 *Vegan options*
i *Eat-in (Counter service) &Takeaway*

This is a remarkable bargain basement vegetarian eaterie on one of Covent Garden's busiest thoroughfares. Forget the couple of tables as you go in, the main event is all downstairs. First you'll have to join the queue on the stairs, a time-honoured tradition that goes back to '74. However, the queue moves fast and before you can say 'Cauliflower and Dill Quiche' you're at the serving counter being ladled up stir-fry veg Tagine with cous cous and leek soup. Laden with your meal, search for a space among the 40 places available but it's always tight, so expect to share a table.

The menu changes daily and each evening there's a special. The Thai Plate Special (£6.90) is generous and comes with fragrant white rice. The 'special' bit is that on the same plate you get a starter of cold bean sprout salad, spring rolls and chilli sauce. Green Spinach and Chick Pea Savoury Crumble (£4.40) is a substantial hunger buster of chick peas, spinach, aubergine and courgettes in a sundried tomato sauce with a parsley and cheese crumble topping which on my last visit was of variable temperature but otherwise quite good.

Recently I went for the vegan Butternut Squash and Lentil Tagine (£4.40), which tasted good and came with brown rice. For another £3 there's an accompanying mixed salad of lettuce, celery, green beans and coriander that was great, although very slightly let down by an unusual spaghetti. Fresh Fruit salad dessert looks better than the Strawberry and Banana Scrunch, but I can vouch for the decadent looking Scrunch as a really yummy treat.

The atmosphere is informal, very friendly and the place is a magnet for blue-jeaned vegetarian students, backpacking tourists and even the odd business-type getting a veggie pre-theatre bite.

Whilst the food is not organic, their mantra is 'they never knowingly use GM foods in any of their dishes'. Still, I manage to bag a Smoothie (£1.80), certified by Soil Association, that was delicious. Food For Thought is a bit rushed, but for a really cheap bite, in the middle of London's theatreland, it's tough to beat.

Just Falafs Covent Garden
Falafels, modern

<table>
<tr><td>⌨</td><td>27b Covent Garden Piazza, WC2</td></tr>
<tr><td>☎</td><td>020 7240 3838</td></tr>
<tr><td>🖱</td><td>www.justfalafs.com</td></tr>
<tr><td>🚌</td><td>Covent Garden LU 3 min walk</td></tr>
<tr><td>🕐</td><td>Mon-Fri 8am-9pm, Sat 10am-9pm, Sun 10am-7pm</td></tr>
<tr><td>🥕</td><td>Vegan options</td></tr>
<tr><td>i</td><td>Counter service, Eat-in/takeaway</td></tr>
<tr><td>☀</td><td>Outside seating for 60</td></tr>
</table>

Vegetarian ★★★★
Organic ★★★★
Taste ★★★★
Price £

Soak up Covent Garden's vibrant atmosphere with good veggie and organic mood food at Just Falaf's. Inside it's a matchbox, so you order your food at the counter and collect your falafel meal deal at the pick-up window. Check out the salad station for free-styling your own falafs.
A much bigger sister branch is at 155 Wardour Street, Soho, W1
(tel 020 7734 1914). For the food review see page 54.

Leon The Strand
Mediterranean and English

<table>
<tr><td>⌨</td><td>73 The Strand, WC2</td></tr>
<tr><td>☎</td><td>020 7240 3070</td></tr>
<tr><td>🖱</td><td>www.leonrestaurants.co.uk</td></tr>
<tr><td>🚌</td><td>Charing Cross LU, 5 min walk</td></tr>
<tr><td>🕐</td><td>Mon-Fri 7.30am-10.30pm, Sat 9.30am-10.30pm, Sun 11am-6pm</td></tr>
<tr><td>🥕</td><td>Vegan options</td></tr>
<tr><td>🍼</td><td>Child friendly</td></tr>
<tr><td>i</td><td>Takeaway and eat in</td></tr>
</table>

Vegetarian ★★★
Organic ★★★
Taste ★★★
Price £

For food review see Leon Spitalfields (page 222). Other local branch at:33 Villiers Street, WC2

Le Pain Quotidien Aveda Institute
French, classic

<table>
<tr><td>⌨</td><td>174 High Holborn,</td></tr>
<tr><td>☎</td><td>020 7486 6154</td></tr>
<tr><td>🖱</td><td>www.lepainquotidien.co.uk</td></tr>
<tr><td>🚌</td><td>Covent Garden LU or Tottenham Court Road LU, 5 min walk</td></tr>
<tr><td>🕐</td><td>Mon-Fri 8am-7pm, Sat 9am-6pm, Sun 11am-5pm</td></tr>
<tr><td>🥕</td><td>Vegan options</td></tr>
</table>

Vegetarian ★★★★
Organic ★★★★★
Taste ★★★★
Price ££

This branch of Quotidien is within the Aveda Hairdressing Institute, and is frequented by beautiful, high-maintenance people seeking a post-cut chow down. As befits such a fashionable location, this is an ultra-chic and modern café serving a quality selection of veggie and vegan options. Lunchtimes are busy, especially late week, but the ambience remains relaxed.

For food review see page 41.

Other branches at:

75 Marylebone High St, W1; 9 Young Street, W8; 201-203 King's Road, SW3; Upper Festival Walk, SE1; 18 Great Marlborough St, W1; Exhibition Road, SW7; St Pancras Station, NW1.

Mela
Indian, Country Style

Vegetarian ★★★★
Taste ★★★★★
Price £££

- 152-156 Shaftesbury Avenue, WC2
- 020 7836 8635
- www.melarestaurant.co.uk
- Leicester Square LU, Tottenham Court Road LU, 10 min walk
- Mon-Fri 12noon-11.30pm, Sat 1pm-11.45pm, Sun 12noon-10.30pm
- Vegan options
- Children-friendly
- i Eat-in & Takeaway menu; function room available

A large and popular Indian restaurant serving highly creative and delicious country-style dishes. Mela has an established reputation and is a former winner of the Indian Restaurant of the Year Award.

The menu has three vegetarian starters, four tandoor dishes, nine mains, three rice dishes and seven breads. Dishes are rich in aroma and a magnificent treat to the taste buds. There's a wonderful tandoor main, Subz Thaal, a mix of peppers stuffed with cumin flavoured vegetables, tomatoes with spiced dal, cottage cheese skewered with capiscums, stuffed potatoes and other veg – all served with a mint chutney.

Mirch Baingan Ka Salan is a deliciously traditional spicy aubergine dish with red chillies in a peanut flavoured yogurt sauce. The Jeero Pulao (basmati rice with cumin), naan and Roomali Roti (a fat-free flat bread) are all excellent. The set, three course, vegetarian menu for two people is £29.95 and there are meat dishes to please your carnivore friends.

Those after a veggie bargain should look out for the Paratha Pavilion Menu for £2.95-£5.95. Your lunch comes in a box with pickle and chutney accompaniment – all you do is choose your bread and curry and leave the rest to the chef.

Mela also has sister restaurants, Chowki and Soho Spice.

Neal's Yard Salad Bar
Brazilian and International, classic

Vegetarian ★★★★
Taste ★★★
Price £

📧 8-10 Neal's Yard, WC2
☎ 020 7836 3233
✏ www.nealsyardsaladbar.com
🚌 Covent Garden LU, 5 mins walk
🕐 Daily 8am-11.30pm
🥕 Vegan options
🍼 Child friendly
☀ Outside tables
i Eat-in & Takeaway, premises can be booked for private parties

Home-made vegetarian/vegan international food with an emphasis on Brazilian dishes. Pick a sunny day and loll around under the parasols. Otherwise, upstairs there's a rather splendid informal dining room with modern paintings on white, orange and pink walls, Buddha heads, and an artistic light installation. Mid-afternoon it's quite busy with a young crowd, Brazilian music playing, just the vibe to go with their speciality Pao De Qeijo – warm vegetarian Brazilian cheese bread, flavoured with garlic and herb – which is not to be missed.

The Brazilian vegan dish of choice is Feijoada, a big plate of black beans, minced soya, pumpkin, finger tapioca, fried bananas and brown rice (£11.50). There are also daily specials such as a vegan risotto of runner beans, spinach, carrot, parsnip, cauliflower and potato, served as either small (£9) or large (£10) portions. Other choices include veggie pastas, pizzas, veggie burgers, quiches and five types of salad. This is also a good place for teatime treat, having eleven desserts of which five are vegan as well as an excellent choice of coffees and Brazilian fruit juices. Across the yard at 1-2 Neal's Yard there is another older part of Neal's Yard Salad Bar which is much quieter.

Sarastro
Mediterranean, classic

Vegetarian ★★★
Taste ★★★
Price ££

⌨ *126 Drury Lane, WC2*
☎ *020 7836 0101*
✎ *www.sarastro-restaurant.com*
🚌 *Covent Garden LU 2 min walk, Holborn, LU 5 min*
🕐 *Daily, Lunch 12noon-3pm, Dinner 5pm-11pm*
🥕 *Vegan options*
◯ *Child friendly*
i *Booking essential*

Sarastro

Calendar Girls film star, Celia Imrie, introduced me to Sarastro in London's Covent Garden Theatre district, and I love it. Inside it's opera themed, so go in a group and reserve an upstairs semi-private opera box and toast the other diners in their boxes who will toast you back. The décor is exuberant with wall-mounted opera boxes draped with gold lamé, crushed velvet tablecloths and napkins, gilt furnishings and brocade upholstered chairs. At ground level, there's more seating for dating couples and a central area for parties of 20 or more.

Upbeat, loud recorded Bizet, Mozart and Verdi opera anthems, cheerful service, birthday party groups, and smiles all round announce this is hedonistic dining with a vengeance. There's even erotic wallpaper in the toilets – don't say you haven't been warned!

Chilli sauce, ginger and tomato dip with olive bread is a complimentary and rather good overture from the management. Asparagus starter with olive oil and lemon is recommended, as is the Cheese Borek, warm triangulated pasties filled with cheese. The Hummus, here, is also done well.

There are three veggie mains of which the Pancake Special filled with stir-fried spinach, cucumber, mushroom and creamy sauce slides down easily. The vegetarian pasta is fussili with mushroom, onion, red and green pepper and seasonal salads are also available. Among the desserts the Seasonal Fresh Fruit Selection (a biggie), makes a fitting finale to the feast. There are plenty of choices for omnivore dining partners too.

Every Sunday and Monday evening, Sarastro hosts an Opera Cabaret Dinner that includes performances from young talented opera singers at £25 and Sunday Matinées from 1.30pm at £19.50, with children half price. Recommended is The Tenor Menu, two courses for £12.50 and definitely something to sing about.

Sister branch at Papageno Restaurant & Bar, 29-31 Wellington Street WC2; Tel: 020 7836 4444.

Sofra Covent Garden
Turkish, classic,

Vegetarian ★★★
Taste ★★★
Price ££

▢ *36 Tavistock St , WC2*

☎ *020 7240 3773*

🚌 *Covent Garden LU (5 min walk)*

🕐 *Daily 12noon-12midnight including Bank Holidays*

🥕 *Vegan options*

🍼 *Child friendly*

This branch of Sofra has seating for 120 with a bar area, plus a roof garden for a further 80, making it an agreeable venue for the summer. *See Özer, Oxford Circus for food review (page 44).*

Thai Square Covent Garden
Thai, classic

- 166 Shaftesbury Avenue, WC2
- 020 7836 7600
- www.thaisquare.net
- Leicester Square LU
- Mon-Thurs 12noon-3pm, 5.30pm-11.30pm, Fri-Sat 12noon-12midnight, Sun 12noon-3pm, 5pm-11pm

The latest of the Thai Square chain and similar in size to the one in Trafalgar Square with some additional veggie dishes and the same pre-theatre special deal.

See opposite for food review.

Thai Square The Strand
Thai, classic

- 148 The Strand, WC2
- 020 7497 0904
- www.thaisquare.net
- Charing Cross LU/BR
- Mon-Sat 12noon-3pm, 5.30pm-11.15pm

Another branch of Thai Square offering good Thai vegetarian choices for pre-and post-theatre goers.

See opposite for food review.

Thai Square

Thai Square Trafalgar Square
Thai, classic

Vegetarian ★★★
Taste ★★
Price £££

⌗ 21-24 Cockspur Street, SW1
☎ 020 7839 4000
✉ www.thaisquare.net
🚌 Trafalgar Square LU, 3min walk or Charing Cross LU
🕐 Mon-Thurs 12noon-3pm and 5.30pm-11.30pm, Fri and Sat 12noon-3pm
and 5.30-12midnight, Sun 12noon-3pm and 5.30pm-10.30pm

A stone's throw from Nelson's Column, this huge Thai restaurant has an attractive traditional décor and serves a short vegetarian menu as well as a pre-theatre, three-course deal for just £14.50 (5.30pm-7.30pm).

The restaurant is on two floors, with the ground floor pretty full by 8pm and the upstairs also getting crowded by 10pm. At the back of the ground floor dining room tables are set up for larger parties.

Portions here are big and it may be quite adequate for two people to split a starter and order a main each and one portion of rice. The starter of Corn Cakes (Tod Mun Koaw Pod) is substantial, spicy and enjoyable and comes with curry paste, chopped lime leaves and a sweet dipping sauce.

Mains, however, are disappointing and I was forced to ask for more soya sauce, ginger, mushroom and spring onions with the Fried Beancurd with ginger (Pad Khing Toa Hoo). On a good note, The Pineapple Rice, served in half a pineapple, is well presented and of quite reasonable taste. The service certainly is attentive but technically leaves something to be desired. Whilst the white wine came suitably cold it was not kept so and waiting staff were over eager to clear your plates before you had finished. If the food could match the place's good looks it would be an even bigger hit.

The Thai Square club downstairs holds 200 and is a huge basement cavern bar with dancing which gets very busy on Friday and Saturday nights from 11pm onward with a mainly Chinese and Japanese crowd. Admission is free for women and £10 for men – although if you dine you will most certainly get in for nothing, space permitting.

Thai Square is a chain with restaurants at the Strand, Oxford Circus, South Kensington, Soho, St Pauls, Aldwich, Putney, Shaftesbury Avenue and the Minories in the City. See relevant reviews for address and contact details.

Thai Square at the Wig and Pen
Thai, tapas

Vegetarian ★★★
Price £££

⌨ *229-230 The Strand, WC2*
☎ *020 7353 6980*
✎ *www.thaisquare.net*
🚇 *Temple LU, 5min walk*
🕐 *Mon-Fri 12noon-11pm*

Opposite the Royal Courts of Justice, how times have changed. The historically famous Wig and Pen Club that survived the Great Fire of London has now become a Thai small plate tapas restaurant. Still, the legal eagles from the Royal Courts of Justice continue to frequent the place along with hungry tourists.

To compliment this grand venue, Thai Square have created a whole new menu that includes veggie dishes such as the intriguingly named Golden Bag – a recipe of diced chestnut, potato and lotus seed encased in a golden dumpling bag, a Vegetable Tempura of deep fried veg with plum sauce and Noodles Roll with beansprouts and mushrooms. The menu looks a lot less vegetarian than other Thai Square branches but they will convert several dishes such as the Thai curries to vegetarian on request. This place is particularly popular at lunchtime with bargain deals including two dishes, rice and veg for £8.95.

For list of other Thai Square restaurants see Thai Square, Trafalgar Square for address and contact details on page 31.

Woodlands
South Indian, Classic

Vegetarian ★★★★★
Taste ★★★★
Price £££

⌨ *37 Panton Street, W1*
☎ *020 7839 7258*
🚇 *Leicester Square LU, Piccadilly Circus LU, (5min walk)*
🕐 *Daily 12noon-11pm*

Situated just off the Haymarket, the Panton Street Woodlands has more of a quick service menu. Still, with a modern beige décor and lots of tables, it's certainly worth a whirl.

See Woodlands, Chiswick (page 190) for food review.

Other Woodlands are at 77 Marylebone Lane W1; Tel 020 7486 3862

World Food Café
International, classic

Vegetarian ★★★★★
Taste ★★
Price ££

- 🖃 *First Floor, 14 Neal's Yard, WC*
- ☎ *020 7379 0298*
- ✎ *www.worldfoodcafenealsyard.com*
- 🚌 *Covent Garden LU, 5 min walk*
- 🕐 *Mon-Fri, 11.30am-4.30pm, Sat 11.30am-5pm*
- 🥕 *Vegan options*
- 🍼 *Child friendly*

Vegetarian world food by the plate at this spacious upstairs eaterie overlooking Covent Garden's famous Neal's Yard. An open plan kitchen at the back isn't worth the look, whilst pinewood tables with yellow plastic chairs are merely okay – try to snag a window seat with a courtyard view.

On the blackboard is Turkish Meze, Mexican, West African, Egyptian falafels, Spicy Indian Vegetable Masala and Special Stir-fry salad at £7.25 each. No table menus are provided.

Dishes change seasonally and recipes can later be tried at home from their own cookbook: *World Food Café 2* by Chris and Carolyn Caldicott (Frances Lincoln publishers, £20).

World Food Café attracts a mixed crowd of veggie new-age tourists and local shop and office folk. It has a pleasant enough atmosphere and often plays vibrant Brazilian music to accompany the food.

The Mexican and Spicy Indian dishes taste fine but with a bit too much of the cheap staples such as tortilla crisps and naan rather than the main ingredients. Likewise, Mango Cheesecake (£3.45) whilst tasting okay, was a small slice topped with foamed cream to make it look bigger. Overall, eating here is regrettably not great value for money, but then it is a great tourist vantage point.

Marylebone, Mayfair & Baker Street

Restaurants

1) Carluccio's Caffé
   St Christopher Place p.35
2) Carluccio's Caffé
   Market Place p.36
3) Carluccio's Caffé
   Fenwick of Bond Street p.36
4) Eat and Two Veg p.36
5) El Pirata p.38
6) Getti Jermyn St p.38
7) Getti Marylebone High St p.39
8) Gordon Ramsay at Claridges p.40
9) Le Pain Quotidien p.41
10) The Natural Kitchen p.42
11) Noura Mayfair p.43
12) Özer Oxford Circus p.44
13) Rose Bakery p.45
14) Sketch p.46
15) Sofra Mayfair p.47
16) Sofra Oxford Street p.47
17) Thai Square,
    Hanover Square p.48
18) Wagamama p.48
19) Woodlands p.49

Shops

a) Bateel p.245
b) Marylebone Farmers'
   Market p.245
c) The Natural Kitchen p.245
d) Stella McCartney p.246

Carluccio's Caffé
Italian, classic

Vegetarian ★★★
Taste ★★★★
Price ££

🖼 *St Christopher's Place, W1*
☎ *020 7935 5927*
✎ *www.carluccios.com*
🚐 *Marble Arch LU, 7 min walk*
🕐 *Mon-Fri 7.30am-11.30pm, Sat 9-11.30pm, Sun 9am-10.30pm*
🥕 *Vegan options*
🍼 *Child friendly, high chairs*
☀ *Excellent outside tables*
i *Booking advised in evenings*

This relaxed Italian restaurant/café serves several good value vegetarian choices. It is the second largest in this popular chain of cafés conceived by superstar chef Antonio Carluccio and his wife Priscilla.

The place is ideal for alfresco dinning in the summertime, despite occasional guest appearances from the local pigeon community. Inside ground floor window tables offer the best views, while downstairs there's a bustling bar.

By 8pm it's crammed to the rafters, with a 40 minute wait for non-reservations, but the service is on the ball. If you explain to the staff that you're vegetarian they will rattle off all the options and specials. Gals outnumber fellahs three to one, with many of the salad-pasta-and white wine binge brigade out for a good time.

Antipasto di vendure, is a fab Italian veggie starter of roasted peppers, pesto, green beans, roasted tomatoes and olives, while the savoury bread tin (£2.85) is substantial enough for two. Even more delicious tomatoes feature on the Brushetta, this time with oregano and basil, which is strongly recommended.

The Egg Pappadelle with Wild Mushrooms main is a perfect pasta/mushroom ensemble – as expected from Carluccio – a world expert on mushroom dishes. I can vouch for the Calzone Imbottito, a fantastic deep fried pastry stuffed with peppers, spinach, aubergine and cheese. I loved it, even without the recommended green salad. Pesche All'ammareto dessert is a bright red peach marinated in Dolcetto wine and amaretti pureé and served with vanilla cream and a small amaretti biscuit. Amaretti fans will love it: others may declare it a bit of a mess. Ice cream is suitable for veggies but the Panna Cotta contains gelatine.

They also offer basic breakfasts of muesli, yogurts, breads and eggs. The most expensive item on the menu is the Trasporti Piaggo Vespa (£1650), a fully automatic scooter imported from Italy!

Carluccio's Caffè
Italian, classic

⌨ *Market Place, W1*
☎ *020 7636 2228*
✎ *www.carluccios.com*
🚇 *Oxford Circus LU, 5 min walk*
🕐 *Mon-Fri 7.30am-11.30pm*
   Sat 9-11.30pm, Sun 9am-
   10.30pm
🌶 *Vegan options*
☀ *Outside tables*
☖ *Child friendly, high chairs*
i *Booking advised in evenings*

One of the smaller Carluccio's Caffès. It is particularly popular in the summer with lots of outside tables and a lively crowd from the fashion showrooms and offices nearby.

Carluccio's Caffè
Italian, classic

⌨ *Fenwick of Bond Street, W1*
☎ *020 7629 0699*
✎ *www.carluccios.com*
🚇 *Bond Street LU, 5 min walk*
🕐 *Mon-Sat 10am-6.30pm, Thurs*
   10am-8pm, Sun 12noon-6pm
🌶 *Vegan options*
☖ *Child friendly, high chairs*

A popular stop off for Bond Street shoppers and ladies that lunch. Go through this exclusive store to the lower ground floor and relax. Service is slow and you may have to wait a bit for your bill.
See Carluccio's Caffè, St Christopher's Place for the food review (page 35).

Eat and Two Veg
Mock Carnivore, American diner-style

⌨ *50 Marylebone High Street, W1*
☎ *020 7258 8599*
✎ *www.eatandtwoveg.com*
🚇 *Baker St LU, 4 min walk*
🕐 *Mon-Sat 9am-11pm, Sun 10am-10pm*
🌶 *Vegan options*
☖ *Child friendly*
i *Booking advisable at weekends*

Vegetarian ★★★★★
Organic ★★★★★
Taste ★★★★
Price ££

One of the hippest vegetarian and organic restaurants in London, this well-designed, New York style eaterie serves incredibly good soya burger sandwiches and classic English and Italian dishes. Run by Simone Cimignoli and David Kranz of Racing Green and Blazer menswear fame, the joint is big, the atmosphere fast, the diners exuberant.

At the windowed front is a small bar with high stools and a few tables serving 10 pre-meal cocktails, six non-alcoholics, a choice of smoothies and vegan shakes in strawberry, banana and mocha flavours. Further inside, there's a hectic open kitchen with metal ceiling plumbing,

Eat and Two Veg

exposed brickwork, good size tables and a row of red leather banquettes, the best seats in the house.

The menu is big, bold and clear and changes every 2 months. They try to use organic and GM free products across the menu. The average price per head is £25 with drinks and service, which is provided courtesy of a t-shirted young waiting staff who are hyper-attentive.

No less than eight salads are on offer here and the Not Nicoise is recommended. In starter portion size it's still big and comes with marinated organic tofu, tiny pieces of avocado, leaves, green beans, potatoes, delicious capers and a free range organic hard boiled egg. The EatV Burger looks just like a real chargrilled burger with a good sesame bun, caramelised onions, tomatoes, lettuce and matchstick french fries – the best mock burger in London.

There are eight main dishes with English faves such as Sausage and Mash and a variation on Lancashire Hot Pot called Marylebone Hot Pot, that's pretty good. The vegan Seasonal Fruit Crumble with berries, rhubarb and thin soya custard is unfortunately not so good, but the Bread & Butter Pudding is well worth a try.

Sunday breakfasts are busy with locals reading the papers and a veggie Sunday Roast is available from 1pm. The front bar is quite good for anytime drinks and features four vegetarian wines and the *Casa de La Ermita* wines are vegan as is the *Samuel Smiths* beer.

El Pirata
Spanish tapas,

Vegetarian ★★★
Taste ★★★★
Price ££

⌨ *5-6 Down St, Mayfair, W1*
☎ *020 7491 3810*
✎ *www.elpirata.co.uk*
🚌 *Hyde Park Corner LU, 5 min walk or Green Park LU*
🕐 *Mon-Fri 12noon-11.30pm, Sat 6pm-11.30pm*
☀ *Seating outside*
i *Evening booking advisable*

El Pirate, offers good value for money Spanish tapas up a backstreet in super expensive Mayfair. The place oozes with relaxed joyful charm. The walls are patriotically festooned with Picasso and Miró prints and there's a good bar on the right hand side as you go in. The ground floor is the most popular – although I like the modern basement with large tables for parties and secret alcoves for romantics. In the afternoon, a vegetarian can drink and snack in calm ambience. At night the atmosphere can be crowded and manic.

The menu is well explained and there is a separate vegetarian section of 10 tapas. In addition there are veggie choices on the starter menu such as Grilled Wild Asparagus or Gazpacho soup. Six tapas choices between two people should be enough and if you fancy a drink there are four organic wines.

Enjoyable vegetarian dishes include aubergine stuffed with veg and topped with cheese and the Chick peas, baby spinach and raisins. Tortilla here is excellent and the cous cous salad is also delicious.

The set lunch menu comprises of two tapas, bread with alioli and a glass of wine or soft drink and is good value for £8. This menu has six vegetarian choices.

Getti Jermyn Street
Italian, modern

Vegetarian ★★★
Taste ★★★★
Price £££

⌨ *16-17 Jermyn Street, SW1*
☎ *020 7734 7334*
✎ *www.getti.com*
🚌 *Piccadilly LU, 2min walk*
🕐 *Mon-Sat, Lunch 12noon-3pm, Dinner 6pm-11pm*

Modern Italian restaurant well located for pre- and post-theatre meals and those wonderful classic Jermyn Street menswear shops. The service is friendly and the upstairs sports some good views over Jermyn Street.
See Getti, Marylebone High Street for food review (page 39).

Getti Marylebone High Street
Italian, modern

⊞ *42 Marylebone High Street, W1*

☎ *020 7486 3753*

✎ *www.getti.com*

🚌 *Baker Street LU, 10min walk*

🕐 *Mon-Sat 12noon-11pm*

🥕 *Vegan options*

🍼 *Child friendly with high chairs*

☀ *Outside seating*

Vegetarian ★★★
Taste ★★★★
Price £££

With Sicilian and Sardinian influences, Getti does a choice of simple but high quality Italian, vegetarian dishes with a modern twist in a large, chic venue.

Inside, it's cruise liner décor. White and blue walls with smart cherry wood tables and porthole windows want you to believe that you are sailing around Lake Como (from where the owner's family come from). Downstairs are some alcoves perfect for a romantic evening for two. In the centre of the dining room there's ample room for big parties. On the ground level there's further seating and outside tables too.

There are four vegetarian antipasti of which the Buffalo Mozarella, roasted plum tomatoes with basil and olive oil is very good. Getti has a reputation for making good risotto and their Risotto with Wild Mushrooms and Chives will not disappoint. Penne pasta with broccoli, tomato and mozzarella is also of good quality. If you're looking for great value, Getti does a set menu meal deal – two course for £15.50 or three courses for only £18.50.
See also Getti, Jermyn Street (page 42).

Gordon Ramsay at Claridges
French, modern,

Vegetarian ★★★★
Price £££££

🕯 *Claridges Hotel, Brook Street, W1*

☎ *020 7499 0099*

✏ *www.gordonramsay.com*

🕐 *Mon-Fri 12noon-2.45pm, 5.45pm-11pm, Sat 12-3pm, 5.45pm-11pm*
Sun 6pm-10.30pm

🚌 *Bond Street LU, 5min walk*

i *Booking advised*

Some top notch vegetarian choices are on the menu at TV celebrity chef Gordon Ramsay's opulent Art Deco designed restaurant in the world famous Claridge's Hotel. The atmosphere here in the evening is pleasantly exuberant and as you walk through the elegant foyer you'll hear live piano music wafting over the hotel lounge where guests linger over their tea or sip champagne. Towards the right of the lounge can be found the restaurant bar, perfect for pre-meal drinks and canapés. Tell the maitre d' that you are vegetarian and he'll give you the special vegetarian menu with a choice of three vegetarian starter, three main courses and a choice of desserts.

From the bar you enter an impressive spacious dining room with long lanterns. Starters may include a tortellini of chanterelles and turnips with white bean velouté, celeriac remoulade or celery and watercress salad with crystallised walnuts. Some menu changes are made every couple of weeks and mains may include dishes like poached Burford brown egg, purple sprouting broccoli, pomme mousseline and trompettes de la mort or Roasted root vegetables, braised red cabbage, creamed pearl barley and ceps. Three courses in the evening cost £45, whilst you can enjoy exactly the same meal at lunch for a very reasonable £30. The six course Vegetarian Menu Prestige is £65. Despite the reasonable prices there is a dress code with Jeans, T-shirts and sportswear not permitted.

Le Pain Quotidien
French, classic

Vegetarian ★★★★
Organic ★★★★★
Taste ★★★★
Price ££

☒ *72-75 Marylebone High Street, W1*
☎ *020 7486 6154*
✎ *www.lepainquotidien.com*
🚌 *Baker Street LU, 10min walk*
🕓 *Mon-Fri 7am-9pm, Sat 8am-9pm, Sun and holdays 8am-7pm*
🥕 *Vegan options*
i *Table service & Takeaway*

This Belgium café chain has a strong commitment to organic produce and ample vegetarian choices. Visiting on a Bank Holiday when many cafés and restaurants are closed, the queue was long and moved slowly. People wait patiently here, it's that good. Dining is largely bench style with a relaxed and friendly atmosphere. Popular is the soup and bread deal and intriguingly one young couple had decided to drink the soups and save the breads to have with the complimentary jams that Le Pain is so famous for.

The organic Moroccan Vegetable soup was flavoursome with lots of chunky vegetables and very good bread. I enjoyed the five grain so much I bought a loaf from their store counter to take home. Other soups include Tuscan Bean and veg and Curried cauliflower and many of the soup options are suitable for vegans. Warm quiche with mesclun salad is very good and they also do a vegetarian tartine of organic roasted vegetable with mozarella, sundried tomatoes and basil. A lot of people go for the small vegetarian cheese board as a light snack or in the evening the Vegan Pot of mushroom, lima bean, and tomato with sweet potato and broccoli.

All the wines and beers here are organic and the house red is quite good and a bargain at £3.75 a glass and there is a selection of fifteen organic wines from which to choose. Organic lemonade is available and coffees here are good but a touch on the expensive side. There's a big selection of vegetarian pastries and cakes and the muffins are vegan.

Although not all the products are yet organic, planned certification is expected in the very near future. They also try to source produce as local as possible.

Other branches are at 75 Marylebone High St W1; 9 Young Street W8; 201-203 King's Road SW3; Upper Festival Walk SE1; 18 Great Marlborough St W1; Exhibition Road SW7; St Pancras Station, NW1.

The Natural Kitchen
English, classic

Vegetarian ★★★
Organic ★★★★
Taste ★★★★
Price ££

▢ 77-78 Marylebone High Street, W1
☎ 020 7486 8065
✎ www.thenaturalkitchen.com
🚌 Baker Street LU, 10min walk
🕐 Mon-Fri 8am-8pm, Sat 9am-7pm, Sun 11am-6pm
🥕 Vegan options
🍼 Child friendly / Baby changing facility
☀ Outside seating
i Eat in (table service) and Takeaway

Amongst the best veggie organic, artisan food in London and with a commitment to top notch fine foods, this upstairs café set within this modern triple level store is rapidly making a big name for itself.

On the blackboard the 'Soup of the day' (always vegetarian) was Broccoli and Vegetable soup. Having overeaten the veggie tasting menu at Zaika the night before, starters were skipped. Terrific comfort food was the Mushroom with Baby Onion Pie with smoked cheddar mash, peas and gravy (£7.95), for the same price was the Warm Roasted Root Vegetables which had a beautiful medley of flavours and came with salad and herb vinaigrette and a quality multi-grain organic bread and butter. Natural Kitchen also do a tofu burger with a crispy coleslaw that looks a delight to the eye and an All Day Full English Veggie Breakfast (£7.95). Stop Press: Natural Kitchen have just upgraded their menu to have a fuller vegetarian offer! Now also on the menu is Butternut Squash Risotto, and Spring Vegetable Quinoa Salad.

Large chunky communal wooden tables and the informal atmosphere make this a pleasant place enjoy quality food and relax. The customers tend to be a mix of casually dressed locals, students and people from the nearby BBC.

For desserts, you'll need to check out the serving counter that displays a rather exceptional homemade passion fruit cake, although the Cherry and Almond cake was pretty memorable too and the smaller apple tart good quality.

On drinks, don't miss their fresh Carrot, Apple and Ginger juice or failing that try the Acai Berry Smoothie. There is a short organic wine list with quite a few wines served by the glass as well as a variety of organic beers and lemonades.

For organic store review see page 245.

Noura Mayfair
Lebanese, classic

Vegetarian ★★★★
Taste ★★★★★
Price ££££

🖃 *16 Curzon Street, W1*
☎ *020 7495 1050*
🖉 *www.noura.co.uk*
🚌 *Green Park LU (5 min walk)*
🕓 *Daily 9am-11.30am*
🌶 *Vegan options*
🍼 *Child friendly*
i Takeaways and deliveries also available

An abundance of mirrors adorn the walls of this bistro-styled upstairs eaterie which is popular for lunch and dinner. Downstairs has a more lively atmosphere with Lebanese live music and song, belly dancing and a special menu of eight mezzes, vegetarian main course, dessert and coffee or tea for £40 per person. The place has proved a great success, making it a good idea to book at the weekends. On other nights, friends meet for drinks in the funky restaurant lounge area.

For food review see Noura Piccadilly, the flagship restaurant (page 59).

Noura

Özer Oxford Circus
Turkish, classic

Vegetarian ★★★
Taste ★★★
Price ££

⊡ 5 Langham Place, W1
☎ 020 7323 0505
✉ www.sofra.co.uk
🚌 Oxford Circus LU, 4 min walk
🕓 Open 365 days 12noon-12midnight
🥕 Vegan options
🍼 Child friendly, high chairs
☀ Outside tables
i Booking advised

A large, lively Turkish restaurant serving an appealing medley of vegetarian choices. The front of house bar area is a low seated, cushioned affair where customers can sprawl out and enjoy snacks before being seated. The main evening dining area is at the back. For a Turkish eaterie it's quite modern and spacious, dark and moody with a sophisticated sculptured ceiling.

Özer has dispensed with the running buffet deals but does have a huge choice of veggie dishes. Your best bet is to tell them right away that you are veggie and they will organise a substantial mezze platter for just £7.95 – great value for this part of town. The mixed nuts and vegetable salad is refreshing and comes with nutritious bulghur wheat which is perfect for a summer's day. Falafel, humus and flat bread are also good and the Börek – a delicious feta cheese and spinach filled filo – is highly recommended. To finish there are a variety of desserts including a type of Turkish rice pudding called Sutlak, fruit salad and a variety of Baklava.

The à la carte is served till midnight with cold mezzes such as Tabbouleh, Mutabel, Lentil Köfte (lentil balls with onion, olive oil and herbs) whilst on the hot mezzes there's Patlican Kizartma (fried aubergine, green pepper with a thick tomato sauce). Three vegetarian mains are on offer: Silk Route (a mediterranean mixed-veg stir fry with rice), Penne Dolce Latté and a Vegetarian Moussaka. Özer, however, will convert their carnivore dishes to vegetarian if you ask. About 20% of their diners are vegetarian and they are used to serving big parties of diners where some are pure vegetarians.

Özer's Oxford Circus is the flagship for the Sofra chain whose sister restaurants are Sofra Mayfair (page 47), Sofra Covent Garden (page 29), Sofra St Christopher's Place (page 35), Sofra Exmouth Market (page 102) and Sofra St John's Wood (page 159).

Rose Bakery
English, classic

Vegetarian ★★★★★
Organic ★★★★
Taste ★★★★
Price ££

🖃 *Top floor, Dover Street Market*
    17-18 Dover Street, W1

☎ *020 7518 0680*

🚍 *Green park LU, 5 min walk*

🕘 *Mon-Sat 11am-5pm*

i   *Eat-in & Takeaway*

This small chi-chi organic café is where the fashionable and beautiful people hang. If one could bottle the waft of freshly baked bread as you approach from the fourth floor lift, you'd make a mint. In Summer, grab a much coveted outside table on the veranda, otherwise the inside benches are fine.

The long metal serving counter will leave you drooling. The menu is short and it's best to let them know you are vegetarian as they will convert quite a lot of the dishes for you and over 90% of the ingredients are organic. We began by splitting the Vegetable Plate of roasted fennel, cherry tomato in balsamic vinegar, chickpea, lentil, cauliflower and broccoli that came with a beautiful French dressing and was excellent. The Red pepper and Courgette Tart is of good flavour and comes with crispy lettuce with a simple oil dressing. Available too was a butternut squash and ricotta tart and a sweet potato version. The Lentils, Chickpeas and Tomato stew was one of the vegetarian conversion dishes which was also very good.

Carrot cake comes in a fairly small portion, like a muffin, but was the best I've tasted in London. Also popular is the semolina pudding and the fruit crumbles. The squeezed orange juice and coffees are also of a high quality.

The café draws in many visitors from the nearby art galleries and hotels which makes it a place where fashion and excellent organic food mingle. It is no surprise that the owners of the Rose Café have also opened another equally fashionable branch on the Rue de Martyrs in Paris. Having enjoyed their London branch so much it is not hard to see this formula proving popular with a demanding French clientele.

Sketch
European, modern

Vegetarian ★★★★
Price £££££

⌨ 9 Conduit Street, W1
☎ 020 7659 4500
✎ www.sketch.uk.com
🚌 Oxford Circus LU 5 min walk,
🕑 Library Restaurant: Tue-Fri 12noon-2.30pm, Tue-Sat 7pm-10.30pm,
   Tea Parlour: Mon-Fri 8am-2am, Sat 10am-2pm

Sketch

Splash the cash with the Vegetarian Tasting Menu at London's most expensive and possibly most imaginatively designed gastronomic destination. The lobby displays modern art pieces and the bathrooms are encrusted with crystals. The menu changes seasonally and has a good selection of vegetarian dishes.

The seven course menu at £65 begins with Patty Pan, a type of squash in a lemon balm marmalade, seasonal vegetables, wild fennel and fresh coriander jelly with herb salad. To follow is Pink Roscoff onions and mustard served with black wheat pancake and grilled cauliflower. The other five courses are equally inventive and there are petit fours to finish. Organic produce is used where possible and sourced from suppliers in England, France and Peru. Portion sizes are fairly substantial throughout the menu but will leave you satisfied without feeling overfed. Dishes can be matched with a selection of vegan wines from £24.50 per bottle.

For something lighter, the Parlour on the ground floor does a Croque Monsieur vegetarian club sandwich of mozzarella, basil oil, tomato, courgette and black bread for £8.50. Forget your bank account and savour the fabulousness of the Sketch experience.

Sofra Mayfair
Turkish, classic

Vegetarian ★★★
Taste ★★★
Price ££

- 📖 18 Shepherd Street, W1
- ☎ 020 7493 3320
- ✍ www.sofra.co.uk
- 🚌 Green Park LU (5min walk)
- 🕐 Daily 12noon-midnight

See Özer Oxford Circus for food review (page 44).

Sofra Oxford Street
Turkish, classic

Vegetarian ★★★
Taste ★★★
Price ££

- 📖 1 St Christopher's Place, W1
- ☎ 020 7224 4080
- ✍ www.sofra.co.uk
- 🕐 Daily 12noon-12midnight

This branch has good food and outside seating on St Christopher's Place precinct.

See Özer Oxford Circus for food review (page 44).

Thai Square
Thai, classic

Vegetarian ★★★
Taste ★★★★
Price £

    5 Princes Street, Hanover Square, W1

☎   *020 7499 3333*

   www.thaisq.com

🕐   *Mon-Sat noon-3pm, 6pm-11pm*

Busy in evenings, quiet at lunchtime.

See Thai Square Trafalgar Square for food review (page 31).

Wagamama
Japanese, modern

Vegetarian ★★★
Taste ★★★★
Price £

   101a Wigmore Street, W1

☎   *020 7409 0111*

   www.wagamama.com

🚇   *Marble Arch, 5 min walk*

🕐   *Mon-Sat 11.30am-11pm, Sun 11.30am-10pm*

🌶   *Vegan options*

Excellent value for money modern eaterie. Located in a brightly lit basement. It's a short stroll from swanky department store Selfridges and the upscale boutiques of St Christopher's Place. Outside, queues of youthful urbanites wait to be assigned seating and it gets manic around the 7-8pm slot. Inside the décor is beige 'n' benches–minimalist. The menu is informative with 16 vegetarian dishes. Staff with hand-held computers take your orders and before you know it's on the table.

A noodle or rice dish and a side order leaves you full, which is just as well as there are no starters here – although for the super hungry there are four vegetarian desserts. Saien Soba, a vegetable soup with noodles, courgettes; and stir fried tofu with ramen noodles and spring onions are both warming and satisfying. Alternatively, try the Yasai Cha Han, an egg fried rice and tofu dish with snow peas, sweet corn and mushrooms alongside a veggie miso soup. A side order of the Yasai Gyoza, grilled vegetable dumplings filled with cabbage, carrots and served with chilli garlic soy sauce is substantial and a great accompaniment to your meal. They also do a raw food juice selection for health foodies.

Other branches at:

Camden, NW1 (see page 132), Bloomsbury, WC1 (see page 18).

Woodlands
South Indian, classic

Vegetarian ★★★★★
Taste ★★★★
Price £££

- 77 Marylebone Lane, W1
- ☎ 020 7486 3862
- Bond Street LU or Baker Street LU
- 🕒 Mon-Thurs 12noon-3pm, 6pm-11pm, Fri-Sun 12noon-10.30pm
- Vegan options
- i Eat in (table service) & Takeaway available

There's fine vegetarian dining at this classic–style Indian restaurant, the first of the Woodlands to open in London.

See the food review for Woodlands, Chiswick (page 190).

Restaurants

Shops

SOHO

Great eating places can be found in London's night-life area famed for hot night-clubs, hip bars, music venues and red light strip joints. Daytime, check out the unique boutiques. VitaOrganic, Mildreds, and Red Veg are vegetarian trailblazers. There is great world-food at Beatroot, bargain Indian at Govinda's, falafels at Just Falafs and Maoz and healthy takeaway salads at Flavour. In the evening, Pizza Express on Dean Street offers great veggie pizzas often accompanied with live jazz.

Beatroot
Café, International

Vegetarian ★★★★★
Organic ★★★
Taste ★★★
Price £

🖾 *92 Berwick Street, W1*
☎ *020 7437 8591*
🖎 *www.beatroot.org.uk*
🚍 *Tottenham Court Road LU, 10 min walk*
🕒 *Mon-Sat 9am-9pm*
🌶 *Vegan options*
🍼 *Child friendly*
☀ *Outside seating for 20 people*
i Counter service

Beatroot

It's vegetarian-to-go at this popular street-wise small café bang in the middle of Soho's thriving Berwick Street Market. The meal-deal is a pick 'n' mix in a box from ten hot dishes and nine cold salads and good value at £3.90 (small), £4.90 (medium) and £5.90 (large). Food is laid out canteen style and servers are pretty helpful. Wised-up diners, however, first get the day's menu sheet by the till that explains all.

The new oak floors and beechwood tables are a big improvement on the old brassy orange/green décor and cumbersome green plant interior of yesteryear. Seating now is much more comfortable but difficult to get at lunchtimes when it gets crowded with a mix of local market traders, media office types and tourists.

Food is served in a cardboard box with plastic fork, fine for takeout but a bit mean for eating in. Nevertheless, lunchers munch delightedly despite the diverse dish choices running into each other in the box. Evening is more chilled except Fridays when it revs up with out of visitors, mooching around for pre-night-on-the-town cheap eats. That said, I went past on a Monday night and it was packed.

The Dal Curry and Organic Rice has good flavour, the spicy Moroccan Veg Tagine is even better, whilst veggie sausage and broccoli are fine. My medium-size world food box left me full, but most people seemed to be grazing contentedly on the large-size. My lunch partner's Tofu Stir-fry was yummy and that day's Bean Hotpot looked tempting.

Beatroot is to be applauded for offering a good veggie menu, which uses about 30% organic ingredients, on a tight budget. Homemade cakes, several vegan, are highly inviting and all the hot drinks are organic and Fair Trade. If you're looking for a healthy vitamin boost try one of their made-to-order smoothies and juices.

The Cafe at Foyles
International, modern

Vegetarian	★★★★
Organic	★★★
Taste	★★★
Price	£

🖼 *113-119 Charing Cross Road, WC2*

☎ *020 7440 3207*

✐ *www.foyles.co.uk*

🚇 *Tottenham Court Road LU, 2 min walk*

🕐 *Mon-Sat 8am-9pm, Sun 10am-6pm*

🥕 *Vegan options*

i *Alcohol served with main courses, Counter service (eat-in table service)*

🎵 *Regular live music*

There is a great atmosphere at this upstairs café, situated amongst possibly the best jazz and blues record selection in London with a good meal-list of light vegetarian and vegan choices. On the evening I dropped-by a band called *Naciente Quartet* were playing live. The place was packed with people listening, drinking or eating at the many wooden tables. At other times there's a good play list, people in conversation and a notably friendly ambience.

The mozzarella, red pepper, tomato and red onion panini made with an oregano flavoured quality bread was delicious and good value at £3.50. All the sarnies are made fresh on the premises including the inviting hummus, avocado, tomato and spinach sandwich. Other tasty meals included spinach and goats cheese quiche, and the aubergine and goat's cheese salad. Particularly popular are the vegan flapjacks that come in fruit, plain or chocolate flavour and they also offer millet munchies. One big favourite is the Pear and Nut Loaf (£2), although on a recent visit lots were tucking into vegan chocolate cake topped with almond flakes. Organic Monmouth Street coffee is available and for chocoholics there's Green & Blacks hot chocolate.

The Café at Foyles is popular with vegans with a few regulars coming for their favourites, rubbing shoulders with the more numerous passing tourists that are visiting one of the world's most famous bookshops.

Govinda's Vegetarian Restaurant
Indian and International, classic

Vegetarian ★★★★★
Taste ★★
Price £

▫ 9 Soho Street, Soho, W1
☎ 020 7437 4928
🖱 www.govindasvegetarianrestaurant.org
🚌 Tottenham Court Road LU, 5 min walk
🕐 Mon-Sat 12noon-9pm
🌶 Vegan options
i Counter service, Unlicensed

Old-style 100% vegetarian cuisine in a friendly but blandly decorated Hare Krishna canteen. A stone's throw from bustling Soho Square, this eaterie tends to be peopled by tranquil diners, meditatively grazing on their food, although it can get busy at lunchtime. The jewel in Govinda's crown is the £6.95 Thali Set ordered before 3pm that nearly everybody seemed to be enjoying. After 3pm it turns into an all-you-can-eat Thali deal for the same price which drops to a mind-boggling £5.95 after 7pm. As Thalis go, it all looks quite reasonable and tastes okay. For those wanting just a lite-bite, vegetable quiche, baked potato and a paneer veggie burger is on the main course list. Govinda's also have quite a few fast food dishes on their menu including a reasonable veggie Lasagne and a Pizza-of-the-day.

Govinda's offers a dozen mainly western desserts, such as lemon or apple pie, cheese cake and flapjack. They also do laddhu, a tasty Indian sweet chick-pea and butter fudge recipe or burfi, a creamy fudge. Coffee here is only decaff and not very good, better is the herbal tea or the lassi (a traditional Indian yogurt drink).

Joi
Thai/Chinese

🖼 *14 Percy Street, W1*

🚌 *Goodge St LU, 5min walk*

🕐 *7 days 12noon-10pm*

🥕 *Vegan menu*

i *Eat in (buffet service) & Takeaway*

Vegetarian ★★★★★
Taste ★★★
Price £

One of the bigger branches of this ever-growing fast food chain offering bargain all-you-can-eat vegan cuisine for £5.50 at lunchtime, £6.50 Sundays and evenings.

For a full food review see Wai Buffet, Goodge Street (page 67).

Just Falafs
Organic falafel cafe

🖼 *155 Wardour St, Soho, W1*

☎ *020 7734 1914*

🖱 *www.justfalafs.com*

🚌 *Tottenham Court Road LU, 10 min walk*

🕐 *Mon-Fri 9am-8pm, Sat12noon-8pm*

i *Counter service, Eat-in/takeaway*

Vegetarian ★★★★
Organic ★★★★
Taste ★★★★
Price £

It's a great name for a falafel café and the food is good as well. The place is a magnet for the Soho young media crowd that often pack out the wooden benches. Service is efficient and there's a small salad station for free styling your own falafel – although plumping for their tried and tested humourously named classics is recommended. Of their top five favourites, the Bean Beenie with tahini, small broad beans, chopped kidney bean, mixed sprout and aubergine in two half wraps is yummy and filling, even at the regular size for £4.50. Who gets through the large wrap at £5.75 beats me – unless of course you're splitting. Car Beet Sale is also very good and substantial with lots of sweetness, from the beetroot and carrot, combined with their own house sauce and served satisfyingly warm. Chickpea balls are organic, as are most salad ingredients as well as the tea, coffee and milk. The salad containers are also biodegradable.

Despite the name, this café also offers a reasonable selection of soups (£3.25) and salad plates (£3.95). The drinks are also good with organic cider, fresh juices and smoothies.

Also at:

27b Covent Garden Piazza, London, WC2 (see page 31)

Le Pain Quotidien
French, classic

Vegetarian ★★★★
Organic ★★★★★
Taste ★★★★
Price ££

⌨   *18 Great Marlborough Street, W1*
☎   *020 7486 6154*
✎   *www.lepainquotidien.com*
🚌   *Oxford Circus LU, 2min walk*
🕐   *Mon-Fri 7.30am-10pm, Sat 9am-10pm, Sun and holidays 9am-7pm*
🥕   *Vegan options*
☀   *Outside seating*
i   *Table service & Takeaway*

One of the larger Le Pain Quotidiens seating ninety people.
For food review see Le Pain Quotidien, Marylebone page (41).
Other branches at:
75 Marylebone High St, W1; 9 Young Street, W8; 201-203 King's Road, SW3;
Upper Festival Walk, SE1; 18 Great Marlborough St, W1; Exhibition Road,
SW7; St Pancras Station, NW1.

Leon
Mediterranean and English, fast food

Vegetarian ★★★
Organic ★★★
Taste ★★★
Price £

⌨   *275 Upper Regent Street, W1*
☎   *020 7495 1514*
✎   *www.leonrestaurants.co.uk*
🚌   *Oxford Circus LU, 2 min walk*
🕐   *Mon-Fri 8am-9pm, Sat 10am-7pm, Sun 11am-6pm*
🥕   *Vegan options*
🍼   *Child friendly*
i   *Takeaway and eat in*

This is one of the smaller branches of the Leon chain of fast food outlets
with three outside tables with a view of Regent Street.
For food review see Leon Spitalfields (page 222.)

Leon
Mediterranean and English, fast food

Vegetarian ★★★
Organic ★★★
Taste ★★★
Price £

🖃 *35 Great Marlborough Street, W1*
☎ *020 7437 5280*
✍ *www.leonrestaurants.co.uk*
🚌 *Oxford Circus LU, 5 min walk*
🕐 *Mon-Fri 8am-10pm, Sat 9am-10pm, Sun 10am-6pm*
🥕 *Vegan options*
👶 *Child friendly,*
☀ *outside tables with Carnaby Street view*
i *Takeaway and eat in*

Opened in July 2004, this natural fast food eaterie and takeaway has proved a great success. With organic leanings and several vegetarian Mediterranean mezzes, salads, hot and cold vegetarian breakfasts, fruit salad, smoothies and organic coffee, Leon has acquired a loyal following of veggie customers.
See Leon, Spitalfields for the food review (page 222).

The Living Room W1
Bar and Restaurant, International

Vegetarian ★★★★
Organic ★★★★
Taste ★★★
Price £££

🖃 *3-9 Heddon Street, Piccadilly, W1*
☎ *020 7292 0570*
✍ *www.thelivingroom.co.uk*
🚌 *Piccadilly LU 5 min walk*
🕐 *Mon-Sat 10am-1am, Sunday 11am-12midnight*
👶 *Childrens menu available*
🎵 *Live music Tue-Sat 8.30-11pm*

For a Central West End venue with vibrant live music and fun quality vegetarian choices, the Living Room W1 is hard to beat. Located just off Regent Street, it has a contemporary décor styled with a colonial twist, there's a great night vibe here as the informal dining tables fill up on the ground floor and the seventeen metre bar at the back gets busy. There is a Georgian-styled staircase leading up to a more formal dining area upstairs that has an open kitchen and gallery for perusing the swaggering clientele in the bar below. The focal point downstairs is the grand piano where some great live music can often be heard.
For food review see The Living Room's sister restaurant in Islington (page 112).

Maoz Old Compton St
Vegetarian falafel cafe

⌸ 43 Old Compton St, Soho, W1

☎ 020 7851 1586

✐ www.maozveg.com

🚌 Tottenham Court Road LU, 10 min walk

🕐 Mon-Thurs 11am-1am, Fri-Sat 11am-2am, Sun 11am-12midnight

☀ Outside tables

i Eat in or take-away.

Soho's falafel hangout. It's a small nondescript place with a mixed bunch crowded at the tables and grazing folk standing around. New initiates get cheap kicks with the £2.50 falafels, moving on to big bowls of Belgian chips for sharing. I joined the chickpea main liners with a £3.50 falafel with hummous in nutritious wholewheat pitta, a quality experience that left my taste buds satisfied. It comes already part filled with veg and then it's over to you to top up and experiment from a varied salad station of cous cous, coleslaw, carrot salad, tomato, pickled cucumber, chillis and sauces.

Mildreds
European, Modern

⌸ 45 Lexington St, W1

☎ 020 7494 1634

✐ www.mildreds.co.uk

🚌 Oxford Circus LU 10 min walk or Piccadilly LU

🕐 Mon-Sat 12noon-11pm

➶ Vegan and wheat-free choices

i Lunchtime takeaway service

A busy, inexpensive restaurant with the best vegetarian private dining room in London. Originally set in the heart of Soho's filmland, Mildreds is named after the waitress Mildred Pierce in the eponymous Joan Crawford film. Mildreds now resides at larger premises on Lexington Street but is as popular as ever. The no bookings policy means by 7pm you're likely to be in for a twenty minute wait for a table. Front of house is a small bar serving wines suitable for vegetarians, many of which are also fine for vegans. The house red has improved considerably.

At the back, the dining room is bright and airy, with modern abstract photos on the wall and pleasant background music. The punters are a gossipy crowd of 20–30 something media types in smart-casual dress, who like to dine with wine.

Mrs Merengos

Stir-fried Vegetables in sesame oil and teriyaki sauce is well cooked with garlic and ginger and comes with tasty organic brown rice. Burrito crammed with re-fried beans, corn and red pepper, topped with guacamole, tomato lime salsa and leaf salad goes down a treat too. Vegeburgers are firm favourites here and there are usually other mock-carnivore dishes such as tofu bolognaise. A completely organic salad with goat's cheese or organic tofu is available and the level of organic ingredients is increasing year by year.

Upstairs, the gracious private dining room with small old photos of naked women on the walls (well, it is Soho) makes a great venue for a party and Mildreds will also help plan your own special party menu. Mildreds have opened a more casual eaterie called Mrs Merengos just a few doors down with bench seating and a takeaway menu:

Mrs Merengos

⌨ *53 Lexington Street, W1*

☎ *020 7287 2544*

🕐 *Mon-Fri 8am-6pm, Sat 12-6pm*

Noura Central
Lebanese, classic

🖃 (Main Entrance) 122 Jermyn Street
    22 Regent Street, SW1

☎ 020 7839 2020

🖉 www.noura.co.uk

🚌 Piccadilly Circus LU (5 min walk)

🕓 Sun-Wed 11.30am-12.30am (last orders), Thu-Sat 11am-1am

♫ DJs playing live music Thu-Sat

🥕 Vegan options

🍼 Child friendly

i Takeaways available

i £2 cover charge per person applied after 7pm

Point your camel and your entourage to London's most luxurious Lebanese dining experience, serving remarkably delectable vegetarian choices. Skip the window tables at the front of house unless you're into street gazing or just stopping for a quick snack and head to the more relaxed and sumptuous tables at the back. The modern décor, gorgeous chandeliers and gracious service from suited Lebanese waiters is perfect for the banquet to follow. The live DJ gives a mix of Lebanese and UK sounds but is not obtrusive.

To be recommended is the Vegetarian Menu consisting of a platter of 10 mezzes, a main of Bamia, Loubieh, or Musaka with rice, a choice of Lebanese desserts, home-made ice cream or seasonal fruits and coffee for £33 per person (minimum 2 persons) – excellent value considering the quality of the food.

The feast begins with a plate of carrot, cauliflower, sliced giant tomatoes topped with herbs, a light mayo-style dipping sauce, olives, and cucumbers, all fresh and delicious. The cold mezzes arrive first and are amongst the best you'll ever have with a wonderful rich Hummus.

The Moutabel, a smoked aubergine dip, is pungently fragrant, whilst the Tabouleh is fresh and delicious. The main course of Foul Moudammus is a tasty dish of green fava beans simmered in tomatoes, garlic and olive oil and the Loubieh – green beans in olive oil and tomato with coriander – were both good.

Next to arrive are the hot mezzes including Warm Potato Kibbeh topped with a light sauce with sesame seed coated falafel balls, Saboussik (small cheese rissoles filled with chopped onions and parsley) and Fatayer (pastry parcels of baked spinach with onion and pine nut kernels) – all of which were delicious and well prepared.

The mains courses included Bamieh with Rice which is an Egyptian stew of okra pods, onions which tasted almost as good as the Msakaa of seasoned aubergine also with rice. Noura has a great selection of Lebanese wines, Araks and beers. The Ka Blanc de Blanc from the Bekaa Valley house wine (they have three) paired well with the mezzes whilst the stronger flavoured mains benefited from an enjoyable Chateau Ksari red.

Desserts are presented on a pretty display stand with five home-made ice-creams. The Lebanese pastry desserts (Baklava) were fresh and sweet and went perfect with a small cup of very good Lebanese coffee. Those looking for a great meal on a budget should try the lunchtime selection of six mezzes, main, desserts and coffee for only £18.

Noura Central is the flagship of a chain of restaurants, see the index for all the London restaurants.

Pizza Express Dean Street
Italian, fast food

Vegetarian ★★★
Taste ★★★
Price £

🖼 *10 Dean Street, W1*
☎ *0871 332 8587*
🖰 *www.pizzaexpress.com*
🚌 *Tottenham Court Road LU, 5 min walk*
🕐 *Mon-Sun 11.30am-Midnight*
🌶 *Vegan options*
i *Tableservice, licensed*

Very popular modern pizza venue in the bustling Soho district. The lunchtime atmosphere here is relaxed with an amiable mix of TV/film folk and West End shoppers. This branch is unique among the Pizza Express chain because of its regular a live Jazz events, but it shares the Pizza Express menu which has seven new vegetarian options.

Red Veg
American, modern mock carnivore

Vegetarian ★★★★★
Organic ★★
Taste ★★
Price £

🖼 *95 Dean Street, W1*
☎ *020 7437 3109*
🖰 *www.redveg.com*
🚌 *Tottenham Court Road LU, 5-10 min walk*
🕐 *Mon-Sat 12noon-9.30pm*
i *Counter service*

Modern veggie fast food take-out with a small eat-in space. With seating for just 12, Red Veg draws in some of the edgiest young characters in Soho yet also gets a peppering of straight dressed local workers.

Burger meal choices are depicted on the wall alongside pics of Lenin, Marx and Che Guevara. But don't be deceived, Red Veg is the real deal... it's Veg Society certified, GM-free and uses strictly vegetarian cheese.

The menu is simple with six burgers from which to choose. The Red Vegburger comes with montery jack cheese and homemade tomato relish whilst the Hickory Smoked Burger comes with a delicious barbecue-style sauce. Both efforts are big boys' portions filled with tomato, pickled cucumber and onion. Those trying the Vegwurst, vegetarian hotdog and the four types of organic falafels seemed to be enjoying themselves and all the food was served with tasty matchstick french fries. Red Veg has definitely established itself in Soho and now has a branch in London-by-the-sea – otherwise known as Brighton.

Sagar
South Indian, traditional

Vegetarian ★★★★★
Taste ★★★★
Price £

🏠 *17a Percy Street, W1*

☎ *020 7631 3319*

🖉 *www.sagarrestaurant.com*

🚌 *Goodge St LU, 3 min walk*

🕐 *Mon-Thurs 12noon-3pm, 5.30pm-10.45, Fri 12noon-3pm, 5.30pm-11pm,*
   Sat 12noon-6pm

🥕 *Vegan options*

🍼 *Child friendly*

☀ *Outside seating*

i *Booking advised at weekends*

Opened in September 2007, Sagar's second London restaurant employs the same highly successful menu formula as its sister branch in Hammersmith (for food review see page 186). The décor is a little more toned down, but in fine weather it has the added bonus of a couple of outdoor tables at the front. For such an attractively designed restaurant, Sagar is very good value and the lunch special for £4.95 is a real bargain.

Also at:

32 King Street, Hammersmith, W6, Tel: 020 8741 8563

27 York Street, Twickenham, Middlesex, Tel: 020 8744 3868

Soho Thai
Thai, classic

    27-28 St Anne's Court, W1

    020 7287 2000

    Tottenham Court Road LU (5 min walk)

    Mon-Sat 12noon-3pm, 6pm-11pm.

Vegetarian ★★★★★
Taste ★★★★
Price £

A very busy pre-and post-theatre Thai restaurant, despite it being one of
the less ornate of the Thai Square restaurant group. Based in the heart of
Soho it also attracts both locals and work people at lunch times.
For food review see the Trafalgar Square branch (page 31).

Tai Buffet
Thai, Chinese, Japanese

    3 Great Chapel Street, W1

    Tottenham Court Road LU, 5 min walk

    Daily 12noon-10pm

    Vegan options

    Outside seating for about 8

Vegetarian ★★★★★
Taste ★★★
Price £

For food review see Wai, Goodge St (Page 67).

V & M Express / V & M Dining

    10 & 11 Greek Street, W1

    www.vandmrestaurants.com

    Tottenham Court Road LU, 5 min walk

    Mon-Tue 11am-10pm, Wed 11am-10.30pm,
    Thurs 11am-11pm, Sat 12noon-11pm

Vegetarian ★★★★★
Price £

V & M Express, at number 10, offers cheap vegan take-away food such
as veggie burgers, veggie nuggets and fries. The food is as uncomplicated
as it sounds and they offer some tasty vegan shakes. For those with a little
more time on their hands, V & M Dining offers a sit down mock meat
menu which includes duck pancakes, pitta with salad and chicken and
some substantial noodle dishes. The food is tasty and good value – ideal
for those looking to refuel on a trip to Soho.

Tai Soho Restaurant

    41 Lexington Street, W1

    Oxford Circus LU, 10 min walk

    Daily 12noon-10pm

Vegetarian ★★★★★
Taste ★★★
Price £

For food review see Wai, Goodge St (Page 67).

Tibits
International, fast food vegetarian

Vegetarian ★★★★★
Organic ★★★★★
Taste ★★★★★
Price ££

🖾 *12-14 Heddon Street, W1*

☎ *020 7758 4110*

🖎 *www.tibits.co.uk*

🚎 *Oxford Circus or Piccadilly Circus LU, 5 min walk*

🕒 *Mon-Fri 8am-12midnight, Sat 8.30am-12midnight, Sun 10am-11pm*

i　*Self service & takeaway*

🌱 *Vegan options*

🍼 *Child friendly*

☀ *Outside seating*

i　*Bookings (parties of 8 or more)*

Tibits is an all day vegetarian restaurant, bar and takeaway restaurant that was first launched in Zurich in 2000. It is the work of three brothers in association with Hiltl, Europe's first vegetarian restaurant founded in 1898.

The London branch is situated along the Heddon Street dining strip, just opposite Momo. It offers a relaxed and casual dining experience, characterised by their help-yourself boat shaped buffet station. It marks the company's first venture outside Switzerland – following their successful vegetarian formula of having over thirty homemade creations with a choice of hot snacks and dips with all dishes priced by weight. There's also a soup of the day with a choice of organic bread roll and a selection of homemade sandwiches made throughout the day with crusty bread.

The cuisine is about 80% vegan and is international with an Indian touch and some typically English classics available. Early risers can enjoy their organic breakfast buffet, while healthy smoothies, wines and cocktails can be drunk till very late at night. All the wines are vegetarian and from small vineyards and a locally produced organic lager is available. All the dairy, tofu and most pastries are organic and there is a strong commitment to introduce even more organic produce.

VitaOrganic
Asian, classic, organic

Vegetarian ★★★★★
Organic ★★★★★
Taste ★★★★★
Price ££

🖼 *74 Wardour Street, W1*
☎ *020 7734 8986*
✍ *www.vitaorganic.co.uk*
🚌 *Leicester Square LU or Tottenham Court Road LU,*
🕐 *Mon-Sat 12noon-10.30pm, Sun 1pm-8pm*
🥕 *Vegan options*
🍼 *Child friendly*
i Eat-in & Takeaway service

A real contender for the best veggie and organic restaurant, café and juice bar in London and the restaurant with greatest improvement in taste since the last edition. Health-orientated Asian vegan, Vita Organic is a raw food paradise at affordable prices.

VitaOrganic opened in 2001 on Finchley Road but now resides in Soho, where it has enjoyed much greater success. The large window frontage reveals an interior of coloured lanterns, bamboo on the walls, and some reasonable wooden seating. There are just ten tables and the place is nearly always crowded. As a lunchtime venue, it's well suited for a casual chow down. In the evenings, when candlelit, the place takes on an altogether more mellow atmosphere. On the night I visited the place was packed by 8.30 and those that hadn't pre-booked were being turfed out of reserved seats.

With an attractive buffet and an extensive and well explained menu, there's definitely something for everyone. The Buffet Meal Deal isn't all-you-can-eat, but calculated by volume working out at £3.50–£8.50 with a £1 discount at lunchtime. I had a mixed plate of steamed Vegetable Moussaka, Black Bean stew, Cauliflower in 'cream' substitute sauce, Shitake Mushroom Stew, some multi-grains of brown quinoa, millet, red and white rice and Scrambled Tofu – all of which was excellent and came with carrot, green pea and five spices. From the menu the Warm Thai green curry is mild in flavour and comes with chunky vegetables. The Cold salad of beetroot, apple, ginger, red cabbage and coriander all tasted first-rate and the buckwheat salad was good too.

The temperature of dishes is variable but this is intentional as VitaOrganic cooks to keep the food proteins intact and preserve vital vitamins and essential fatty acids. The restaurant is 98% organic and is in the process of going through Soil Association Certification. The very few non-organic items are marked on the menu.

Specialities at VitaOrganic include their own recipe 'Live-food' for £5.80 a dish. Nothing is cooked above 40 degrees Fahrenheit to produce an 'enzyme-rich' menu. The Live Sprouted Buckweat Pizza with sun dried tomato and basil comes up as a mini pizza with 'seed cheese' made from flax, sesame, pumpkin and sunflower. It was a real treat, laden with lots of good flavours.

At VitaOrganic no dough is used, so really novel dishes are created. Golden Flaxeed Crisp with guacamole on lettuce comes as two portions and is delicious and great for splitting. Grain-free Yellow Squash Noodles with a coconut curry arrives as a neat cylinder and has a very hot aftertaste. On the Living Salads menu, the favourite is Green Veg Lasagne with pesto that contains courgette, fennel, seaweed and onion. I'm not a great seaweed fan, but this was well crafted in layers and tasted as good as it looked. Alternatives to other traditional dishes abound including a cheeseless cheesecake dessert that is very popular.

The Juices here are made without added sugar and I can recommend the Golden Pina Colada made with pineapple, soya and coconut yoghurt. The Pink Mermaid Tonic – a lassi of pear, strawberry, raspberry and rosewater – tastes good for £3.80.

The over enthusiastic health claims on some of the juices are the only thing about this small restaurant that I found worthy of criticism. VitaOrganic, under the enthusiastic management of chef Phong, continues to innovate, making this a great place to enjoy new and healthy taste sensations.

Veg

🖼 *33 Old Compton Street, W1*
🚌 *Leicester Square LU, 10 min walk*
🕐 *Mon-Thurs 12noon-10pm, Fri-Sat 12noon-11pm*
   Sun 12.30pm-10pm
🥕 *Vegan Menu*
🍼 *Child friendly*
i *Eat in (buffet service) and Takeaway*
For food review see Wai, Goodge St (below)

Vegetarian ★★★★★
Taste ★★★
Price £

Veg

🖼 *39 Great Windmill Street, W1*
🚌 *Piccadilly LU, 5 min walk*
🕐 *Mon-Thurs 12noon-10pm, Fri-Sun 12noon-11pm*
🥕 *Vegan Menu*
🍼 *Child friendly*
i *Eat in (buffet service) and Takeaway*
For food review see Wai, Goodge St (below)

Vegetarian ★★★★★
Taste ★★★
Price £

Wai

🖼 *32 Goodge St, W1*
🚌 *Goodge St LU, 2 min walk*
🕐 *Mon-Thurs 12noon-10pm, Fri-Sun 12noon-11pm*
🥕 *Vegan Menu*
🍼 *Child friendly*
i *Eat in (buffet service) and Takeaway*

Vegetarian ★★★★★
Taste ★★★
Price £

Bargain £5.50 all-you-can-eat vegan Thai/Chinese cuisine that goes up to £6.50 after 5pm and on Sundays. They offer a marvellous Takeout Box deal for only £3. Opened early 2003 the place is a modern oriental café with eight tables and plenty of options at the hot and cold buffet.

Moderately busy at 8pm, I re-filled my plate several times with a selection of good black bean soya chicken, chow mein, special fried rice, ginger tofu and very reasonable spicy potato. Of particular note was the sweet and sour sauce with luscious pineapple chunks and the small spring rolls were yummy. On the cold section, worth a whirl is the crispy aromatic veg duck, cucumber, plum sauce and roll-up pancake, as well as Northern Style carrot and mushroom dim sum, mushroom and cucumber salad, seaweed and crackers. Staff are friendly, attentive, keep the place immaculately clean, but don't speak much English. For a healthy bargain meal in the centre of town, this place is great value.

Restaurants

Southwark & Waterloo

This district is home to Borough Market, London's finest gourmet food market. Here you can find organic and vegetarian speciality foods and juices at The Veggie Table and Total Organics, falafels at Arabica, tarts, cakes and pastries at Artisan Foods, fab tomatoes at Isle of Wight Tomatoes and more general organic fruit and veg at Only Organic. Other culinary treats in the area include Coopers and branches of Leon and Le Pain Quotidien.

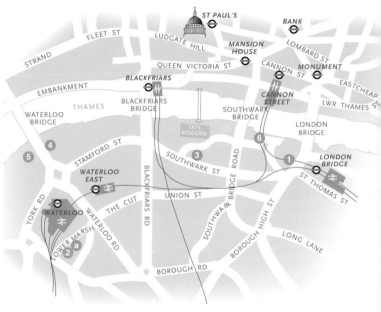

Restaurants
1) Borough Market p.69
2) Coopers p.70
3) Leon Bankside p.71
4) Le Pain Quotidien p.72
5) Wagamama- Royal Festival Hall p.71
6) Wagamama-Clink p.71

Shops
a) Coopers p.249

Borough Market

⌨ *8 Southwark Street, SE1*
🖋 *www.boroughmarket.org.uk*
🚇 *London Bridge BR/LU, 5 min walk*
🕐 *Thur 11am-5pm, Fri 12pm-6pm, Sat 9am-4pm*

This gourmet food retail market is well worth a visit, offering high quality vegetarian and organic produce and prepared foods.

Total Organics, one of the largest operators in Borough Market, is all organic and vegetarian with as much produce as possible being UK sourced. At the front they sell an organic vegetarian salad box for £4.50. I chose a bean and chickpea salad with sliced cucumber in mint sauce, tomato, lettuce and rice. It was quite filling and fresh, but over chilled to diminish some of the flavour. Their 'Borough' omelettes are very tempting for £2.50 per slice. Further inside, Total Organics is a juice bar designed like a pub bar that does brisk trade in wheat grass shots, super food juices and has a few high stools for customers. Owner Gary Green says, 'We opened up at Borough Market in 2000, when it was all foods for carnivores. We wanted to give a veggie option. We just started with a stall and it just grew and grew. Borough Market is now so popular it's here on Thursdays as well. The customers who come to us don't like supermarkets – they want to come and see what they are eating'. Total Organics is a family run business and all of them are committed vegetarians. **The Veggie Table** serves three veggie organic burgers made from twelve different vegetables without soya or 'pretend meat' products. The most popular is the Haloumi Burger that's made with vegetarian rennet, carrot, courgette, coriander and mint. The Quinoa Superstar is frequently bought to take home and then warmed up. Although the burgers are small they're quite filling. Coming two in a box for £3.80 they're great for vegetarian kids. Eight salads are available as is a lentil curry. The Veggie Table is also at Whitecross St Market EC1 on Thursday and Friday (11am-4pm), Broadway Market E8 on Saturdays (9am-5pm) and The Oval Farmers Market, SE11 on Saturdays (10am-3pm).

Dark Sugars is a vegetarian cakes stall with some tempting creations – although it is not organic. They also sell at Notting Hill Market on Sundays. **Isle of Wight Tomatoes** is a specialist fruit stall with organic large plums and Aranca tomatoes. They are working towards getting all their tomatoes organically certified.

Amazing looking tarts and quiches are at **Artisan Foods** that is 90% vegetarian. They also have a good selection of vegetarian cakes. **Neal's Yard Dairy** have a shop near the market and has good selections of top notch cheese suitable for vegetarians. Those unsuitable are clearly labelled as having animal rennet. **Arabica** serves organic falafels and gets very busy with takeaways. Also, in Borough Market is biodynamic vegetable specialist **Fern Verrow Vegetables**. It is certified biodynamic and organic and is run by a family with a smallholding on the Welsh border. More recently, Harriet Booth and her husband Paul have started their stall, **Only Organics**, selling exclusively organic fruit and veg. **Flour Power City,** artisan bakers, do a fabulous tasting wholemeal bread. This London based company offers breads that are certified by the Organic Food Federation (OFF). They also supply lots of London's wholefood stores and have stalls at many London Farmer's Markets.

Coopers
Vegetarian café, international

🏠 *17 Lower Marsh, Waterloo, SE1*

☎ *020 7261 9314*

🚇 *Lambeth North (5min walk)*
Waterloo LU & BR, (5 min walk)

🕐 *Mon-Thurs 8.30am-4.30pm, Fri 8.30am-4pm,*

🥕 *Vegan options*

☀ *Outside seating*

i *Eat-in (counter service) & Takeaway*

Vegetarian ★★★★★
Organic ★★★
Taste ★★★
Price £

This friendly, family run neighbourhood snack café has been serving wholesome veggie food at Lower Marsh for over twenty five years and has now improved it's food and café facilities. The market that was once a feature of the street is not up to much these days and most customers are lunchtime Waterloo Station commuters and mostly office staff.

Coopers now seats 26 inside with a further 30 seats available in a good outside setting. The various soups on offer include the Spicy Oriental, and the tangy Apricot and Lentil, both served with an olive roll and a bargain for £3.80. Baked tortilla, various quiches, savoury tarts, pizzas and hummus are freshly made on the premises and there's plenty of choices for people with strict diets. One of the improvements is that much of the pre-packed snacks, such as the spring rolls, are no longer stocked; instead there's vegetarian sushi and Hoxton Beach's organic falafel wrap with spicy aubergine. The sandwich choice is good too with Organic Tomato and Feta Focaccia with veggie ham and free range egg and Organic White Baguette with mozzarella, tomato and pesto. The Coffee is also organic and they offer Lavender Rose and Lavender Orange cakes, croissants and very good scones,

For a review of the shop see page 249.

Leon Bankside
Mediterranean and English, fast food

Vegetarian ★★★
Organic ★★★
Taste ★★★
Price £

🏠 7 Canvey Street, The Blue Fin Building, SE1

☎ 020 7620 0035

✎ www.leosrestaurant.co.uk

🚌 Southwark LU, 5 min walk

🕐 Mon-Fri 7.30am-10pm, Sat 10am-9.30pm, Sun 10am-7pm

🥕 Vegan options

🍼 Child friendly

i Takeaway and eat in

Situated just behind Tate Modern and a short distance from the Globe.
For food review see Leon, Spitalfields (page 222).

Le Pain Quotidien
French, classic

Vegetarian ★★★★★
Organic ★★★★
Taste ★★★★
Price ££

🏠 Units 12&13, Upper Festival Walk
Belvedere Road, Royal Festival Hall
South Bank, SE1

☎ 020 7486 6154

✎ www.lepainquotidien.com

🚌 Waterloo LU, 5min walk

🕐 Mon-Fri 7.30am-11pm, Sat 9am 11pm, Sun and holdays 9am-10pm

🥕 Vegan options

i Table service & Takeaway

Great venue for the Festival Hall or a pit stop for a leisurely Bankside
walk. This place is very busy at weekends in the Summer.
For food review see Le Pain Quotidien, Marylebone (page 41).
Other branches at:
75 Marylebone High St W1; 9 Young Street W8; 201-203 King's Road SW3;
Upper Festival Walk, SE1; 18 Great Marlborough St, W1; Exhibition Road
SW7; St Pancras Station, NW1.

Wagamama
Japanese, modern

🏠 1 Clink Street, SE1

☎ 020 7403 3659

✎ www.wagamama.com

For food review see Wagamama, Wigmore Street (page 48).
Other branches at
Royal Festival Hall, SE1, Tel: 020 7021 0877

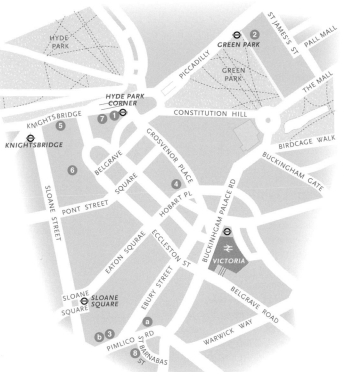

Restaurants

1) Apsley's at The Lanesborough p.73
2) Le Caprice p.75
3) Daylesford Pimlico p.76
4) Noura Belgravia p.79
5) Noura Knightsbridge p.79
6) Ottolenghi Belgravia p.79
7) Pizza on the Park p.80
8) Roussillon p.80

Shops

a) Pimlico Farmers' Market p.287
b) Daylesford Pimlico p.263

Hyde Park Corner, Victoria & Pimlico

With cash to splash in the heart of Central London, Roussillon, Nahm, Le Caprice and The Lanesborough are amongst four of the best restaurants in the capital. Next door to the Lanesborough, there's Pizza on the Park for veggie pizzas. For stylish but casual organic lunching and shopping there's Daylesford Pimlico and an excellent vegetarian Mediterranean at Noura. Another excellent veggie culinary experience can be found at the City Inn Hotel, home to the City Café, where there's veggie gastronomic art on a plate – well it is only a few yards from Tate Britain!

Apsley's at The Lanesborough
Italian, classic

⌨ *1 Lanesborough Place , Hyde Park Corner, SW1*
☎ *020 7259 5599*
✎ *www.lanesborough.com*
🚇 *Hyde Park Corner LU,*
🕐 *Daily 12noon-12midnight*
🥕 *Vegan options*
i *Booking highly recommended*

Vegetarian ★★★
Organic ★★★
Taste ★★★★★
Price *££££*

One of the classiest and romantic settings in London, serving exceptional Italian vegetarian food. Arrive by car at this five star Hotel's entrance and let the head porter valet park it for you. Inside, an opulent hallway leads to the Conservatory, a mouthwatering art deco candle-lit chinoiserie restaurant, with several hideaway dining sections for more private dining. The atmosphere is relaxing with celebratory couples in smart casual wear and some parties a little bit more formal.

Although the executive chef for the whole of the Lanesborough is Paul Gayler, Apsley's head chef is Nick Bell, whose prestigious pedigree includes Zafferano and Cecconi's and who has created an impressive new menu with perhaps the most delicious pasta dishes in London. Apsley's new menu still has a great many dishes suitable for vegetarians. Altogether there are two antipasti, two soups, three main courses and seven desserts from which to choose and many of the non-veggie dishes can be converted. Each day Bell creates an off the menu vegetarian special available on request. Telling your waiter on arrival that you are vegetarian is advisable as they can offer further options according to seasonal availability of ingredients.

Complimentary breads, with herbed and plain olive oils and the balsamic vinegar are delicious. The Antipasti of tomato and buffalo mozzarella salad is substantial, with bags of flavour, whilst the Artichoke salad is much lighter with pecorino cheese and broad beans, garnished with sweet potato peel and rocket. The Sardinian vegetable broth with red pesto as a primi dish is a triumph, while the Chilled Courgette and basil soup is quite refreshing although the salted ricotta a little difficult to negotiate. For secondi dishes, the pappardelle with broad beans and rocket is to be recommended. All the pasta here is made fresh on the premises. I can also vouch for the off the menu daily special of warm Ricotta parcels with asparagus – a labour intensive dish made with semolina, egg yolk and extra virgin olive oil. Gnocci at the Lanesborough has always been a firm favourite and the Potato and Ricotta Gnocci is no exception and beautifully flavoured. The recommended dessert is the floating summer prosecco fruits with apricot sorbet. Also a treat is the banana semi freddo with toffee sauce which is a delicious banana mousse affair. Apsley's are building a fine organic wine list, and their organic vegetarian Chardonnay Waterford Stellenbosch paired well with all our dishes. Some petit fours and a special limoncello completed a wonderful meal. With attentive but friendly service, Apsley's and The Lanesborough are a world class vegetarian venue. An Italian regional lunchtime set menu is also available at £24 for three courses.

Breakfast at the Lanesborough

Daily 7am-11.30am

The Lanesborough Hotel is notable for providing vegetarians a top class service 24/7 and it's breakfast and room service menu deserve special mention, showing that this is an excellent venue for the discerning vegetarian traveller.

Breakfast is served at a leisurely pace. The freshly squeezed passion juice is very good and refilled as you wish, as is the exceptionally good Columbian coffee. The Lanesborough Vegetarian Breakfast is carefully made with two mild flavoured lentil cookies that look like slices of veggie sausage, grilled tomatoes, a couple of eggs, small mushrooms and a wonderful flavoured large hash brown. It's pleasantly filling and one of the best vegetarian breakfasts in London. Lemon ricotta pancakes with seasonal berries is also a great choice and is delicately cheesy with good lemon vibes. For those with larger appetites, the bakery basket has freshly made breads and pastries and top notch marmalade and honey. Budget for about £27 per person, service included. For a review of the hotel rooms see page 304.

Le Caprice
Fast Food, Italian

Arlington House, Arlington Street, SW1

Vegetarian ★★★
Taste ★★★★
Price ££££

- 020 7629 2239
- *www.le-caprice.co.uk*
- *Green Park LU, 3 min walk*
- *Mon-Sat 12noon-3pm, 5.30pm-12midnight, Sunday 12noon-11pm*
- *Vegan options*

A venerable and formal restaurant, adored by the stars, the rich and the famous. Beautifully mirrored and with a sumptuous bar and dining area, this is a place to relax extravagantly, soak up the pleasurable atmosphere and enjoy the impeccable service. Ask for the Vegan and Vegetarian menu that has at least six vegetarian starters and eight mains – all of high quality with the risotto and linguines being particularly memorable. Le Caprice has a following who return again and again and is part of the same group as the Rivington Grill (see page 94).

City Café
British, Modern

Vegetarian ★★★★★
Taste ★★★★
Price £££

- *City Inn Westminster, 30 John Islip Street, S*
- 020 7932 4600
- *www.citycafe.co.uk*
- *Pimlico or Westminster LU, 10 min walk*
- *Breakfast: Mon-Fri 6.30am-10am, Sat 7am-11am, Sun 7am-11am*
  Lunch: Mon-Fri 12 noon-3pm, Sat-Sun 1pm-3pm
  Dinner: Daily 5.30pm-10.30pm
- *Child-friendly*
- *Outside seating*

Ultramodern hotel with a new luxuriously refurbished restaurant serving a complete vegetarian menu and well worth visiting after the Tate. Opened in September 2003, it's located off the Embankment at the back of the Tate Britain. Art lovers come in along the special 'Side Street' into the restaurant or from the main entrance.

Al fresco diners spill out onto 'Side Street', the capital's first ever street conceived as a work of art by acclaimed artist, Susanna Heron. Side Street is 80 metres long and seven metres high and features monumental five metre-high slate engravings, the result of 12 months carving in Heron's studio. A vast textured, mirrored wall reflects light and views from beyond the street.

The restaurant is big and decorated in grey-blues and beiges with chandeliers constructed for cookery whisks – a touch of light culinary humour! It is now a popular destination for hotel non-residents and the evenings are by far the busiest time.

The Vegetarian Garden Menu conceived by Bank executive chef Peter Lloyd is three starters, three mains, seven desserts with top quality complimentary breads to start. Salad Caprice of sliced tomatoes and buffalo mozzarella with rocket and cress is a well presented appetiser. Artichoke-based dishes have always been a forte of the City Café and the Artichoke Florentine main will not disappoint.

Chocolate desserts have always been a particularly strong suit here and the Valhorona Chocolate, with it's chocolate tear drop, chocolate mille-feuille and panacotta, is heaven on a plate. The British Strawberry Short Cake with vanilla ice cream was wonderful too

For breakfast, there's soya based vegetable sausages, various cereals, organic baked beans and organic free range eggs. If you fancy something sweeter to start the day then sample the fresh fruit bowls, nuts and seeds, crumpets or French toast.

Daylesford Pimlico
International, modern

| Vegetarian ★★★ |
| Organic ★★★★★ |
| Taste ★★★★★ |
| Price ££££ |

- 🖃 *44b Pimlico Road, SW1*
- ☎ *020 7259 4900*
- ✐ *www.daylesfordorganic.com*
- 🚇 *Sloane Square LU, 4 min walk*
- 🕐 *Mon-Sat 8am-7pm, Sun 10am-4pm*
- 🥕 *Vegan options*
- 👶 *Child-friendly*
- ☀ *Outside seating*

One of the biggest names in English organic foods, while also catering for carnivors, has some of the best vegetarian dishes in London. Their café in Kingham, Gloucestershire is a former winner of the Soil Association Organic Restaurant of the Year Award and this smart London off shoot offers the same quality and attention to detail.

The long marble communal table on the ground floor seats twenty with everybody polite and content with the arrangement. At the front window the ten bar stalls were also popular with another double communal table downstairs in the wineshop where people were discussing business and socialising. The décor is grey and white, the music jazz and classical.

It's best to tell a member of staff that you are a vegetarian and they will guide you through the short menu of veggie choices and importantly explain ways that other dishes can be adapted. Some regulars opt for two veggie starters as their main, which is also a good idea.

Begin with the freshly baked Daylesford bread from Gloucestershire – the Seven Seeds and the Sourdough with olive oil are both outstanding. There are three veggie starters of which the delicious Beetroot Soup is an unusual golden-coloured beetroot topped with liquidised red beetroot. The Thai-styled Mango Spring Rolls adapted to vegetarian proved tasty and the main of Vegetarian cheese and herb omelette (£9.95) had great consistency with a superb cheese flavour. Mains often come as works of art. The Marinated Cauliflower with curry oil and red grapes (£9.95) looked beautiful. Arriving on a black wooden slab it was white with raw puree of cauliflower. The sweet wine jelly was excluded as it was non-vegetarian. The dish tasted as good as it looked.

Four of the desserts are vegetarian and the Daylesford apple and plum crumble (£4.95) is full of fruit and of very good taste. The Chocolate Fondant with vanilla ice cream is also good quality.

There are a few organic wines including a celebratory pink Prosecco, an excellent biodynamic wine and a Léoube which is less expensive and from their own estate in Provence. A full selection of Luscomb organic soft drinks is available and Monmouth Coffee and organic soya milk.

Service is good but can run a bit slow when extremely busy. They are quite amenable about you choosing vegetarian food options from the shop that can be served at table.

For casual lunching, freshness of organic produce and beautiful presentation of dishes, Daylesford Pimlico is a remarkable experience.
For Daylesford Pimlico's organic shop review see page (263).

Nahm
Thai, modern

🖼 *The Halkin Hotel, Halkin Street, SW1*

☎ *020 7333 1234*

🚌 *Hyde Park Corner LU, 10 min walk*

🕐 *Lunch: Mon-Fri 12-2.30pm, Dinner: Mon-Sat 7pm-11pm,*
Sun 7pm-10pm

🥕 *Vegan options*

Vegetarian ★★★★★
Organic ★★★
Taste ★★★★★
Price ££££

The Halkin is one of London's leading boutique hotels and Nahm, its top class Thai restaurant, offers exemplary vegetarian dining. Forget notions of a traditional Thai dining room lavished with gilded buddhas and artefacts, at Nahm, the look is classy modern chic with gleaming gold and russet walls, gold columns and teak tables. Overall, the place exudes style – even the staff wear Armani.

Opened in 2001, Nahm was the first Thai restaurant in Europe to get a Michelin Star. Australian chef, David Thompson, prepares all the dishes freshly so let them know that you are vegetarian or vegan and the staff will put together a fantastic meal according to your preference. Although there are only a few vegetarian choices on the menu, all the dishes can be converted to vegetarian. At lunchtime, there's a set menu for £26 with a tasting menu for £55 in the evenings. Vegetarian breakfasts of a high standard are available, although these are prepared in the Halkin Hotel itself.

The meal begins with four superb Pineapple and mandarin canapés topped with sugar beet and coriander. Next, a well presented tray of wafers with a green curry sauce and lychees wrapped with ginger. All this was a prelude to the main event of a fantastic Smokey Red Curry, rich in complex flavours of galangal, mace and tofu which gave the dish a 'meaty' consistency. Served simultaneously is a cucumber and coriander salad, that works well with the curry. The Starfruit, red chilli and red onion salad is absolutely excellent and the stir fry of cornichons, spring onion and asparagus was very good too. The Spicy Coconut Soup flavoured with lemongrass, coconut slices, mushroom and green chilli was a accompaniment to the main meal. The meal ends with Banana Dessert grilled with sticky rice and a small bowl of lychees.

Much of the food is sourced directly from Thailand being delivered in one and half days from Bankok. About 40% of the menu is organic and they are striving to increase the use of organic ingredients.

Noura Belgravia
Lebanese, classic

Vegetarian ★★★★
Taste ★★★★★
Price ££££

🖼 16 Hobart Place, Belgravia, SW1
☎ 020 7235 9444
🖥 www.noura.co.uk
🚌 Hyde Park or Victora LU (10 min walk)
🕒 Sun-Wed: 11.30am-12midnight, Thu-Sat: 11am-12night
🥕 Vegan options
☖ Child friendly
i Takeaways also available

Sleek and modern, at lunchtimes this Noura offers a brasserie for informal dining, as well as the traditionally restaurant menu.
For food review see Noura Central (page 59).

Noura Knightsbridge
Lebanese, classic

Vegetarian ★★★★
Taste ★★★★★
Price ££££

🖼 12 William Street, Knightsbridge, SW1
☎ 020 7235 9444
🖥 www.noura.co.uk
🚌 Knightsbridge LU (3min walk)
🕒 Mon-Sun: 07.30am-12.00am (last orders)
🥕 Vegan options
☖ Child friendly
☀ Outside seating

Popular al fresco café with some inside tables and a terrific delicatessen.
For food review see Noura Central (page 59).

Ottolenghi Belgravia
International, modern

Vegetarian ★★★★
Taste ★★★★★
Price ££££

🖼 13 Motcombe Street, Belgravia, SW1
☎ 020 7823 2707
🖥 www.ottolenghi.co.uk
🚌 Knightsbridge LU, 10 min walk
🕒 Mon-Fri 8am-8pm, Sat 8am-7pm Sun 9am-6pm
🥕 Vegan options
i Eat-in & takeaway

Opened in Spring 2008, this is similar to their highly successful pattisserie and shop in Notting Hill. It has a small communal table at the back, ideal for a delicious quick bite.
For food review see Ottolenghi Notting Hill (page 181).

Pizza on the Park
Fast Food, Italian

Vegetarian ★★★
Taste ★★★
Price £

⊞ 11 Knightsbridge, SW1
☎ 020 7235 7825
⌥ www.pizzaonthepark.co.uk
🚌 Hyde Park Corner LU exit 4, 5 min walk
🕐 Mon-Sat 11.30am-10.45pm, Sun 12noon-9.45pm

This is a celebrated pizza venue that was formerly known for its live jazz music, but has abandoned this side of its business to concentrate on the whole pizza and pasta thing. It's a pity for those that like Jazz, but the pizzas are still very good with plenty of veggie options.

In addition to a classic pizza menu there's vegetarian canneloni, mushroom raviolia and a good choice of salads. The Pesto Bufalita is a very interesting veggie pizza of buffalo mozzarella and beef tomatoes that are added after cooking and seasoned with garlic, basil leaves and rocket. The pizzas here are good and they will cater for special requests such as a cheeseless vegetarian pizza asked for by a friend of mine.

Roussillon
French, modern

Vegetarian ★★★★
Taste ★★★★★
Price £££££

⊞ 16 St Barnabas Street, SW1
☎ 020 7730 5550
⌥ www.roussillon.co.uk
🚌 Sloane Square LU, 5 min walk
🕐 Lunch: Mon-Fri 12noon-2.30pm, Dinner: Mon-Sat 6.30pm-10.30pm
🍼 Children-friendly

An amazing vegetarian tasting menu from chef Alexis Gauthier who worked with Alain Ducasse in Monte Carlo. Alexis has Michelin star cred and creates dazzlingly inventive dishes. Set in suave Pimlico, down a short residential side-turning, its premises are a converted pub – although you would never guess it once inside. Two adjoining rooms on ground level are cool and crisp and delight the the eye with spaciously arranged tables, smart Guy Degrenne cutlery, immaculate white tablecloths, abstract paintings and lush flower arrangements. Rousillon is now becoming a magnet for a younger more exuberant dining set than in former years. Downstairs is a private dining room with its own bar and lounge for parties up to 26.

The Menu Légumes is eight courses with a lacto-ovo vegetarian focus, but easily adaptable for non–egg eaters. It begins with complimentary warm Goat's Cheese Canapés, Chick Pea Beignets with dark mustard sauce and throughout the meal eight fabulous breads are available, of which the Sundried Tomato and Olive Breads are highly recommended. Light Cauliflower and Truffle Cream, Truffle Royale and Deep Fried Leek tastes as great as it sounds. Better was yet to come with a gorgeous warm Lettuce and Tomato Tempura, Sage with Quails Eggs and incredibly good black olives, perfectly matched with a 2006 Voignier, Vin de Pays des Coteaux de l'Ardèche. The small Winter Truffle & Risotto was good quality and was not at all heavy on the stomach and was matched well with a 2002 Grenache Blanc. The Green Bean and Almonds is deliciously crisp and crunchy and a great prelude to the attractive and delicious Green Ricotta Gnocci that comes with beetroot, sprouting purple broccoli and parsley jus garnished with beetroot shavings.

At lunchtimes, some time-poor diners belt through the courses in a single hour, but this food is worth taking time to enjoy. Whilst there is a cheese course none is vegetarian. The first dessert course, a small vegetarian Fourme D'Ambert Soufflé was perfect. This was followed by a wonderful Rhubarb Compote accompanied by an absolutely superb Brioche Pain Perdu with a dab of Maple Ice Cream. A final dessert of Tarte Tartin with Green Apple Sorbet leaves you completely satisfied. The meal at £60 plus 12.5% service is expensive but bearing in mind the intensive labour and skill involved it is very good value.

Roussillon is proud of its wine. The wine tasting menu is picked by the talented sommelier, Roberto Della Pieta. Eight small glasses from the 400 bin selection matches each course and is a veritable adventure. Of particular note was the 2006 Sauvignon Blanc, Côtes du Duras – a fab tasting organic wine from South West France. Regrettably there are no veggie wines but there are several organic champagnes, wines and a few biodynamics. The wine tasting menu is £42 and highly recommended, although wines can be bought individually by the glass. A special mention is given to Roberto's outstanding service and wine matching explanations.

During the Chelsea Flower Show in May there is the Special Flower Menu. Warm Fuschia and tofu sandwich with lovage and tomato dressing, Chrysanthenum Soufflé with a light infusion of it's leaves, are just a few examples. Definitely a place to revisit time and again.

City of London

The most historical setting in London for a vegetarian eaterie and hugely popular with city workers is The Place Below in a real Norman Crypt! Maybe they should build a small monument for Futures! The pure vegetarian takeout food here deserves some sort of accolade. The newest additions to this part of town are of a remarkably high standard with visually thrilling vegetarian food at Vanilla Black, and remarkable organic vegan food and drink at Saf Restaurant and Bar just a short ride away from Liverpool Street. For splendid speciality organic afternoon teas seek out Tea which is near St Pauls.

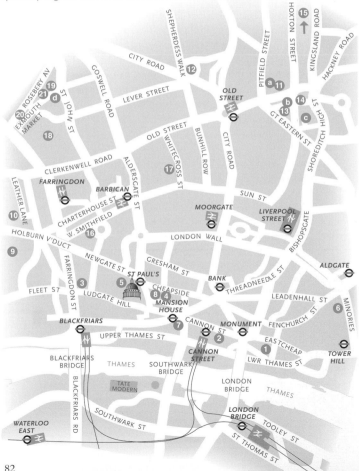

Futures!
International, classic

⌨ 8 Botolph Alley, Eastcheap, EC3
☎ 020 7623 4529
🚇 Monument LU, 1 min walk
🕐 Breakfast: Mon-Fri 8am-10am, Lunch: Mon-Fri 11.30am-3pm
🥕 Vegan options available
i Counter service, Takeaway only

Vegetarian ★★★★★
Taste ★★★★
Price £

The tiniest takeout in town for pure vegetarians and, considering the price, the food served here is remarkable. Found down a City back alley, the 12.30pm lunch-rush manifests itself as a queue of twelve office workers. The all-vegetarian take-out menu that changes daily. and has an established following. Tourists visiting the nearby Monument should try and include a visit here for breakfast or lunch.

The daily choice format is soup, hot pot, bake, savoury, quiche/pizza, four salads and desserts. Chilli Mexcaine, a vegetable chilli bake topped with tortilla crisps, is a sheer delight, substantial in size with lots of cauliflower, beans and other veg – a meal on its own and a bargain. The Thai Green Curry is splendid with oodles of butternut squash, courgette, green beans, coriander, lime and lemon grass on a bed of brown organic rice. Both these mains come in sturdy biodegradable cartons with the food at perfect temperature. The Apple and Blueberry Crumble sells well here, although there's also a scrummy looking fresh fruit salad. Delivery is free for orders over £15.

Best on the Breakfast Menu is the toast (three different breads are made on the premises) and Futures! own blend muesli. The service is slick and fast, making this a real veggie treat for those visiting the City.

Leon Cannon Street
Mediterranean and English, fast food

⌨ 86 Cannon Street, EC4
☎ 020 7623 9699
🖱 www.leonrestaurants.co.uk
🚇 Cannon St LU, 2 min walk
🕐 Mon-Fri 7.30am-9pm
🥕 Vegan options
🍼 Child friendly
i Takeaway and eat in

Vegetarian ★★★
Organic ★★★
Taste ★★★
Price £

See Leon Spitalfields for food review (page 222)

Leon Ludgate Circus
Mediterranean and English, fast food

Vegetarian ★★★
Organic ★★★
Taste ★★★
Price £

- 🖼 12 Ludgate Circus, EC4
- ☎ 020 7489 1580
- 🖱 www.leonrestaurants.co.uk
- 🚇 Blackfriars LU, 5 min walk
- 🕓 Mon-Fri 8am-11pm
- 🥕 Vegan options
- 🍼 Child friendly
- i Takeaway and eat in

One of the larger Leon's that also serves cocktails.
See Leon Spitalfields for food review (page 222)

The Place Below
International, classic

Vegetarian ★★★★★
Taste ★★★
Price £

- 🖼 St. Mary-le-Bow Church, Cheapside,, EC2
- ☎ 020 7329 0789
- 🖱 www.theplacebelow.co.uk
- 🚇 St Pauls LU, 3 min walk
- 🕓 Mon-Fri 7.30am-3pm, Lunch served 11.30am-2.30pm
- ☀ Outside tables in courtyard
- i Counter service, eat in, eat out, takeaway
  Vegetarian catering service available

The Place Below

London's most historic venue for vegetarian food is deep down in a voluminous Norman crypt. This is a Christopher Wren Church with beautiful stained glass windows and it's almost surreal to see smart city guys in shirts and ties eating their meals off serving trays in this most unusual of city eateries. Established since 1990, The Place Below is run by Crypt Restaurants, a private firm that supports some of the church's projects.

It's a friendly, well run sort of place with the staff knowing many of the customers by name. At lunchtime the place is thronged with queuing diners. First timers should take the main church entrance and stairs downwards, otherwise you'll be walking around the church perimeter forever (you can tell I've done it!).

Once in, on the right is a coffee and cake counter serving sandwiches and focaccia Brie de Meaux, Neal's Yard Mature Cheddar, Roast Aubergine with red pepper salad, croissants and smoothies. At the far end is the main serving station with the selection written on the menu notice board. Indonesian casserole of couscous, broccoli and roasted peanuts in a mildly spicy sauce that tastes fine and includes courgettes, carrot, onion and baby corn. The Healthy Bowl, a very filling whole grain rice salad of puy lentils, mushroom, courgettes, tomato, green beans and carrots garnished with coriander was even better. Other choices may include a potato, watercress and orange soup, whilst on mains there may be a baked potato or quiche and salad. Fruit salad dessert here is good as is the warm Apple and Blackberry Crumble with clotted cream or Greek yogurt.

The best place to eat to get the real crypt feel is the large dining room. In the middle is a large communal table with other smaller tables dotted about. On the tables are large jugs of water and you can bring your own wine (no charge for corkage) – although few do.

The recipes here are devised by director and owner Bill Sewell and on sale are his two veggie cooking books *Food from the Place Below* (Bill Sewell with Ian Burleigh and Frances Tomlinson) and *Feasts from the Place Below* (Bill Sewell).

In the mornings it's busy here with porridge eaters reading the morning newspapers and you can smell the freshly baked bread rolls that are made on the premises

For those on a budget there's an off-peak lunch deal from 11.30am-12noon and 1.30pm-2.30pm, where you pay takeaway prices for eat-in on quiches, main salads and hot dishes with a saving of about £1.50.

Tea
British, classic

⌨ *1 Paternoster Square, St Paul's Churchyard, EC4*

☎ *020 7248 6606*

✐ *www.wearetea.com*

🚇 *St Paul's LU, 1 min walk*

🕐 *Mon-Fri 7am-7pm, Sat &Sun 11am-6pm (Summer)*
Mon-Fri 7am-5pm, Sat &Sun 11am-5pm (Winter)

☀ *Outside seating 6 tables*

i *Counter service*
Eat-in/Takeaway

The best organic afternoon tea shop in London was opened in May 2007 by tea specialist owners Daren Spence and Suzanne Connolly. Located in the shadow of St Paul's Cathedral, Tea has the look of an old English pantry with a modern twist. The outside tables boast a terrific view and inside there are old rustic wooden tables and chairs, whilst on the walls there's modern abstract designs and, oh yes, an intriguing five gallon giant tea cup and saucer – lest you forget why you are there!

Ordering at the counter, knowledgeable staff will help you navigate the tea menu on the wall. The place attracts sophisticated tea cognoscenti but is also popular with tourists visiting St Paul's.

Organic Gunpowder Supreme is a clean refreshing and sweet green tea, although I found even better was the Organic Mao Jian – the best organic tea that I have tasted in London. On the black organic teas there is a bergamot scented Earl Grey Supreme and a Bohea Lapsang. Quite likeable is the infusion of Organic Honeybush, a reddish caffeine-free herbal that goes down well with their delicious organic scones. All the muffins are organic too and I can vouch for the pecan and toffee that is served in generous portions. Also available is a Rooibos infusion.

The owners use organic where possible in the food. At breakfast there is organic muesli and at lunch, sandwiches, wraps and rolls are made with organic bread. Sandwichs include hummus with spinach, red pepper and pine nut, free range egg and mustard cress, and Somerset cheddar with pickle. A great place for afternoon tea.

Thai Square City
Thai, classic

Vegetarian ★★★
Taste ★★
Price £££

🖼 *136-138, The Minories, EC3*

☎ *020 7680 1111*

✐ *www.thaisq.com*

🚌 *Aldgate or Tower Hill LU*

🕙 *Mon-Fri 12noon-10pm (Bar till 2am)*

Part of the Thai Square chain of restaurants, this follows their traditional ornate Thai design format with seating for 250 and a license for a further 240 people in their basement bar until 2am. This place is popular for business lunches or an after work chow down.

See Thai Square, Trafalgar Square for meal review (page 31).

Thai Square Mansion House
Thai, classic

Vegetarian ★★★
Taste ★★
Price £££

🖼 *1-7 Great St Thomas Apostle, EC4*

☎ *020 7329 0001*

✐ *www.thaisq.com*

🚌 *Mansion House LU(30 seconds walk)*

🕙 *Mon-Fri 12noon-3pm, 5.30pm-10pm*

This is one of the smallest of the restaurants in the Thai Square chain.
See Thai Square, Trafalgar Square for food review (page 31).

Le Pain Quotidien
French, classic

Vegetarian ★★★★
Organic ★★★★★
Taste ★★★★
Price ££

🖼 *1 Bread Street, Unit 5, Ground Floor*
   Bow Bell House, EC4

☎ *020 7486 6154*

✐ *www.lepainquotidien.com*

🚌 *St Paul's LU, 5min walk*

🕙 *Mon-Fri 6am-10pm*

✦ *Vegan options*

Opened in June 2008, this 90-seater is similar in size to the one in Great Marlborough Street W1.

For food review see Le Pain Quotidien, Marylebone (page 41).

Vanilla Black
English, modern

🖼 *17-18 Tooks Court, Holborn, EC4*
☎ *020 7242 2622*
🖥 *www.vanillablack.co.uk*
🚋 *Chancery Lane LU, 5min walk*
🕐 *Mon-Fri 12noon-2.30pm, 6pm-10pm*
🥕 *Vegan choices on request*

Vanilla Black

This restaurant offers visually sensational vegetarian cuisine that also provides a wonderful palette of flavours. Situated in the heart of London's legal district, near the Royal Courts of Justice, Vanilla Black's chef, Andrew Dargue, has done a magnificent job introducing his innovative recipes from his York restaurant and also creating a formidable array of new ones.

Stylishly designed with crystal chandeliers, 1950's mirrors and light jazz in the background, Vanilla Black exudes an expensive ambience that appeals to the discerning barristers and financial high rollers that it attracts. The menu, however, is reasonable value taking into account the quality of the food and Vanilla Black is definitely a place for vegetarians to visit when they are after something a little bit special.

The meal begins with a complimentary plain roll of excellent quality with a choice of saffron or salted butter followed by an amuse-bouche of tiny eclairs filled with black olive paste. The starter of Tomato Terrine with Whipped Mustard comes as a sculptured red cube of tomato, a light hearted take on raw tuna and salmon starters – it tasted wonderful with a creamy mustard topping and surrounded by a few fried chickpeas. The oblong Saffron Potato with Black Olive fragments inside came with five micro servings of almond muesli and tomato paste that were satisfying.

Service is attentive, effective and knowledgeable and the savoury and sweet signature mains are to be recommended. Steamed Cabbage and Longmans' Matureman Cheddar arrives on an oblong plate with a neat cabbage parcel at either end filled with the strong cheese that pairs superbly with the sweetish port and raisin sauce. A small mound of braised beans in the plate's middle completes this beautifully tasting composition. A gloriously rich Baked Blue Vinny, comes with a sweet tasting Celery Meringue, topping two pastry profiter rolls, filled with a milder cheese. The accompanying sweet flavoured small apple turnover worked well with the dishes cheese flavours.

The dessert of Rum Raisin Curd Cake looks similar to a small scone and tastes wonderful and comes with a tomato ripple ice cream that is intentionally underpowered to impart the slightest tomato taste. Warm Lemon Sponge is an easy going comfort food finish and comes with almond cheese and a delightful ginger butterscotch sauce. The bottle of organic vegetarian, Rioja Biurko Graciano 2003 was enjoyable and robust enough to pair well throughout our meal. Most of the reds are vegan and the all the whites and champagnes vegetarian. A two course lunch is £18, three courses £24 and in the evenings two courses are £24, three courses £30. A wonderful treat.

Zen Garden
Thai, Chinese, classic

Vegetarian ★★★★

Price £

🖃　88 Leather Lane, Moorgate, EC2

☏　0871 971 6995

🚌　Chancery Lane or Farringdon LU 8min walk

🕐　Mon-Fri 12noon-10pm

🥕　Vegan menu

Bargain £5 all-you-can-eat vegan Thai/Chinese cuisine. Independent from the VegVeg chain but offering a similar choice.

For food review see Wai, Goodge Street (page 67).

Hoxton & Shoreditch

Cay Tre
Vietnamese, classic

Vegetarian ★★★
Organic ★★★
Price £

⌨ *301 Old Street, EC1*
☏ *020 7729 8662*
🖰 *www.vietnamesekitchen.co.uk/caytre*
🚌 *Old Street LU, 5 min walk*
🕑 *Mon-Thurs 12noon-3pm, 5.30pm-11pm*
  Fri-Sat 12noon-3.30pm, 5.30pm-11pm, Sun 12noon-10.30pm
🥕 *Vegan options available*
🍼 *Children-friendly*

Possibly the best bargain Vietnamese eaterie in London. The former dowdy décor has now improved remarkably with black tables and smart black and white oriental wallpaper, mirrors and multi coloured lights. The Sunday lunchtime I visited it was packed with a mixed crowd of locals, while at night it's popular with clubbers and on weekdays there are lots of city slickers slurping down a swift soup meal.

Vietnamese family-run, service here is pretty good. Do let them know you are vegetarian as your wait person will reveal a lot more options than the six choices on the vegetarian section of the menu. Furthermore, they will also convert several dishes to veggie on request.

Vietnamese Pizza is one such conversion, a traditional warm pancake starter dish where you cut a slice, add some fresh Vietnamese watercress, marjoram, dipping sauce, wrap it in lettuce and let the wonderful medley of flavours melt in your mouth – delicious!

The veggie version of Canh chua, a popular aromatic soup containing pieces of fresh tomato, pineapple chunks, tofu strips, celery slices and accented with basil, produces a delightful mix of flavours and is recommended.

Other tempting choices include crispy seaweed starter, veggie Special Pho and the Braised Aubergine in black bean sauce. All the desserts are vegetarian although most people are too full to bother. The fresh pineapple juice is good quality and only £1.20.

Eating at Cay Tre (that incidentally means bamboo) is an enjoyable experience and for the budget conscious the best veggie bet in Hoxton/ Shoreditch. Go for it!

Fifteen
Italian, mediterranean, modern

🖼 *15 Westland Place, N1*

☎ *0871 330 1515*

🖉 *www.fifteen.net*

🚌 *Old Street LU 5 min walk,*

🕐 *Trattoria restaurant: Mon-Sat 7.30am-11pm, Breakfast: 8am-11am*
Lunch: 12noon-3pm, Dinner: 6pm-10pm, Sun 12noon-5pm
Fifteen restaurant (booking essential)
Daily, Lunch: 12noon-4.30pm, Dinner: 6.30pm-11.30pm

🌱 *Vegan options*

⬡ *Child-friendly*

This place made famous by the TV series 'Jamie's Kitchen' is a magnet for fans of TV chef Jamie Oliver. The food is great and mostly organic, and there are now two eateries to choose from, one with a complete vegetarian tasting menu that changes daily. Granted, it all comes at a pukka price, but profits go to the Fifteen Foundation, a charity that takes on 30 unemployed youngsters a year to train to become the next new wave of chefs.

The actual place is a dreary walk from Old Street Tube and the venue is a dull looking warehouse surrounded by equally boring office blocks and more grim warehouses. However, one could say it's just a New York style restaurant: crap on the outside but everything you could wish for on the inside.

Once in, you're into Jamie's world. There's a small bar area packed with punters waiting with a drink for their table. Expect a fifteen minute wait unless you arrive early. On the ground level is the Trattoria, in the basement, Fifteen. The Trattoria offers more menu flexibility for vegetarians and it's cheaper, but Fifteen is more contemporary in design and the atmosphere more electric.

Most people venturing here are making a one-off visit to have the 'Jamie Oliver Experience'. Expect cameras flashing and videos recording as dads capture the family on safari in the Trattoria and frenzied friends take party pics on their mobiles down in Fifteen.

Most of the food is organic. However, one ingredient in a dish may not be – so there's no mention of organic on the menu. Organic and bio-dynamic wines are here, but you will need to quiz the sommelier to find out what's what. Similarly, double check the menu with a waiter for what is vegetarian.

Fifteen Trattoria

Vegetarian ★★
Organic ★★★★
Taste ★★★★★
Price £££

The décor is less striking than it used to be and no longer has the shocking pink graffiti scrawled on the back wall that gave so much character. Comfortable wooden benches, tables and chairs, chandelier lights and a large Venetian mirror creates a pleasant informal atmosphere.

All the food is well presented and those complimentary breads with olive oil are superb and not to be missed. Tortellini with three cheese, figs and orange gremolata, is excellent, although portion size is more starter than main. Spinach and Ricotta Gnocci comes in a light buttery sauce and avoids being gummy; it's delicious without being mind blowing although it too is on the small side. Small portion sizes are great news for young kids and dieters but those with an appetite will need three courses. On other days choices maybe include a pasta and bean soup, salads, ravioli of artichoke, penne pasta or hand-cut tagliatelle, chilli, purple figs and goat's curd.

Half the tables can be booked, the other half of the space is kept for those without reservations. This eaterie is now so popular it is best to book ahead.

The Restaurant at Fifteen

Vegetarian ★★★★
Organic ★★★★
Price £££££

Downstairs is so rich in personality you'll want to buy it by the pound. The open kitchen, the brown banquettes, black columns and funky graffiti artwork all provide a burst of vitality. At lunch it's fab with a swanky dressed crowd who want to be 'seen'. For more privacy and romance book a booth. Book well in advance as this restaurant is red hot.

The lunchtime á la carte choices may include a starter of Mozzarella with Peaches, Basil, Mint and Rocket followed by a main of Gnocci with Chanterelles or one of Jamie O's speciality risottos.

In the evening everything turns set menu downstairs. The Vegetarian Tasting Menu is six courses and costs a whopping £50 per person with a special wine package to match the courses for another forty quid. As vegetarian tasting menus go the choices are not as exciting as Roussillon or Morgan M, but the ambience of the place will certainly make it a night to remember.

Rivington Grill
British, modern

Vegetarian ★★★
Price £££

⬚ 28-30 Rivington Street, EC2
☎ 020 7729 7053
🚍 Old Street LU 5min walk
🕑 Breakfast: Mon-Fri 8am-11am, All day Menu: Daily 11am-11pm,
Lunch: Mon-Fri 12noon-3pm, Brunch: Sat-Sun 11am-4pm

Tuck into modern Brit comfort food at this smart, buzzy and bright eaterie in the heart of the Hoxton and Shoreditch warehouse district. Grungy clubbers, leave your smelly jeans and trainers at home – this place exudes well-heeled nouveau riche neighbourhood residents, city boys and chic professional women. Immaculate white walls, wooden floorboards, comfy large leather sofas, good size tables with crisp white tablecloths defines a look far superior to most gastro pubs leaving one with the expectation of high quality food.

A short vegetarian menu of three starters, three mains and four desserts was initiated in August 2004, following a surge in demand from local vegetarians. For starters there's Squash Salad with Ragstone Goats Cheese, Vegetarian Broth or Welsh Rarebit. The most tempting main is a modern veggie version of the traditional English dish, Bubble and Squeak accompanied by fried egg and wild mushrooms. Other mains are Eggs Florentine and Glamorgan Caerphilly Veggie Sausages with creamed leeks. A further six veggie side dish choices including the likes of minted potatoes, mixed greens, heritage carrots and mash – adds versatility to this somewhat limited menu. Desserts, however, make a strong showing with Apple and Bramble Crumble with Jersey Cream, Chocolate Mousse and Rice Pudding with Prune Jam.

With bags of personality and some unique menu choices, Rivington Grill is a likeable eaterie and a comfortable place to relax.

SAF
Organic Vegan, modern

Vegetarian ★★★★★
Organic ★★★★★
Taste ★★★★★
Price ££££

⬚ 152-154 Curtain Road, Shoreditch, EC2
☎ 020 7613 0007
🖉 www.safrestaurant.co.uk
🚍 Old Street LU, 7min walk
🕑 Mon-Sat 12noon-3.30pm, 6.30pm-11pm,
◻ Child friendly
☀ Outside seating
i Eat in(table service) & Takeaway 11am-5 pm

SAF

London's most innovative upscale vegan organic restaurant and bar. It serves remarkable vegan raw food with top class organic vegan cocktails and wines and is probably the best organic cocktail bar in London with fourteen botanical cocktails and four non-alcoholics. The Avenue is a very decent cocktail mix of organic calvados, bourbon, passion fruit and grenadine. The ladies favourite is the Lacey Langston, enormously rich in taste and made from local organic green apple, pear juices and a hit of organic cava, framboise and fresh raspberries.

Past the bar, the restaurant's exposed concrete and solid oak furniture aptly complements the rawness of the cuisine. Anna McNeil's floor-to-ceiling paintings of flowers, water, sunlight and the earth, reflect the use of natural ingredients. Modern vertical 'figure-eight' ceiling lighting is charming and constructed from a medley of porcelain and oak. At the oak dining tables and banquettes expect sophisticated, casually dressed diners rather than suits from the City. The 'Chef's Table' gives the best view of the open plan kitchen and is good if you opt for the tasting menu with wine pairings, although all the tables in the place are pretty good and outside there's a terrific al fresco dining terrace where many of the herbs and flowers for the menu are grown.

Executive chef, Chad Sarno, excels in artistic presentation and balance of flavours and has a celebrity following of raw foodists that include Charlize Theron and Woody Harrelson. With a well explained menu, an approach of starter, mains and salad together, cheese dish and a dessert to finish, gives an excellent range of Sarno's capabilities leaving one gastronomically delighted and comfortably full.

The signature starter of Beetroot Ravioli with cashew herb ricotta, early asparagus salad, balsamic figs and pumpkin seed oil is as fascinating to look at, as it is delicious. 'Caviar' starter is a gastronomic creation of green chive pearls, sweet potato latkes, apples and sour cream – an interpretation of five caviar blinis, beautifully presented, that tastes excellent in itself but dissimilar to authentic caviar. Similarly, afficinados of traditional Caesar Salad's may have mixed opinions on the authenticity of taste, however, this cos lettuce, kalamata almond crouton, lightly seasoned leaf dulse and miso interpretation is a wonderful creation. I took the Caesar with the Buddha Bowl, the most popular main on the menu that to my mind was the best tofu dish in London. It takes the form of two generous slabs of green tea glazed tofu, with kimpira (sliced carrots), gomasio (ground roasted seame seeds and sea salt), sambal and garlic greens. Substantial, it could be enough for a light meal in itself and was paired well with a glass of organic Chilean Sauvignon Blanc.

An even better main, however, is the modestly named 'Mushrooms', a delicate dish of rich tasting croquette, excellent wild mushroom, truffle alfredo and rosemary with a side dish of Greens & Flowers.

SAF's cheese course choices deserve attention as they are specially created from almond, cashew and pine nut milks cultured and fermented in the same style as their dairy counterparts. Macadamia Caprese comes on a long narrow plate with sliced rouleaux speckled cheese made from macadamia nut with rocket accompanied semi-dried tomato – wonderful. For desserts, the Caramelised Apple Cheesecake made from cashew nut cheese and coconut lemon crust was quite good, whilst the Ganache Tart was of excellent quality.

Of the twenty-three à la carte menu choices, seventeen are under 48 degrees whilst those cooked above are clearly marked on the menu. Five and seven course tasting menus are also available from £35 plus £15 for five matching wines. Dining at Saf is an amazing experience and a place to return to many times.

Water House
London, Modern

⌨ *10 Osman Road, N1*

☎ *020 7033 0123*

🖰 *www.waterhouserestaurant.co.uk*

🚌 *Old Street LU Exit 2,*

🕐 *Mon-Fri 9am-4pm, 6pm-10pm, Sat 10am-4pm, 6pm-10pm,*
Sun 10am-4pm

🥕 *Vegan options*

◌ *Child-friendly*

☀ *Outside seating*

Vegetarian ★★★★
Organic ★★★★★
Taste ★★★★
Price *££££*

Water House

Don't forget to tip your gondolier well as you pull into this innovative canal-side restaurant at London's first truly eco-friendly restaurant, offering praiseworthy organic and veggie options. Regrettably there's no great palazzos to admire nor a vaporetti water bus service in sight. Instead, there's a good London bus service running nearby and a reasonable urban canal offering the best alfresco in Shoreditch with seating for sixteen outside and sixty-four inside.

Attracting a fashionably informal dining set, inside there's a large attractive bar serving organic cocktails and juices and although the grey chairs and wooden tables are quite nice, overall, there's a canteen feel about the place. One good thing is that the restaurant uses renewable hydroelectric power from the canal, reducing carbon emissions down to a minimum and also produces it's own filtered, chilled water.

Owned by the Shoreditch Trust, the executive chef is Arthur Potts Dawson who set up Acorn House at King's Cross. He is absolutely passionate about organic food, including his domestic life where he uses organic wherever possible.

As with Acorn House, tell staff that you are vegetarian and they will direct you to the veggie options and conversions from non-veggie. The menu is short with a different special daily. Perry & Parsnip Soup is crammed with delicious organic parsnips that are spicy with bags of flavour and substantial. Also yummy was the starter of Burrata di bufala, a soft young cheese that comes with chopped olives and a drizzle of olive oil on toasted bread.

On mains, the fully organic Artichoke and Thyme Barigoule – a kind of veggie stew – doesn't look too appetising but tasted good, especially the curly kale and potatoes. The Ravioli with white truffle oil and parmesan, comes filled with potato and somehow needed some extra ingredient to boost the taste. That said, those who love their pasta mild would find this perfect, especially matched with the very enjoyable organic Touchstone Pinot Grigio sold by the glass (£5), whilst the Touchstone Shiraz paired well with the Barigoule stew.

To finish, of the four vegetarian desserts the Sticky Lemon Cake and sweet crème fraîche was delectable and the Poached Pear in red wine & vanilla ice cream slid down extremely well.

At lunch there is also an eat-in/takeaway deli menu of paninis and vegetarian soups and bread (£4) and salads plates (£8.50) and hot & cold antipasti for £7.

Great care is taken to source supplies as locally as possible with lots of produce from Kent and Hertfordshire. This kind of care for the quality of the food and its environmental impact is certain to become more widespread, particularly when the results taste so good.

Smithfield, Barbican & Farringdon

Veggie lunchtime food is to be had at Wheatley Vegetarian Café near the Angel. In West Smithfield enjoy informal Italian food at Carluccio's, whilst tucked away in the depths of Clerkenwell, there are good veggie organic lunches at The Clerkenwell Kitchen. Further north, there's a Sofra in Exmouth Market offering excellent Turkish cuisine with plenty of veggie options. For distinctly well-prepared Mediterranean cuisine in the Old Street area there's always Carnevale.

Carluccio's Caffé
Italian, classic

Vegetarian ★★★
Taste ★★★★
Price ££

- 🖼 *12 West Smithfield, EC1*
- ☎ *020 7329 5904*
- 🖱 *www.carluccios.com*
- 🕐 *Mon-Fri 8am-11pm, Sat 9am-11pm, Sun 9am-10.30pm*
- 🌱 *Vegan options*
- 🍼 *Child friendly, high chairs*
- ☀ *Excellent outside tables*

Another Carluccio eaterie, this one with attractive outdoor seating. *For the food review see Carluccio's, St Christopher's Place (page 35).*

Carnevale
Mediterranean, modern

Vegetarian ★★★★★
Organic ★★
Taste ★★★★
Price ££

- 🖼 *135 Whitecross Street, EC1*
- ☎ *020 7250 3452*
- 🖱 *www.carnevalerestaurant.co.uk*
- 🚌 *Old Street LU, 5 min walk or Barbican LU*
- 🕐 *Mon-Fri 12noon-11pm*
- 🌱 *Vegan options*
- 🍼 *Child friendly*
- ☀ *Outside tables*

Despite a change in ownership, this small pure vegetarian restaurant continues to serve well conceived Mediterranean dishes using fresh seasonal and many organic ingredients. The black painted entrance opens into an enticing deli-counter with takeaway sandwiches and tempting jars of gourmet produce. The restaurant is further inside and has a small conservatory. The atmosphere is relaxed with evenings candlelit.

The set menu is an absolute gift at £13.50 that offers three courses or two with a glass of wine or non-alcoholic drink (12noon-3pm and 5.30pm-7pm). The short á la carte menu has seven starters, five mains and six desserts and is quite inviting with Carnevale happily catering for vegans and those with special nutritional needs.

Leek, courgette and basil soup comes up thick, rustic and flavoursome with a delicious walnut bread. Even better is a very well presented Grilled Halloumi that comes with superb oven roasted plum tomatoes and baby spinach with balsamic honey dressing. One of the favourite mains is Potato Cakes with Fennel, Lemon and Basil with Provencale Vegetable casserole and a mixed rocket salad, which comes in generous proportions and is delicious. Homemade Vegetarian sausages here are a million miles away from the usual meat-free supermarket substitutes – made with a unique recipe that includes nuts, bread crumbs, apricot and sultana. It is nicely presented on a rich bed of mash potato with a red wine rosemary gravy – a real comfort food treat.

For dessert, the Cinnamon crusted English Pear comes well presented, stuffed with a good fruit compote and spiced red wine and vanilla cream sauce. It went very well with a Vino Santo dessert wine. Raspberry Crème Brulee, a firm favourite, continues to be of the same cool, thick and creamy high standard.

At £21 a head from the á la carte menu, Carnevale is good value for what you get. Most ingredients come from a local Surrey farm and the menu changes every six weeks to take advantage of seasonal produce. Much of Carnevale's trade comes from its takeout lunch counter where freshly prepared sandwiches and salads are very popular.

The Clerkenwell Kitchen
English, modern

	Vegetarian ★★★
	Organic ★★★★
	Taste ★★★★
	Price ££

🖃 *The Clerkenwell Workshops*
   27-31 Clerkenwell Close, EC1
☎ *020 7101 9959*
✎ *www.theclerkenwellkitchen.co.uk*
🚌 *Farringdon LU 5min walk*
🕐 *Mon-Wed & Fri 8am-5pm, Thurs 7am-11pm*
🥕 *Vegan options*
🍼 *Child friendly*
☀ *Outside tables*
i *Counter service (Eat-in table service) & /takeaway service*

One of the best kept secrets in the City, this modern, informal dining room serves delicious dishes with an emphasis on organic, seasonality and the environment. Found in the courtyard of a modern workshop/office complex, at midday the dining room is filled with smartly dressed-down creatives and IT types, discussing projects around well designed beech wood tables and enjoying vegetarian sandwiches made with artisan breads or tucking into a bowls of leek and potato soup.

The blackboard menu changes daily and there are at least two veggie choices, plus a small veggie plate to choose from. Spinach Cheese Tart was a memorably attractive warm wedge, oozing with the flavour of feta cheese from Neal's Yard, crunchy green beans sprinkled with Maldon salt, accompanied by a good potato salad, pickled red onion and balsamic vinegar – marvellous value at £7.50. Side dishes of Buttered Kale and Green Salad are available for £2.50. The Butternut Squash risotto and Frittata also looked substantial and well made. Vegan dishes are made-to-order for the select few who are toiling away in the work units.

They also offer a private events and weddings catering service which offers a fantastic range of veggie dishes and the restaurant space can be hired for these especial events. The efficient kitchen is run under the watchful eye of former Mildreds chef, Emma Miles, and her imagination and zeal are reflected in the quality of the food.

The drinks list has four organic wines from £4 a glass and a tempting organic cox apple juice from Chegworth Valley in Kent, as well as an array of organic teas, chocolates and herbals.

The Clerkenwell Kitchen is worth beating a path to for the quality of it's food and ethical stance. It's advisable to book a few days in advance for lunch.

Rye Wholefoods
Café and Organic Shop

Vegetarian ★★★★★
Organic ★★★★
Taste ★★
Price £

- 35a Myddleton Street, EC1
- 020 7278 5878
- Angel LU, 10 min walk
- Mon-Fri 10am-3pm, Sat 12noon-5pm
- Vegan options

Small and simple vegetarian and vegan provisions shop with a couple of tables for eating-in. The menu tries to use as many organic ingredients as possible but the place is geared up more for takeaway.

Sofra Exmouth Market
Turkish, classic,

Vegetarian ★★★
Organic ★★★
Price ££

🖾 *21 Exmouth Market, EC1*

☎ *020 7833 1111*

✑ *www.sofra.co.uk*

🚌 *Farringdon LU & Rail*

🕓 *Mon-Sun 12noon-11.30pm (including Bank Holidays)*

See Özer, Oxford Circus for food review (page 44).

Wheatley Vegetarian Café
Café, British

Vegetarian ★★★★★
Taste ★★★
Price £

🖾 *33/34 Myddleton Street, EC1*

☎ *020 7278 6662*

🚌 *Angel LU, 10 min walk*

🕓 *Mon-Fri 8am-3pm*

i *Eat-in (counter service &takeaway)*

✦ *Vegan options*

☀ *Outside seating*

Excellent informal lunchtime al fresco eaterie with food that has bags of wholesome personality. With no credible veggie eats on Exmouth Market apart from Sofra, it's worth taking a stroll to Wheatley's, which sits on a small parade of shops just five minutes away.

The bright, spacious, no-thrills interior seats 20 with large tables for sharing, whilst outside the back garden gets packed in the summer. Trainee barristers, students and workers from nearby Amnesty International are among the regulars here enjoying dishes such as the thick homemade lentil, carrot and coriander soup accompanied by chunky sunflower seed bread – a filling meal deal just in itself.

The blackboard menu changes daily and there's a choice of mock carnivore standards such as an interesting Veggie Burger Sandwich with vegetables, beans, salad tomato chutney and mayo. It's a doorstop and very popular. There's also two veggie lasagne options made with roasted veg or spinach and ricotta. The Spinach Wrap crammed with hot roasted root vegetables, curried chick pea and feta cheese salad comes as a huge portion and is quite excellent with three homemade salads. There's also some low fat organic cakes and 90% of the food is vegan. A little gem of a veggie café and well worth going out of your way to visit.

North London

Restaurants

Islington

Islington has been transformed in the last twenty five years from a modest local neighbourhood into a major shopping and eating area with numerous restaurants along Upper Street. Among the super-bargain vegetarian places to eat are the Indian Veg Bhel-Poori House and Tai Buffet. For great Turkish food there are several Gallipoli restaurants and the buzzing Italian, Carluccio's Caffé on Upper Street. The area also has exemplary French vegetarian haut cuisine at Morgan M and the best organic pub in London, The Duke of Cambridge. For vegetarian food in a unique atmosphere, Candid Café is a great alternative to more mainstream eateries. Just the other side of the junction is Bliss – which is a firm favourite with the locals. A branch of Planet Organic has also recently been established on Essex Road which proves that Islington is definitely a very smart part of London.

Bliss
French, Pattiserie, modern

Vegetarian ★★★★★
Organic ★★★
Price £

- 🖼 *428 St Johns St, EC1*
- ☎ *020 7837 3720*
- 🚌 *Angel LU, 5 min walk*
- 🕐 *Mon-Sat 9am-6pm, Sun 9am-2pm*

This café has been on St John Street for over 20 years which makes it one of the oldest establishments in this fast changing, high rent part of town. After a quick look at the fresh pastries, pizzas, quiches and tarts on display it is easy to explain the longevity of Bliss who pride themselves on the quality of their food, most of which is made on the premises using vegetable fat. The croissants are considered by many to be the best in London and I know of one friend that would still make the journey here after leaving the area just to enjoy one of their delicious almond croissants, washed down with a strong cappuccino. Not all the sandwiches and food here is vegetarian, but the staff are keen to differentiate those foods containing meat or fish and about 80% of the menu is suitable for veggies. On my last visit I enjoyed a wonderfully fresh mushroom quiche and finished off with a deliciously sweet strawberry flan – Bliss...

Café Gallipoli
Turkish

Vegetarian ★★★
Taste ★★★★
Price ££

⌨ *102 Upper St, N1*
☎ *020 7359 0630*
✎ *www.cafegallipoli.com*
🚌 *Angel LU, 5 min walk*
🕐 *Sun-Thurs 10.30am-11pm, Fri-Sat 10.30am-12midnight*
☀ *Outside seating*

Party-on at this good value traditional Turkish café. Situated on Upper Street, cheap eats central for North London, Gallipoli gets crammed to rafters in the evenings with the out-for-a-good-time 20-40 year old crowd. Friendly and obliging waiters always manage to find you a table no matter how full they are.

Rickety old tables, wobbly chairs, lively Turkish music, pictures and ornaments recreate a noisy informal bazaar atmosphere. Front of house is very lively in the evenings with bigger birthday parties who dance on the chairs, whilst the back room is only slightly quieter. During the day the mood is a lot more sensible with people enjoying a mezze or falafel sandwich without feeling the need to dance in a ecstatic manner.

The choice of seven main vegetarian dishes includes Vegetarian Moussaka, Imam Bayildi - fried aubergines stuffed with an onion mushroom mix – and very filling falafels. For the full works we took the delicious Set Meal that included a big veg mezze selection, any main dish off the menu, coffee, tea and a light milk pudding with apricots. The wine is reasonably priced and there are meat and fish dishes for your non-veggie friends.

Sister cafés are Café Gallipoli Again, 120 Upper Street (see below).
Also there's Gallipoli Bazaar, 107 Upper Street (see page 110)

Café Gallipoli Again
Turkish

Vegetarian ★★★
Taste ★★★★
Price ££

⌨ *120 Upper St, N1*
☎ *020 7359 1578*
✎ *www.cafegallipoli.com*
🚌 *Highbury Islington or Angel LU, 5 min walk*
🕐 *Sun-Thurs 10.30am-11pm, Fri-Sat 10.30am-12midnight*
☀ *Tables outside*

Sister café to Café Gallipoli with the same menu. Here though, the place is smaller and less frenzied.

Candid Café
International, classic

🖼 *3 Iorrens Street, EC1*

☎ *020 7278 9368*

🖊 *www.candidarts.com*

🚌 *Angel LU*

🕐 *Mon-Sat 12noon-10pm, Sun 12noon-5pm*

☀ *Outside seating*

Candid Café

A popular haunt for young arty vegetarians. Located in the Candid Arts Trust building, the café is just minutes away from the main Islington dining strip and identifiable by the half horse statue sticking out of its front wall. Various contemporary art and design exhibitions and fairs are held here as well as line drawing classes.

Once up the old warehouse-style stairs, order at the counter and crash out on one of the comfy green velvety sofas, now in a mild state of disrepair. The Sunday afternoon I visited, the spacious main dining room was packed. Around the big communal wooden dining tables in the centre, diners ate and chatted cheerfully. On the perimeter, young couples sipped coffee on small tables with gilded banquet room chairs. At night the place is romantically candlelit. I really liked the genuine friendliness of the people here who were up for relaxed conversation with anyone in the room. I visited one evening when some great trance music was playing, the sun was setting, the place was candlelit, some girls were drinking wine and a guy was writing a novel on his laptop. I thought, hey, this is a really cool place.

On the blackboard menu, there's always a vegan, organic soup such as carrot and coriander or pumpkin that comes with a crusty brown bread and butter – a comfort food lite bite. The selection of sandwiches is also pretty good and they are all pretty substantial – if a bit basic.

Of the three veggie main choices, Vegetable Lasagne is a safe bet whilst the Spinach and Ricotta Quiche comes nicely warm, but is a little let down by a sad lettuce and tomato side salad. The Cauliflower Cheese was reasonable but accompanied with the same side salad. A Greek salad is also available. Desserts are also on the large size. Apple pie comes with custard or cream with a sprinkling of cinnamon and was quite good. If the food gets as good as the atmosphere in this place it will be a real winner, but with bags of atmosphere it's still a good place to go for a veggie bite.

Carluccio's Caffé
Italian, Classic

Vegetarian ★★★
Taste ★★★★
Price ££

- 📖 305–307 Upper Street, N1
- ☎ 020 7359 8167
- 🖱 www.carluccios.com
- 🚇 Angel LU, 5 min walk
- 🕐 Mon-Fri 8am-11pm, Sat 9am-11pm, Sun 9am-10.30pm
- ☀ Two outside tables

Although it's one of the smaller eateries of the ever expanding Carluccio Caffé chain, every time I visit it's always packed – even on a Sunday evening. People come here for anything from a strong cappuccino to a substantial three course meal.

For a quick hearty bite I can recommend the nourishing Pasta E Fagioli soup, a thick bean and veg soup that you can almost stand your spoon up in. They drizzle it with olive oil and it comes with a chunky square of foccacia. Ice-creams here are really intense and creamy.

For the restaurant review see Carluccio's, St Christopher's Place, W1 (page 35).

Duke Of Cambridge
Organic, British &.
Mediterranean, modern

Vegetarian ★★★★
Organic ★★★★★
Taste ★★★★
Price ££

▭ 30 St Peters St, N1
☏ 020 7359 3066
✎ www.thedukeofcambridge.co.uk
🚎 Angel LU, 5-10 min walk
🕐 Lunch: Mon-Fri 12.30-3.00pm, Sat and Sun 12.30pm-3.30pm
    Dinner: Mon-Sat 6.30-10.30pm, Sun 6.30pm-10pm
🖋 Vegan options available
👶 Child friendly

The mother of organic gastropubs with knock-out list of organic fine wines and draught beers. A capacious corner pub, it's a short stroll down a gentrified street away from Islington's manic main dining strip. Large old wooden tables with non-matching chairs and stripped wooden flooring create an informal setting. At the back, a candlelit conservatory dining room exudes a New Age vibe. Weekday evenings attract eco-conscious affluents, weekends are more family centred. Booking is advisable especially on Sunday.

The short blackboard menu changes daily. Food here is as organic as can be and so are the drinks except whiskey, tequila and rum. There are four organic real ales, Pitfield Brewery's Eco Warrior, Shoreditch Organic Stout, St Peter's Organic ale and Singhboulton (named after the pub owners) and all of them are well worth a try.

The complimentary warm crusty bread is very good and comes with olive oil. Baked brushetta, with roast celery, cherry tomatoes, courgette and mozzarella is tasty and substantial. Spaghetti with herb pesto, garlic and olives with a vibrant tang of lemon bread crumbs made a delicious vegetarian main course. There are appealing organic choices for carnivore friends too.

A very reasonable £6.50 lunch deal of a main course plus a half pint of draught Freedom beer, ale, fruit juice or wine is available every weekday. It goes some way to explain why this gastropub continues to be so popular.

Gallipoli Bazaar
Turkish

Vegetarian ★★★
Taste ★★★★
Price ££

🖃 *107 Upper Street, N1*
☎ *020 7226 5333*
✎ *www.cafegallipoli.com*
🚌 *Highbury Islington LU & Rail or Angel LU (5 min walk)*
🕐 *Tues-Thurs 5.30pm-11.30pm, Fri 5.30pm-12midnight,*
   Sat-Sun 1pm-12midnight

The latest edition to the Gallipoli empire, featuring the same menu (see page 106) plus a few Moroccan specials. Set on two floors, the ground floor is a souk sofa chillout zone – Islington's answer to Momo on Heddon Street. It serves cocktails and is about 10% pricier than the other branches of Gallipoli.

Gallipoli Bazzar

Indian Veg Bhel-Poori House
Indian

Vegetarian ★★★★★
Taste ★★
Price £

🖼 *92/93 Chapel Market, London N1*
☎ *020 7837 4607*
🚇 *Angel LU, 5 min walk*
🕐 *Daily 12noon-11.30pm*
🥕 *Vegan*

Bargain-priced, pulse-based restaurant that proudly wears it's veggie heart on it's sleeve, promoting cruelty-free food, world hunger issues and vegetarian health benefits. Based on Islington's competitively price-driven street market dining strip, the jewel in the crown is the eat-as much-as-you-like lunch and dinner buffet at £3.50. At lunchtime it attracts stall holders and local office workers while in the evening the customers are a mix of voraciously hungry well-mannered 18-25's and budget-conscious, middle-aged locals.

Atmosphere is friendly, chatty and without music. Décor is old-style Indian restaurant with mint walls, worn carpets, small chandeliers and assorted self-promoting posters and cuttings. Good tablecloths, decent plates, knives and forks and dignified service are pleasant features at this incredibly cheap restaurant.

The self-service buffet changes weekly. Most diners don't have a clue what they are eating as there are no dish descriptions, yet delighted in refilling and piling their plates high. On offer are two okay tasting vegetable curries and two good varieties of rice. The deep fried onion, cauliflower and potato were disappointing with more fry than veg, and the wheat flour puri was not warm and the papadom came as small broken bits rather than whole. Some of the dishes looked bland and unappetising and were not as hot as they should be, a problem frequently encountered with buffet-dining in general.

On the salad station, the choice is a bit limited but there's a decent shredded cabbage with mango chutney, two onion salads and three reasonable sauces of mango, mint and spiced tomato ketchup. All the food is vegan, except on occasions when they do panir (cheese) in the curry.

There are lots of soft drinks including five non-dairy lassis, (traditional sweet or savoury yoghurt drinks). The Soya Mango Lassi is to be recommended although it doubles the price of the meal! There's also a good selection organic canned drinks but, if you're on a budget, they also serve tap water. It's the cheapest veggie eaterie in town.

The Living Room
Bar and Restaurant, International

Vegetarian ★★★★
Taste ★★★★
Price £££

🏠 *18-26 Essex Road, Islington, N1*
☎ *020 7288 9090*
✑ *www.thelivingroom.co.uk*
🚌 *Angel LU 5 min walk*
🕐 *Mon-Wed 12noon-11.30pm, Thurs 12noon-12midnight, Fri 12noon-2am*
   Sat 11am-2am, Sun 11am-11.30pm
🍼 *Childrens menu available, high chairs*
☀ *Outside tables*
♫ *Live music & DJ*

Having had a great time here at a recent post-launch party I am really impressed with the Living Room's ability to lay on a fantastic celebration. This is the place where vegetarians have a tipple, hang out and party. The upmarket bar and restaurant opened in 2002 and has never looked back. The restaurant is dark wooden, colonial style, revolving ceiling fans and leafy plants. The best tables are the banquettes, big, brown leather. The menu is long, with eight veggie small plates and bread choices, three vegetarian starters, two veggie salads, two or three mains and always one veggie special. Soup of the day when I visited was Leek and Potato.

The Living Room does a good choice of alcoholic concoctions and a Chauffeur's Choice of alcohol-free cocktails, where the big faves are 'Virgins Kiss' and 'Sea Biscuit'.

It's more an evening spot than lunchtime place and the Thursday evening I went, there was live piano in the bar with some very impressive renditions of Elton John, Queen and jazz classics being played by one of the regular performers here. It's particular vibrant in the Summer when the place opens out onto the pavement.

Starter-size veggie Caesar Salad turned out to be a very good choice, crispy, delicious and with good flavour. Goat's Cheese and Baby Spinach Tart with beetroot is enjoyably mild and paired well with a generous portion of red onion jam to elevate the dish's flavour. On mains, the special was Roasted Butternut Squash in a gorgeously flavoured Red Thai Curry sauce, laden with red peppers, green beans and courgettes and served with steamed rice, is strongly recommended. A glass of peachy apricot Voignier went well with it. Mains arrive in massive dishes and the Potato Gnocci with tomato and basil topped with parmesan and rocket was no exception, although the actual portion size itself was not overly generous. The gnocci was a little cool by the time it reached the table, but otherwise it was of good quality. The Belgian Waffles are always excellent

– warm in a succulent sweet maple syrup and served with ice cream. Also a very good effort is their new 'Banofee in a Bag' that comes in a brown and silver lined paper bag that you slice open with a knife and pour ice cream and gingersnaps into. The Eton Mess is also another favourite here which will never disappoint.

The ambience of the Living Room is lively and fun, particularly on Friday and Saturday nights with several groups enjoying a private party and couples wining and dining. If you've moved on from the courting stage, the children's menu has three veggie starters, one veggie main, a macaroni cheese and a good choice of desserts. Of note is the selection of organic baby foods for main course and desserts.

Some of the staff are vegetarian and are adept at handling dietary questions. Artificial coloured and flavoured products are avoided as much as possible and data sheets are available. Service is attentive and friendly, making this a great place to seek out for relaxed veggie dining.

The Living Room's, sister restaurant is in Heddon Street, W1 (see page 56).

Living Room

Morgan M
French, modern

⌨ *489 Liverpool Road, N7*

☎ *020 7609 3560*

✍ *www.morganm.com*

🚌 *Highbury and Islington LU, 5-10 min walk*

☺ *Lunch: Wed-Fri & Sun 12.30pm-2pm*

   Dinner: Tue-Sat 7pm-12.30am, last orders 10pm

i *Food allergies and intolerances catered for*

Vegetarian ★★★★
Organic ★★★
Taste ★★★★★
Price £££££

Vegetarian haut cuisine six-course set menu that's amongst the best in London. The formal dark green exterior speaks serious dining. Inside, there are white and burgundy walls with modern paintings, gracious high backed chairs and spaciously arranged tables laid with modern Robert Welch cutlery. The service is elegant, the atmosphere refined, the clientele discerning foodies from Canonbury, Hampstead and Highgate. Evenings are busy, lunchtimes much quieter.

The 'From the Garden' menu costs £36 (£39 evenings) and changes seasonally and four different delicious wines by the glass are suggested to match the courses for £24. I would recommend this, although an extensive wine list is available. Cream of Girolles infused with thyme and Pumpkin Beignet begins what is a series of small dishes, each sparkling with different and delightful tastes. The Chestnut Sorbet, Wild Mushroom Caviar and Jerusalem Artichoke 'Barvois' that comes divided into three by thin vertical tile biscuits over layed with a further tile of herb salad, is a sumptuous creation. The Tarais Bean Ragoût with hazelnut, parsley root soubise and butter onions, was a medley of wonderful tastes – an absolute triumph. Glazed Quince on a sweet potato purée followed and was also excellent. A pre-dessert of a tiny orange tuile edible cup complete with a handle of Vanilla Rice Pudding was refreshing.

Desserts here are exemplary and the Pineapple Soufflé with a Pina Colada sorbet is inspired, although the Roasted Fig Tarte with lemon thyme ice cream and red wine syrup was quite incredible too. Allow two and half hours to enjoy this wonderful dining experience that will leave you satisfyingly full. A meat and fish set menu is also available if you are dining with omnivore friends.

Ottolenghi (Islington)
Mediterranean, classic, modern

Vegetarian ★★★★
Organic ★★★★
Taste ★★★★
Price Lunch ££
Price Dinner £££

- 🖼 *287 Upper Street, N1*
- ☎ *020 7288 1454*
- 🖉 *www.ottolenghi.co.uk*
- 🚌 *Angel LU, 7 min walk*
- 🕐 *Mon-Sat 8am-10.30pm, Sun 9am-7pm*
- 🥕 *Vegan options*
- 🍼 *Child friendly*
- ☀ *Outside tables*
- i *Takeaway*

Ottolenghi

115

Ultra cool minimalist dining room, serving high quality, well-crafted dishes just across the road from the Almeida Theatre. Islington foodies are forever peering in through the window at the fabulous pastries, tempting breads and the two long dining tables that are seductively candlelit in the evenings. These are the only tables in the place, a major plus for socialisers, movers and shakers – a minus for diners who prefer a bit of privacy. Personally, I liked it.

The Friday night I dropped in the place was half full of sophisticated diners who knew what they were in for – a unique dinner party with chance encounters with strangers who, like themselves, are ever intrigued by new gastronomic experiences.

The short Dinner Menu changes daily with five to six veggie starters, at least two hot veggie mains and four desserts and is mostly organic. Allow £25 per head for three courses without drinks. The meal begins with a selection of inviting complimentary breads that include sourdough and white Italian. To be sure of eating at the time you want, booking is advised for the evening meal on one of the long tables. The other bar tables with stools are for walk-ins on a first come first serve basis – perfect for a quick bite.

At lunch there are ten veggie salads (see Ottolenghi Notting Hill on page 181 for food review) and vegetarian patisserie are available day and night. Ottolenghi also have a takeaway-only service in Kensington at 1 Holland Street, W8 (see page 171) for details.

Ottolenghi has become an established favourite on the Islington foodie scene with a justified reputation for imaginative and fresh cuisine and a stylish dinning environment.

Planet Organic Islington
Organic, Vegetarian, International

Vegetarian ★★★★	
Organic ★★★★	
Taste ★★★	
Price £	

🏛 *64 Essex Road, N1*

☎ *020 7288 9460*

🖂 *www.planetorganic.com*

🚇 *Highbury and Islington LU, 5-10 min walk*

🕐 *Mon-Fri 8am-9pm, Sat 8.30am-9pm, Sun 10am-9pm*

This new Planet Organic opened in the autumn of 2008 and is a reasonable size with an in-store café.

See Planet Organic Westbourne Grove for food review (page 182).

Tai Buffet
Northern Chinese, classic

Vegetarian ★★★★★
Organic ★★★
Price £

⌨ *11 Islington High Street, N1*
🚌 *Angel LU, 1 min walk*
🕐 *Daily 11am-12midnight*
🍴 *Vegan cuisine*
☀ *Outside tables*

On the former site of Tai Noodle, Tai Buffet moved from a couple of doors away to this site. This chain of bargain Thai restaurants are certainly hard to pin down with telephone numbers and the name constantly changing. They do offer good value and the Thai buffet box is well worth a try. This particular branch seems to be a big hit with Islingtonians, it's packed at lunchtimes, with queues often extending onto the street. The £5.50 buffet (£6.50 after 5pm and Sundays) deal is unbelievably good value and includes a fresh fruit salad. The décor is a bit of a mish mash and the service is brisk, but at this price no one is complaining.
For a detailed food review see Wai on page 67.

Thai Square Angel
Thai, classic

Vegetarian ★★★★★
Organic ★★
Price £££

⌨ *347-349 Upper Street, N1*
☎ *020 7704 2000*
🖂 *www.thaisquare.net*
🚌 *Angel LU, 5 min walk*
🕐 *Lunch: Mon-Fri 12noon-3pm,*
   Dinner: Mon-Thurs 6pm-11pm, Fri till 11.30pm
   Sat 12noon-11.30pm, Sun 12noon-10.30pm
🍴 *Vegan options*
i *Table service/takeaway*

With 18 vegetarian Thai dishes to choose from and one of the most beautifully designed restaurants in Islington, this Thai Square is developing into a big Islington favourite especially in the evenings. Its basement bar can hold 100 and is licensed to 2am.
For a full food review see Thai Square, Trafalgar Square (page 31).

Restaurants

1) Café Seventy Nine p.119
2) Camden Market p.120
3) Carluccio's Caffé, St Pancras p.121
4) Chutneys p.121
5) Diwana p.122
6) Whole Foods Market p.132
7) Greens & Beans p.123
8) Green Note p.124
9) Gigi Hut p.125
10) Ha Ha Veggie Bar p.126
11) Inspiral Lounge p.126
12) Manna p.128
13) My Village p.130
14) Ravi Shankar p.130
15) Tai Buffet, Euston p.131
16) Veg, Kentish Town p.131
17) Wagamama p.132

Shops

a) Ambala Foods p.252
b) Braintree Hemp Store p.252
c) Whole Foods Market p.253
d) Greens & Beans p.253
e) Gupta Confectioners p.253
f) Sesame p.253

Camden Town, Primrose Hill & Chalk Farm

This area of London is one of the most vibrant, dominated as it is by Camden Market which has a vast selection of veggie food to choose from including the Ha Ha Veggie Bar. Just South of the market is Camden's live music hotspot, Green Note, which offers great veggie café cuisine. Further North is Cafe Seventy Nine in Primrose Hill which has a more relaxed atmosphere and Manna is a great innovative organic vegetarian restaurant in the same neck of the woods. If you fancy something spicy there are great value restaurants on Drummond Street, the best of which are reviewed below. Also of interest is Liz Heavenstone's Guest House (see accommodation section on page 304).

Café Seventy Nine
Modern, English

⌨ *79 Regents Park Road, NW3*
☎ *020 7586 8012*
🚌 *Chalk Farm LU, 5 min walk*
🕓 *Mon-Fri 8.30am-5pm, Sat 8.30am-6pm*
🥕 *Vegan options*
🍼 *Child friendly*
☀ *Outside Seating*

Vegetarian ★★★★★
Organic ★★★
Taste ★★★
Price £

Despite the des-res surroundings, the menu prices here are very reasonable. There's a delightful ambience where diners can enjoy all-day veggie breakfasts and get a caffeine boost with cafetière coffees and expressos. The place is a favourite neighbourhood eaterie with a mix of artists, writers and locals amongst its patrons.

All day breakfasts are the thing here and the special is particularly recommended. Scrambled eggs, mushrooms and toast with two veggie sausages is well worth a whirl. The home-made Veggie burger ensemble with salad, mayo and wholemeal pitta bread is a popular light option compared to the heavier Bagel Burger served with vegetarian Cheddar and deep fried new potatoes. All of the food is made using organic free range eggs in their own kitchen. The soup and a roll deal changes daily and is always organic.

Café Seventy Nine is not an in your face vegetarian eaterie and there's no mention of it's veggie credentials outside or even on the menu. Yet, this one of the best veggie café's in London. A swell place to visit when around Primrose Hill.

Camden Market
International, traditional

🚇 Camden Town or Chalk Farm LU, 5 min walk

🕐 Sat-Sun 9am-5pm

If you've worked up an appetite haggling over clothes purchases at London's most youth orientated market, then the food stalls of The Stables (one of several markets along Camden High Street) is the place to set your sights. Expect no-frills street food with many international cuisines represented: English, Indian, Chinese, Japanese and Thai. It's cheap and cheerful take-away food but there are also some old outdoor benches if you want to take a more leisurely approach to eating.

Carluccio's Caffé
Italian, modern

Vegetarian ★★★
Taste ★★★★
Price ££

- 🖼 *St Pancras International Station, Pancras Road, NW1*
- ☎ *020 7278 7449*
- 🖥 *www.carluccios.com*
- 🚌 *King's Cross/St Pancras LU, 2min walk*
- 🕐 *Mon-Sat 8am-11pm, Sun 8am-10.30pm*
- 🥕 *Vegan options*
- 🍼 *Child friendly*
- ☀ *Outside seating*

Popular with the international railway travelling set, it's well positioned on the Rendezvous level near the Meeting Place Statue.
See Carluccio's Caffé, St Christopher's Place for food review (page 35).

Carluccio's Caffé
Italian, modern

Vegetarian ★★★
Taste ★★★★
Price ££

- 🖼 *32 Rosslyn Hill, NW3*
- ☎ *020 7794 2184*
- 🖥 *www.carluccios.com*
- 🚌 *Hampstead LU, 5min walk*
- 🕐 *Mon-Fri 8am-11pm, Sat 9-11pm, Sun 9am-10.30pm*
- 🥕 *Vegan options*
- 🍼 *Child friendly, high chairs*
- ☀ *Outside seating*

A great place to head for after a long lazy stroll across Hampstead Heath – about a ten minute walk away. Set on the ground floor, the place is busy in the evenings with the affluent Hampstead Village set.
See Carluccio's Caffé, St Christopher's Place for food review (page 35).

Chutneys
Indian, classic

Vegetarian ★★★★★
Price ££

- 🖼 *124 Drummond Street, NW1*
- ☎ *020 7388 0604*
- 🚌 *Euston LU&Rail, 3min walk*
- 🕐 *Mon-Sat 12noon-11pm, Daily lunch buffet 12noon-5pm*
  Sunday all day buffet 12noon-10.30pm
- 🥕 *Vegan options*

The first Indian buffet in London, this is now the most up-to-date and biggest of the three Indian restaurants on Drummond Street and makes a big thing of advertising on the exterior that it's a Vegetarian restaurant.

During the week its clientele is mainly European and it is popular with German and Swiss vegetarian tourists. On Fridays, Saturdays and Sundays there's more of a mix with Asian families. With background Bollywood music and a relaxed, sophisticated atmosphere, it's the most upscale of the Drummond Street restaurants.

The most popular choice is the Chutney's Deluxe Thali (£10.50), a complete three course meal although the Kerala Set Menu at £13.95 is worth a try. Thalis here tend to be bigger than at Diwana and Ravi Shankar. The eat-as-much-as-you-like Sunday Buffet is a selection of over 40 dishes and is good value at £6.50.

Diwana Bhel Poori House
Indian, classic

🖃 *121-123 Drummond Street, NW1*
☎ *020 7387 5556*
🚌 *Euston LU &Rail, 1min walk*
🕐 *Mon-Sat 12noon-11.30pm, Sun 12noon-10.30pm*
🌢 *Vegan options*
🍶 *BYO (no corkage charged)*

Vegetarian ★★★★★
Organic ★★
Taste ★★★
Price £

Diwana is the oldest Indian vegetarian restaurant in the UK and has been going strong since 1970 with a classic Bhel Poori House menu and good value lunchtime buffet for £6.95.

The décor consists of bright wooden varnished tables and chairs and a few Indian artifacts, it's a big place with an upstairs for a further 40 people. On the several occasions that I've eaten here service has been okay, but the staff can get a bit abrupt and the service a little slow when it's busy. At 6.15pm the place gets packed with lively chatty office workers and a few veggie tourists. Most go for juices but some take the option to bring their own wine.

The menu is fairly extensive and well explained. Rava Deluxe Dosa is a huge flavoursome lacy, semolina based dosa with seasoned vegetables and comes with a good coconut chutney and okay sambar. The Gujarati Thali, comes with a quite spicy potato and pea curry with reasonable rice, dal and veg. Both these mains are quite sufficient but diners with bigger appetites could opted for starters and savouries as well. The lunchtime buffet (12noon-2.30pm) is popular and can attract 100 people.

Greens & Beans
International, classic

⌨ *131 Drummond Street, NW1*

☎ *020 7380 0857*

🚇 *Euston LU&Rail 2min walk*

🕐 *Mon-Fri, 9am-4pm (buffet 12-3.30pm, breakfasts all day)*

🌱 *Vegan options*

i *Eat-in/Takeaway*

Vegetarian ★★★★★
Organic ★★★★
Taste ★★★
Price £

Opened in 2006, this lovely vegetarian café offers a completely different menu line-up from the many veggie Indian restaurants that have made Drummond Street so famous. There are a few good tables as you go in and the buffet and takeaway counter is at the back, but the best seating is downstairs. The place is pleasantly bright, white and well decorated with smart varnished wooden tables complete with small flower arrangements. The lunchtime I visited the place was packed with veggie regulars from the nearby offices, the hospital opposite and Euston Station, all enjoying their food.

Eighty percent of the food is organic and the buffet changes daily. There are five á la carte choices of which the Lentil and Cheese Nut Roast arrives looking appetising enough with three logs of nut roast mounted on a large bed of mash and a light brown gravy. The overall flavour was hearty and satisfying and the side salad was quite good. Crespelle, a dish of two large paper thin crepes crammed with ricotta cheese and spinach and coriander in tomato sauce was also substantial and one of the most popular dishes on the menu.

The buffet looks good with enchilada, short grain brown rice, carrot, broccoli and roast potato served on a large oval plate and was good value for only £6.50. Takeout meals cost £3.25-£5.25 depending on size. Also available are five veggie pizzas and four pasta dishes. Organic breakfasts include muesli and porridge as well as a traditional full veggie breakfast of scrambled eggs, veggie sausage, tomatoes and toast. Everything is made on the premises and six organic salads are available.

The smoothies here are virtually light lunches in themselves and they offer a good selection of organic vegetable and fruit juices. The Super Skin Smoothie is a pale cream coloured concoction of pear, banana, yoghurt, tahini, pumpkin seed and flax oil and tasted quite reasonable. *For the shop review see page 253.*

Green Note

Cafe Bar, Live music, Vegetarian Menu

Vegetarian ★★★★★
Organic ★★★
Taste ★★★★
Price ££

106 Parkway, NW1
020 7485 9899
www.greennote.co.uk
Camden Town LU, 3 min walk
Wed-Sun 7pm-11pm
Vegan options
Children-friendly, high chairs
i Table service
Live music

This is an excellent music venue offering enjoyable veggie food at reasonable prices. Inside, black and white photos of famous performers line the walls with Billie Holiday and Aretha Franklin looking benignly down upon the mixed crowd of music lovers that tend to hang out in this friendly venue.

The night I visited they had live music and I split the Green Note Tapas Platter for Two (£17.95) which consisted of a selection of the chefs favourite tapas. Individual tapas can be ordered separately at about £3.50 each for those with the munchies, but this was a good way to sample everything.

The Quesdillas filled with mango and pepper came with a good dollop of sour cream and was very good. The Aloo Ki Tikki consisted of three good sized mild flavoured Indian potato patties topped with mint and coriander chutney that were reasonable, while I really enjoyed the dip pots of freshly made humous and tzatziki that came with cut pitta bread. Mock Duck, spring onion and cucumber rolls were nicely covered with lines of hoison sauce and tasted good. The organic falafels had green filling (green bean) and were really tasty, as were the Dolmades – Mediterranean stuffed vine leaves served with cut artichokes for dipping.

On the blackboard menu was Jalepeno Soup (£3.95) and there's a main special that changes daily such as Tofu and Spinach Lasagne £8.95. A salad plate of five different salads served with a good wad of mixed baby leaves, toasted seeds and house vinaigrette is also available for a very reasonable £8.95. The main course special changes daily and all dishes are freshly prepared in their kitchen.

The Green Note always has a good cheese cake on the menu and I finished my meal with the very popular vegan Mango and Apricot cheese cake that was well presented and tasted great. Other desserts available are Fresh Fruit Salad, Chocolate Brownies and organic ice creams.

Along with the 80 other members of the audience, it was a bit of a squeeze but the music was great on the night I visited and the atmosphere electric. Of the vegetarian wines Chenin Blanc and the Chardonnay were both very good and could be bought by the glass. A few organic wines are about to join the wine list and organic Freedom Lager is already on tap. The soft drinks and smoothies are also good with all the coffees and teas organic.

Many shows sell-out in advance, so check before leaving home. Tickets are a few pounds and can be bought in advance. If you are not planning to eat, feel free to show up and grab a bar stool and enjoy the music from the back. Tables are also available away from the live music area for dining without an admission charge.

Gigi Hut
Thai/Chinese, classic

▯	339 Euston Road, NW1
☎	020 7383 3978
🚌	Warren Station Road LU, 2min walk
⊕	Daily 12noon-10pm
✦	Vegan Menu
ⓞ	Kids go half price with free drinks
i	Eat-in buffet & Takeaway
⍓	BYO – no corkage charged

Vegetarian ★★★★★
Taste ★★★★
Price £

A superior quality bargain vegan oriental buffet. The décor could certainly do with a revamp, but make no mistake, Gigi Hut ups the taste stakes in this very competitive bargain arena. Formerly on the CTJ site, this is now independent from the rest of the Tai chain. It still offers a bargain £5 all-you-can-eat vegan Thai/Chinese buffet and the takeaway box is only £3.

The Hot and Sour soup was very reasonable. I went back for several enjoyable helpings of the Black bean soya and the Aubergine Mushroom Tofu with plum sauce. The Singapore noodles and fried Potato, also in a Plum sauce, was very good as well. The Thai Green Curry, although advised as mild, does come up quite spicy.

On the cold bar there was an attractive seaweed and rice salad, curried samosa, crackers, mixed vegetable salad, rice noodle salad, raw peanuts and five sauces. The drinks are also very good value with juices for just £1 and a pot of Chinese Tea for the same price.

Whilst the place has rather dowdy tables and chairs, traditional lanterns and recorded Whitney Huston music, the service is pretty good and it is hard to beat for value for money.

Ha Ha Veggie Bar
International, fast street food

Vegetarian ★★★★★
Organic ★★★★
Taste ★★
Price £

🖼 *Camden Lock Market*
  West Yard Entrance (opposite Gilgamesh), N
🚌 *Camden Town LU, 5 min walk*
🕐 *Daily 10am-5pm*
🥕 *Vegan options*
i *Counter service*

Veggie burger fans should head straight to this well established stall that serves the biggest range of veggie burgers in Camden Market. Standouts are the Hawaiian Burger with Pineapple, mayo, lettuce and onion or the Monkey Burger loaded with banana, peanut butter and salad, both priced for just £3. The Monkey Burger comes up large with an egg-free mayonnaise and tomato ketchup option that is worth trying. The soya burger itself is passable but the bun far too soft so that it easily fell apart and became quite messy to eat. If burger's just aren't your bag, there's always a very reasonable Pitta Bread, Hummus and salad at £3. Some organic drinks are also available and there are a few tables nearby. This place is popular with the market's vegetarian stall holders which is always a good sign.

Inspiral Lounge
International, classic organic vegetarian

Vegetarian ★★★★★
Organic ★★★★★
Taste ★★★★
Price ££

🖼 *250 Camden High Street*
  Camden Lock, NW1
☎ *020 7428 5875*
✎ *www.inspiralled.net*
🚌 *Camden Town LU, 5 min walk*
🕐 *Mon-Thur 10am-10pm, Fri-Sat 10am-12midnight, Sun 10am-11pm*
🥕 *Vegan options*
⊡ *Child friendly*
☀ *Outside seating by canal*
i *Counter service (Eat-in & takeaway)*
♫ *Music (DJ)*

An impressive, informal veggie organic haven for wandering souls, alternative lifestylers and lovers of gourmet live and raw food. Set on the corner of Camden Lock Bridge and Camden High Street, this is a brilliant chill out zone, with excellent electronic play list vibes, making

Inspiral Lounge

it a good place to chill out in style. The menu changes seasonally but with several classics always available. There are several serving stations with warm veggie food none of which is over 40 degrees and also a gourmet live/raw food buffet. The window seats with narrow ironing board shaped wooden tables overlooking the canal are especially good, and the canal side tables downstairs are perfect in the Summer.

Moroccan soup made from tomato, chickpea and courgette is heartily filling and delicious and comes with a multi seeded roll. It is recommended, particularly for a very reasonable price of £4.10. For a warm main, the stuffed aubergine with couscous, mushroom, courgette, garlic and topped with bread crumbs and a squiggle of yogurt was nicely presented. The aubergine was tender with a gently tang of mustard coming through. Accompanied by stir fried seasonal veg of carrot, cauliflower and potato the whole ensemble was quite enjoyable. Better still was a three raw salad selection of Asian Leaf Salad consisting of bok choi, arame seaweed, sesame seed, sliced red pepper, a sliver of spring onion, pickled ginger, cabbage and hemp seed oil that was crispy and refreshing. Love & Light Curry Salad comes mild but flavoursome with a mix of cauliflower, cherry tomato, courgette and garam masala, whilst the mixed leaf salad of lettuces, parsley and basil is above average with touches of rocket and coriander. Of the side sauces, the avocado with mustard is quite mild as is the pine nut and cumin, whilst the Guacamole with Spirulina was deep, rich and top notch.

Inspiral has a good selection of organic wines including a house merlot at a bargain £3, they also offer a good selection of smoothies with the ruby red Berry Bliss arriving in a wine glass and tasting very good. Organic cocktails such as Mojitos are popular too.

All the cakes are vegan and the chocolate and blueberry cake was okay, although a little dry on the outside when I tried it.

'Inspiral combines ethical business with culture' says Sarah Dredzykins, the amiable manager and vegetarian. 'It's not a preachy approach, although we are very much about health. Originally, we started at pop festivals, serving vegetarian food and thought to ourselves wouldn't it be great to carry the experience on for people in Camden'. And what a great idea it's turned out to be. You can even book a boat trip along the canal.

Events: Electonic chillout music Friday 7pm-12midnight
Sat 7pm-12midnight Groovy tempo, electro treats and performance
Sun 4pm-10pm Acoustic Gems, open mic and poetry

Manna
Mediterranean, international, mode

Vegetarian ★★★★★
Organic ★★★★
Taste ★★★★
Price £££

🖳 *4 Erskine Road, NW3*
☎ *020 7722 8028*
✐ *www.mannav.com*
🚌 *Chalk Farm LU, 3 min walk*
🕑 *Daily 6.30pm- 11pm (last orders 10pm), Lunch: Sat-Sun: 12.30-3pm*
🥕 *Vegan options*
⌀ *Children-friendly*
i Booking required

Opened in 1966, Manna is one of the oldest Veggie restaurants in London. It continues to push the boundaries and is a past winner of the Vegetarian Societies, 'Best Vegetarian Restaurant' Award.

Located on a side turning off the main Regents Park Road/ Primrose Hill restaurant drag, it's a popular destination, offering informal dining and strong on organic choices. Madonna, Paul McCartney, Kate Moss, and Woody Harrelson have vegged out here and Manna has done outside catering for Radiohead and Coldplay. Celebrities aside, Manna attracts an affluent, casual-dressed twenty to fortysomething crowd and has a friendly atmosphere with a gentle background sound track of jazz music and 70's-80's progressive sounds adding to the ambience.

The organic drinks range is marvellous. There's an exemplary Organic aperitif selection which includes the Juniper Green Gin and Tonic and also the Utkins Organic Vodka and Cranberry Cocktail (both recommended). There are twenty organic wines with the Argentinian organic Chenin Blanc making a very decent house choice and three organic beers and organic cider. To finish is a selection of eight organic liqueurs.

The short menu is inviting and changes every two months with different specials each day. The Butternut Squash and Coconut soup is to die for and comes with an organic bread selection of which a red and green pepper encrusted white bread is excellent. Organic Ravioli filled with herb ricotta, served on walnut pesto, parmesan and rocket leaves is enjoyably light and subtle, whilst the Tofu Triangles look tantalisingly attractive. The organic Fennel Schnitzel is a big boys portion as are all the mains at Manna. Arriving on a bed of crushed potatoes, a wad of kale with tarragon and pinky-white peppercorn sauce, it works rather well. The Wild Mushroom and flageolet Bean Ragout, is also good and comes on a root vegetable square with caramelised baby onions and baby leeks.

Save room for the desserts. Of the five organic choices, the Organic Fruit Crumble with a choice of dairy or soya cream is recommended. Vegans might like to try the Organic Orange & Amaretto Tiramasu, which although it doesn't taste of traditional Italian Tiramisu, is a landmark recipe in its own right.

Owner and Executive Chef, Matthew Kay and his team have served ground breaking dishes for years and continue to innovate. The service is attentive and staff have an extensive knowledge of vegan, gluten-free, wheat-free cuisine. Given 24 hours notice Manna can knock something up for even the most demanding vegetarian with food allergies.

My Village
Organic food, drink

🖃 *37 Chalk Farm Road, NW1*
☎ *020 7485 4996*
🚌 *Chalk Farm LU (4min walk), Camden LU (8min walk)*
🕐 *Mon-Fri 9am-8pm, Sat-Sun 10.30am-8pm,*
   Bank Holidays 12noon-8pm

This old rustic looking shop is largely organic and has a great selection of sweet treats including vegetarian cakes such as orange & lemon and date & walnut. They even have a vegan carob cake and deliciously soft banana & pecan muffins that are well worth a try. My Village is part organic café and part food store, with the cooler cabinet offering a good range of ready meals for veggies. The small quaint café is at the back and is a great place to relax after the noisy chaos of shopping in Camden.

Ravi Shankar
Indian, Classic

Vegetarian	★★★★★
Organic	★★
Taste	★★★
Price	£

🖃 *133-135 Drummond Street, Euston, NW1*
☎ *020 7388 6458*
🚌 *Euston LU&Rail 2min walk*
🕐 *Daily 12noon-10.30pm*
🥕 *Vegan options*

Ravi Shankar is under the same ownership as the two other Drummond Street Indian restaurants – Diwana and Chutney – and the food is very similar. Ravi Shankar, like Chutney's, doesn't allow you to bring your own booze but they do offer three French organic wines that are suitable for vegetarians and vegans.

A popular Indian eaterie, it's decked out with cream coloured walls and dark wooden furniture with seats on the ground floor and upstairs. The house special is the Shanka Thali, a substantial three-course meal, although lots go for the lovely looking Paper Dosa – a paper thin pancake with veggie filling.

Tai Buffet Euston
Thai/Chinese

Vegetarian ★★★★★
Taste ★★★
Price £

⊞ 337 Euston Road, NW1
🚌 Euston LU&Rai
🕐 Daily 12noon-10pm
🥕 Vegan Menu
i Eat-in buffet & Takeaway

The most modern looking of this ever-growing Thai chain. They offer a £5.50 all-you-can-eat vegan, Thai/Chinese cuisine that goes up to £6 after 5pm and on Sundays. The marvellous takeout box deal is still only £3 and if you are a real bargain hunter visit near closing time, as they do a two-for-one takeout box deal.

See food review on Wai (page 67).

Veg
Thai/Chinese, classic

Vegetarian ★★★★★
Taste ★★★
Price £

⊞ 6 Kentish Town Road, NW1
🚌 Camden Town LU, 30 sec walk
🕐 Daily 12noon-10.30pm
🥕 Vegan options
🍼 Children-friendly

Bargain £5.50 all-you-can-eat vegan cuisine that's just a quid more after 5pm and on Sundays. Opened in September 2003, the place looks definitely alright: modern café interior with twenty options at the buffet table that are regularly replenished.

It's about 80% eat in; 20% takeaway despite the amazing £3 takeaway box offer. I piled a respectable mountain of soya mock beef, soya lamb, sweet and sour soya chicken, soft Singapore noodles, veg chow mein and tofu into my plastic box that was delicious and filling. They've a good spread of salad dishes too and I spotted a rock musician filling his carton with a couple of dozen spring rolls for the band to nosh back at a nearby recording studio. When you taste them you'll know why! This is a great cheap pitstop.

Some food is organic, the policy being that if the buy-in price is a little higher than non-organic they will purchase. Veg is related to a chain of similar outfits that used to be run in conjunction with a Buddhist group. The situation is that they have become less meditative and more commercial and are planning further expansion. The meal deals are great and essentially the same at all these restaurants. Ken Chow, the head honcho, also runs free vegan cookery classes.

Whole Foods Market
Foods, Drinks, Eats,

Vegetarian ★★★★★
Organic ★★★★
Taste ★★★
Price £

- ▣ 49 Parkway, NW1
- ☎ 020 7428 7575
- 🖉 www.wholefoodsmarket.com
- 🚌 Camden Town LU, 2 min walk
- 🕐 Mon-Sat 8am–9pm, Sun 10am–8pm
- ☀ Outside seating

A great place to fill up on organic goodies when visiting Camden Market. It has a buffet/deli counter so you can eat in or out.
See Whole Foods Market, Kensington for shop review (page 265) and restaurant review (page 174).

Wagamama
Japanese, modern

Vegetarian ★★★
Taste ★★★★
Price £

- ▣ 11 Jamestown Road, NW1
- ☎ 020 7428 0800
- 🖉 www.wagamama.com
- 🚌 Camden Town LU, 5 min walk
- 🕐 Mon-Sat 12noon-11pm, Sun 12noon-10pm
- 🍼 Children-friendly

Wagamama is a superb chain of thirteen noodle bars all with the same menu, serving some very good inexpensive Japanese vegetarian choices. What makes this one different, is that it's the only Wagamama with a street level view.
For food review see Wagamama, Wigmore Street (page 48).

Hampstead, Finchley & Golders Green

Golder's Green, the vegetarian 'falafel mile' is fab for snacks, light bites and bakeries with veggie choices. Amongst the best of the fast food Jewish joints is Taboon with Milk and Honey offering a wider choice of sit down menu. The Tasti Pizza on Golders Green Road closed, but is due to re-open at sometime in North London and VitaOrganic has moved uptown to Soho with great success (see page 65). The hot ticket now on the Finchley Road is the Tiki Organic Coffee Shop. Woodlands, the famous Indian chain, has opened a branch in Hampstead, whilst much loved Rani in Finchley Central reigns supreme with it's Indian buffet – perhaps the best in London.

Finchley & Golders Green

Milk 'n' Honey
International, classic, kosher

⌨	*124 Golders Green Road, NW11*
☎	*020 8455 0664*
🚌	*Golders Greens LU, 5 min walk*
🕐	*Sun-Thurs 10.30am-11pm, Sat 7.30pm-11.30pm*
✎	*Vegan options*
☖	*Child friendly*
i	*Counter/takeout service*

Vegetarian ★★★
Taste ★★★★
Price £££

An eclectic mix of kosher Italian, Israeli and Oriental dishes in a big informal dining room. I started the extensive menu at the 'Appetiser - Let the fun begin' section with their very popular Country Style Vegetables, a mix of oven cooked veg with herb and olive oil served with a good cream dip. Mains are big and include staples such as Vegeburger and fries, Stir fry of noodles with peppers, courgettes, mushrooms with soy sauce and a selection of vegetarian pastas and pizzas. To finish there's a healthy Fresh Fruit Salad or the decadent pastries the size of doorsteps and a list of sorbets and sundaes as long as your arm. The Viennese Strudel is delicious and comes either with a good dollop of cream or ice cream. Some canned organic drinks are now on offer and low fat options are now available on some of the mains for those looking after their heart.

Milk 'n' Honey draws a garrulous clientele of Golders Green grannies–who-lunch, local Jewish ladies and young men.

Paradise Bakery
International, kosher

Vegetarian ★★★★
Taste ★★★
Price £

🖃 109 Golders Green Road, NW11
☎ 020 8201 9694
🚌 Golders Green LU, 5 min walk
🕐 Sun-Fri, 12.30pm-1am, or one hour before sabbath on Fridays and one hour after sabbath on Saturday
🥕 Vegan options
i Counter/takeout service

Pastries, cakes, chollahs, bagels suitable for vegetarians. Also, to take away, mini bourakis, pizzas and rolls. The store has undergone a refurbishment with self-service and a higher quality range of cakes.

Rani
Indian, Gujurati

Vegetarian ★★★★★
Taste ★★★★
Price ££

🖃 7 Long Lane, N3
☎ 020 8349 4386
🚌 Finchley Central LU, 6 min walk
🕐 Mon-Sat 12noon-2.30pm, 6pm-9pm,
Sun (Buffet) 1pm-2.30pm, 6pm-9pm
🥕 Vegan options (more than 50%)
🍼 Children-friendly; half price buffet for children under 10
i Eat in (table and buffet service) & Takeaway

Lifelong vegetarian, Jyotindra Pattni, a portly gentleman in a dark suit, stands proudly and content at the reception desk having checked in a full house of evening diners. He and his wife (who is the chef) offer one of the best buffets in London. The dishes are excellently presented, well labelled and all are at the correct temperature. Hygiene standards are of the highest. An attentive waiter stands at the buffet area to assist and check that no used plates are brought into the area so that there is no cross contamination of food.

Rani has been running for 24 years and whilst the service is quite formal the staff are quite friendly. Less than half the clientele are Finchley locals, with vegetarians trekking in from Islington, Camden, St Albans, Harrow and Wembley. Rani serves 100% vegetarian home-style Gujarati just like Jyotindra and his wife had back home.

The restaurant is large and comfortable, with 70's Indian style mango and red décor and green tablecloths. The eat-as-much-as-you-like buffet offers a big choice, and this is what most people go for although there is an extensive á la carte menu which works out more expensive. The buffet choices change weekly so that regulars never get bored.

At the Cold Starter station, there is Dhai Vada, Aloo Papri Chat and Bhel Poori (all good) with an excellent selection of 18 accompaniments – the lime/chilli chutney, apple chutney and mango chutney are particularly recommended. Of the hot starters I had Palak Bhajia (very good) and Rani Mogo (good). For mains, I enjoyed tasty Methi Poori and Banana Methi (v.good), pitch perfect Pilau Rice, Gurati Dal and Liloti Sak. On the desserts front, the Meth Sev is fine whilst the Fruit Shrikand is very good indeed.

The á la carte menu is most informative and wheat, nut and dairy dishes clearly marked for those people with special dietary needs.

Taboon
Jewish, Classic, Kosher

Vegetarian ★★★★★
Taste ★★
Price £

☐ 17 Russell Parade,
    Golders Green Road, NW11s
☎ 020 8455 7451
🚌 Brent Cross LU, 10 min walk
🕘 Sun-Thurs 9am-12midnight, Fri 9am-4pm, Sat 8pm-1am
i   Counter/takeout service
🌶 Vegan options

Kosher falafel filled pittas meet pizza slices and chips in this popular small neighbourhood nosh bar decked out with high stalls and zero décor. Inside, it's a mix of observant north London Jewish adults and school-kids with a few non-Jewish local workman.

Your unsmiling server diligently crams falafels into the pitta pocket leaving you to top it up from the self-service salad station with coleslaw, chopped salad, hummus, green chilli and various sauces – shame you can't get much extra in! Still, it tastes okay, while the pizza slices look just about alright. It's fine for a cheap pit-stop and they do latkas and burekas – a Yemeni speciality in cheese, potato, spinach and mushroom flavours. Drinks are canned and the Israeli Strawberry and Banana Spring Water is good. Taboon also have a branch in Edgware, tel 020 8058 5557.

Tai Buffet
Thai and Chinese, classic

Vegetarian ★★★★★
Taste ★★★
Price £

⌨ 22 Golders Green Road, NW11

🚋 Golders Green LU

🕐 12noon-10pm

Bargain £5.50 all-you-can-eat vegan Thai/Chinese cuisine that goes up to £6.50 after 5pm and on Sundays. The marvellous takeout box deal is still at only £3.

For food review see Wai (page 67).

Hampstead

Good Earth Express
Chinese, classic

Vegetarian ★★★★
Taste ★★★★★
Price £££

⌨ 335 West End Lane, NW6

☎ 020 7433 3111

🖊 www.goodearthgroup.co.uk

🚋 West Hampstead LU & Rail

🕐 Daily 5.30pm-11pm

Takeaway and delivery service only.

See Good Earth Knightsbridge for food review (page 165).

Hugo's
International, modern organic,

🖼️ 25 Lonsdale Road, NW6

☎ 020 7372 1232

🚌 Queen's Park LU, 2 min walk

🕙 Daily 9am-11pm

🍼 Child friendly

☀️ Outside seating

Vegetarian ★★★
Organic ★★★★
Taste ★★★★
Price £££

Sister restaurant to Hugo's in Kensington with essentially the same menu (see page 168). The décor at this organic café is brown rustic and there's live music on Tuesdays and Wednesdays with jazz on Sunday.

Tiki Organic Coffee Shop
International, Classic, Organic

🖼️ 229 Finchley Road, NW3

☎ 020 7317 7070

🚌 Finchley Road LU, 1 min walk

🕙 Mon-Fri 7am-9pm, Sat-Sun 8am-9pm

🥕 Vegan options

🍼 Child friendly

i Counter service/Takeaway service

Vegetarian ★★★★
Organic ★★★★★
Taste ★★★★
Price £

Tiki is one of the best organic cafés in London with a good selection of veggie options. Opened in February 2007, it's a café delight with circular modern lights, cappuccino and cream coloured walls and ceilings, ten tables with comfortable beige leather bucket chairs for street gazing and comfy brown wooden padded chairs. The style continues downstairs where there is a children's play area in the corner.

The serving counter looked a bit like Starbucks but that is where the similarity ceased. The food and drink was a lot better with organic fair trade coffee, including an excellent medium roast cappuccino. On hand too are a good range of teas including suki tea and smoothies. The lunchtime I visited was busy with a mixed crowd including a few laptop wealding urbanites taking advantage of the free wireless connection and a business suit sipping organic lemonade and tucking into a pre packed vegan wedge of a sarnie.

All ingredients here are 99% organic. The mozzarella, rocket, tomato and pesto seeded panini (£3.20) was made on the premises and loaded with good taste and the Brie, sweet green pepper, rocket and pesto plain bread panini was equally good.

Vegan Organic Chocolate Cake topped with almond flakes (£2.60) was the best vegan cake I tasted this year and made from a chocolate sauce that gave a superb rich taste which concealed a moist interior. It was enough for two people to split, but the flavour was so good that you might resent sharing it. Also available was organic carrot cake and an Organic Cranberry & Raspberry cake which was great looking and also suitable for vegans – a group which Tiki do a lot to cater for with a complete listing of their vegan dishes. Also on the counter were shortbreads, cookies, biscuits and Kallo organic rice cakes as well as fruit, nut and oat bars suitable for vegans.

In the chiller section there were bottled soft drinks and juices and in the summertime there is freshly squeezed orange and carrot juice. A pre-packed Celtic Bakery vegetarian mini quiche of leek, mushroom and pepper is available and can be heated up at the counter.

If any criticism can be made, it is that the tables can be a bit of a tight squeeze. That said, I really like this place for its style, presentation and the quality of the food.

A Tiki branch in Hemel Hempstead opens shortly.

Woodlands Hampstead
South Indian, Classic

	Vegetarian ★★★★★
▭ 102 Heath Street, Hampstead, NW3	Taste ★★★★
☎ 020 7794 3080	Price £££
✎ www.woodlandsrestaurant.co.uk	
🚌 Hampstead LU	
🕐 Tues-Sun 12noon-3pm, 6pm-11pm, Mon 6pm-11pm	
➶ Vegan options	
⬡ Child friendly	
i Eat in (table service) & Takeaway available	

Opened in November 2005, Woodlands' vast experience in Indian vegetarian cooking is a most welcome addition to this Hampstead dining strip. With bare brick walls and an interior of stone and marble with water features this is an enjoyable and stylish place to eat. The food is of the same high standard as the other vegetarian restaurants in the group. *For a full review of the food see Woodlands, Chiswick on page 190.*

Archway
The Peking Palace
Chinese, classic

Vegetarian ★★★★★
Organic ★★★
Taste ★★★★
Price ££

▦ *669 Holloway Road, N19*

☎ *020 7281 8989*

🚌 *Archway tube, 1 min walk*

◷ *Mon-Sat Lunchtime Buffet 12.00pm-3.00pm, £4.95*
Dinner 6.00pm-11.00pm, Sunday 6.00pm-11.00pm

✹ *Vegan options*

◊ *Child friendly*

i *Table service/Takeaway*

Speciality mock-carnivore Chinese vegetarian restaurant that will leave you pleasantly full, taste buds intrigued and your concepts of soya-driven cuisine changed forever. Peking Palace has the longest vegetarian menu in London with over a hundred dishes, all vegan except five. The Set Dinners represent good value at £12.50-£18.50 per person. The Set Dinner C is voluminous enough to satisfy a Sumo wrestler while set A or B will suit most appetites. Swop dishes from the other Set Dinners if you fancy.

Complimentary cassava crackers compare well with good prawn crackers in taste and texture. Don't eat too many as you'll need room for your starters! Set Dinner C begins gently with traditional appetisers of mini Vegetable Spring Rolls, Sesame on Toast, Crispy Seaweed and Grilled Dumplings. Nothing too special here until you get to the yummy Satay Veg consisting of mock-chicken pieces with pepper and onion pieces on skewers. The second act is a very reasonable Crispy Aromatic Veggie Duck appearing as strips covered with a 'mock-veggie batter'.

The best comes in Act 3 with the Veggie Beef Steak Peking style, arriving as big succulent slices of Veggie Chicken with Cashew Nuts in Yellow Bean Sauce, Stir-fried Broccoli with Mange Tout in Veggie Oyster Sauce and a good Thai Fragrant Steamed Rice. The big star undoubtedly is the Veggie Fish in Black Bean sauce that I swapped with the Veggie Prawn on the set menu. The best mock-fish dish in London, it has a smoked haddock flavour and texture and comes in three pieces rimmed in seaweed. Dessert choices are limited although the fried banana with sesame and vegan Swedish Glacé ice cream are both good.

Alcohol is now a bit frowned upon here for health reasons, so it's no longer BYO but people seem to be quite happy with the virtually alcohol-free lager, Schloer White Grape drink or a pot of traditional Organic Kukicha Roasted Bancha Twig Tea drunk throughout the meal. Service here is attentive and staff are knowledgeable and helpful.

Highgate & Muswell Hill

This part of London has several great cafés including The Pavilion and Queen's Wood Café and Garden, both of which offer great food in the midst of lush woodland. The Cue Garden gets a special review, just because it is such a great resource for those wanting to garden organically near the capital. Nearby also is Café Theatro and with a new Planet Organic café in Muswell Hill, vegetarians in this area have never had it so good.

Café Theatro
International, Classic

Vegetarian ★★★★
Price £

- 🏠 269a Archway Road, N6
- ☎ 020 8340 5226
- 🚌 Highgate LU, 1 min walk
- ◷ Tue-Sun 10am-8.30pm
- 🥕 Vegan options
- 🍼 Children-friendly
- ☀ Seating outside in Summer
- i Order at counter, food delivered to the table
- i Takeaway

Vegetarian food meets theatre in this busy community arts centre located in a converted Edwardian Church which now has no religious affiliation. Inside, it's looks like a community centre with loads of big tables and ample seating, giving visitors ample opportunity to hang out and chat.

Café Theatro opened in January 2008 and is run single-handedly by Koula Pericleous, who makes all the food on the premises. The café's blackboard menu lists the 'specials' that change daily. These could be Pasta Penne with pesto and pine nuts with or without cheese (£4), grilled halloumi, pitta bread and Mediterranean salad for only £4.50. There's a tempting soup choice of broccoli with blue Brie or alternatively lentil, tomato or leek – all of which come with a roll for £3.50. Other lighter meals include quiches, paninis, jacket potatoes filled with Mediterranean veg or beans. Kids are well catered for with smaller portions for just £2.50 and there's a Pensioners Club also at 12 noon each day.

Always available for tea are eight vegetarian cakes, including chocolate, apple, coffee, banana & coconut and a vegan carrot cake.

Pavilion Café
Mediterranean and English, Classic

Vegetarian ★★★★
Price ££

🖵 *Highgate Wood, Muswell Hill Road, N10*

☎ *020 8444 4777*

🚌 *Highgate LU, 5 min walk*

🕓 *Daily 9am-5pm (winter)*
   9am-till 30min before gates close at Highgate Wood (summer)

🌶 *Vegan options*

🍼 *Children-friendly*

☀ *Seating outside*

i *Counter service/Takeaway*

♫ *Live music Thursday, Friday evenings during May and June*

The Pavilion Café is a pleasant outdoor garden for lunches and snacks and a great place to bring the kids. In the heart of an ancient wood, it's best approached from Gypsy Gate on Muswell Hill Road, although you might have to ask several times for directions.

On a lazy summer's afternoon the place is joyously packed with families, couples and kids sipping, slurping and grazing in the big dining area which can hold up to 150. Particularly good are the tables undercover in the shade, with a view of the roses and wisteria that surrounds the enclosure. In the winter there is less flora to enjoy but they do have outdoor heaters to make it tolerable.

The menu is 75% vegetarian and light snacks include mezzes with hummus, grilled haloumi with flat bread and vegetable couscous. Other favourites include Goat's cheese salad, soups and sandwiches. For hungrier souls there's more substantial fare such as a posh Pasta with Truffle Mushroom Sauce for £9.

There's a further 30 seats inside the café, which is nice to know if it pours with rain. The café is opposite the wood's sports ground that has a cricket and football pitch. The charms of Highgate Wood and the award winning children's playground nearby make this a great place to visit with the family and offers enough delicious cakes and snacks to entice even the most committed couch potato to take a walk.

Planet Organic Muswell Hill
Organic, vegetarian, International

Vegetarian ★★★★
Organic ★★★★★
Taste ★★★
Price £

🖿 *111-117 Muswell Hill Road, N10*
☎ *020 8442 2910*
✍ *www.planetorganic.com*

Planet Organic offers a 30 seater café inside their massive 4,200 sq ft shop on a former building merchants site with parking for 80 cars.
For the food review see Planet Organic, Westbourne Grove (page 182).

Queen's Wood Café and Garden
Mediterranean, English, classic

Vegetarian ★★★★★
Organic ★★★
Taste ★★
Price £

🖿 *Queen's Wood Lodge,*
    42 Muswell Hill Road, N10
☎ *020 8444 2604*
🚌 *Highgate LU, 5 min walk*
🕒 *Mon-Fri 10am-4pm, Sat-Sun, 9am-6pm (till 5pm in winter)*
🥕 *Vegan options*
🐾 *Child and dog friendly*
☀ *Seating outside*
i *Counter service sit in or /takeout*

A woodland haven with a community-run veggie organic café complete with its own organic garden (see next page). A short walk from Muswell Hill Road, this former derelict building now has a charming forest cabin exterior whilst inside the look is cosy-grot with an old sofa, a couple of tatty armchairs, some folding chairs and red coloured tablecloths. Previously open only at weekends it is now open to enjoy seven days a week

At 4pm it's packed with all ages sipping organic tea and coffee and woofing down organic cake. The food here is pure vegetarian and the café is committed to organic on a 'where-possible' basis. There are about eight main meals including Spicy Burrito served with fresh mixed salad and salsa and a very respectable range of toasted ciabatta sandwiches with combinations of mozzarella, roast veg, char-grilled aubergine, avocado and tomato.

The vegetable soup with beans and rice served with a big chunk of bread and butter is one of the favourites here and the organic cakes are freshly made, good and enough for two. The Lemon Polenta is moist and yummy and the Fruiti De Bosco (fruits of the forest pie) is what I'll try next time. There are now a few choices for meat eaters but about 90% of the menu is still vegetarian.

Goblin-themed children's parties, treasure hunts and private functions are held here that also utilise the nearby woodlands. You could almost imagine a performance of *A Midsummer's Night Dream* being performed here. After 6pm sometimes there are wedding parties. What an enchanting idea!

During the week *Friends Of Queen's Wood* use the building and a new literary group meets on a Monday.

Cue Organic Garden

This garden attached to the Queens Wood Café is a must see for anyone interested in urban organic gardening. A working garden, it might not look much aesthetically but is extremely informative and educational with useful printed notices explaining practices like crop rotation and mulching.

There's a good example of Square-Foot Gardening showing how London urbanites can grow a wide variety of organic plants in a very small area comprising usually of 16 tiny units. This system is ideal for children and beginners and on show the day I visited were onions, tomatoes, lettuce that were used in the cafe's salad. There's also a greenhouse to look round as well as a section on Organic Container Gardening where containers are hung up, stood on the ground or in a window box – ideal for Londoners without gardens. Amongst the foods grown that are used in the café are carrot, courgette, tomato, lettuce and potato.

The Cue Organic Garden experiment forms part of a project giving urban solutions to ecological problems. No matter where you live in London there's advice on sustainable development, solar energy and the principles of growing fresh organic fruit and veg.

The Garden runs regular volunteer workdays, an Organic Gardening Course and occasionally education and local community workshops as well as continuing research into environmental problems.

Organic gardening volunteer work varies from delicate plant tending to labour intensive compost heap turning on Thursdays 10am-2pm. A free lunch is provided for volunteers.

Restaurants

1) The Blue Legume p.1145
2) The Dervish p.146
3) Whole Foods Market p.150
4) Higher Taste Vegetarian Patisserie p.146
5) Lemon Monkey p.147
6) Rasa p.148
7) Tasti Pizza p.150

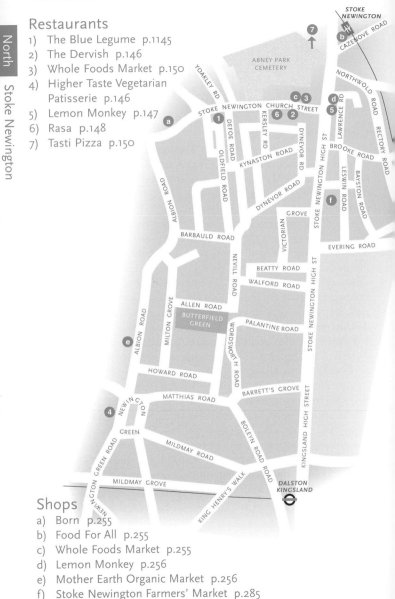

STOKE
NEWINGTON

ABNEY PARK
CEMETERY

Shops

a) Born p.255
b) Food For All p.255
c) Whole Foods Market p.255
d) Lemon Monkey p.256
e) Mother Earth Organic Market p.256
f) Stoke Newington Farmers' Market p.285

Stoke Newington

Stoke Newington is a diverse area with a varied social and racial mix making up its inhabitants. The restaurants of the area are largely concentrated round Church Street with The Blue Legume and Rasa both proving long established favourites, whilst new kid on the block, Yellow Monkey is showing much promise. We have cast our net more widely to Newington Green and the great Tasti Pizza further north on Amhurst parade. The smart branch of Whole Foods Market is a great mainstay to the shops of Church Street and further indicates the affluence of the area.

The Blue Legume
English, Traditional

🖾	*101 Stoke Newington Church St, N16*
☎	*020 7923 1303*
🚌	*Stoke Newington BR 10 min walk*
🕑	*Mon-Sat 9.30am-11pm, Sun 9.30am-6.30pm*
i	*Counter service*

Vegetarian ★★★★
Organic ★★
Taste ★★★
Price £

Relaxed chill out zone serving good value vegetarian breakfasts, snacks and lunches attracting media types, psychologists and laid-back intellectuals. To blend in perfectly bring a newspaper, book, friend or kid and wear bohemian black, grey or beige. Paintings by local artists spice up the walls and there's a totem pole of Punch sitting on a frog (maybe that's why they get so many psychologists). Look up and you'll see a kitsch mock Sistine Chapel ceiling complete with a New Age Sun.

The breakfast of vegetarian sausage, peppery pan fried mushrooms, baked beans, poached egg, grilled tomato and fresh wholemeal toast is tastily satisfying at £5.95. Mushroom on toast with creme fraiche is another delicious option or you could perhaps try the popular organic honey waffles with fresh fruit, yogurt and maple syrup. Organic ginger cordial and lemonades are available.

The blackboard changes daily and among the vegetarian choices there are five salads, quiches, chickpea and tahini burger or leek and gruyère tart. In the evenings things go Mediterranean with the big fave being Gnocci with Vegetables topped with vegetarian Parmesan (£8.95), although Organic Vegetarian Burgers with french fries (£7.95) and Vegetable Moussaka with Goat's cheese (£8.95) are also very popular. Whether you're looking for a substantial meal or a relaxed coffee and cake, The Blue Legume is an established Stokie favourite and well worth a visit.

The Dervish
Turkish, traditional

Vegetarian ★★★
Taste ★★★★
Price ££

🖾 15 Stoke Newington Church St, N16

☎ 020 7923 9999

🚞 Stoke Newington BR 10 min walk

🕘 Daily 9.30am-6.30pm

🍼 Child friendly

☀ Outside seating

The Dervish has the same menu as Gallipoli Again (see page 106) and has now established itself as a favourite in Stoke Newington with a similar lively atmosphere in the evenings.

Higher Taste Vegetarian Patisserie
Turkish Patisserie and Café

Vegetarian ★★★★★
Taste ★★★
Price £

🖾 47 Newington Green, N16

☎ 020 7359 2338

🚞 Canonbury BR 5 min walk

🕘 Mon-Sat 7am-8pm, Sun 9am-6pm

🥕 Vegan options

🍼 Child friendly (but no high chairs)

i Counter/takeaway service

A gem in Newington Green's 'Little Istanbul' dining area. At the back is a small vegetarian bakery making birthday and wedding cakes (£20-£25), cheese and potato pastries, spinach and cheese pancakes, cheese buns and a vast array of traditional Turkish biscuits and sweets. The rest of the place is a narrow greenish strip of a café, seating 15 with a counter serving hummus and hot snacks to hungry lunchtime local Turks and Brits.

The vegetarian Baklava, topped with pistachio nuts and filled with syrup is of good quality and pleasantly soft, whilst also worth a try is Sutlu Bogrek, a pastry filled with custard and Seker Pare, small liquid filled sweets. The butter free Shortcake is quite novel and the coffee surprisingly good.

Lemon Monkey
International, Traditional

Vegetarian ★★★
Organic ★★★★
Taste ★★★
Price £

⊞ *188 Stoke Newington High Street, N16*

☎ *020 7241 4454*

✐ *www.lemon-monkey.co.uk*

🚉 *Stoke Newington BR 5 min walk*

🕐 *Mon-Wed 9am-6pm, Thurs-Sat 9am-9pm, Sun 10am-6pm*

🥕 *Vegan options/Counter service*

☀ *Outside eating area at the back is planned*

Laid back and yummy, this welcome addition to Stoke Newington's organic scene opened in November 2007 and has been busy with mums and kids every weekday ever since. On Sunday afternoons it's more chilled out with a 25-40's crowd, chatting round the large table by the window, whilst others lounge around on the massive sofas upstairs or perhaps peruse an old cookery book off the bookshelf, or read a newspaper. Indeed, the place has a large airy atmosphere, recorded soul music and a regular flow of customers browsing round the wall to ceiling shelving units stocked with food produce – see page 256 for shop review.

In terms of the menu the salads are 100% organic with a choice of three pulse salads suitable for vegans. Another delicious temptation is the Goats cheese and spinach quiche with a side salad for just £4 or for the same price there are rye bread sandwiches with grilled vegetables and Brie, Cheese and Sun dried Tomato or Cheese and Roasted Artichokes, all of which come with a side salad. I can vouch for the organic latte made with coffee from Monmouth Coffee Company and organic soya milk and there's a Poppy seed Cake with ground almonds which is well worth a whirl. Alternatively, for a quick hunger-buster, there's Organic cheese with pumpkin seed crisp bread on the front counter. This place has a great atmosphere and offers equally interesting and fresh food, making it a great place for a veggie bite in Stokie.

Rasa
South Indian

Vegetarian ★★★★★
Taste ★★★★
Price £££

- 📠 *55 Stoke Newington Church St, N16*
- ☎ *020 7249 0344*
- 🖱 *www.rasarestaurants.com*
- 🚉 *Stoke Newington BR 10 min walk*
- 🕐 *Lunch served Daily 12noon-2.45pm*
- *Dinner served Sun-Thurs 6pm-10.45pm, Fri & Sat 6pm-11.45pm*
- 🍴 *Vegan options*
- *i Eat in (tableservice) & Takeaway service, booking essential in evenings*

This is the one everyone talks about. With its totally vegetarian Keralan cuisine and authentic atmosphere Rasa continues to be a hot destination in town. The relaxing rose-pink décor, pictures of tropical South West Indian village scenes and Keralan music creates a comfortable ambience in which casually-dressed, Stokey twenty-fortysomething intellectuals chat the night away.

Rasa's menu gives helpful introductory info on the region's cuisine as well as lucid dish explanations. Friendly, knowledgeable staff dressed in regional apparel explain what's what when they serve up. The 'Kerala Feast' is recommended and represents excellent value at £16.50 per head for pre-meal snacks, starters, side dishes, curry selection, rice, breads and sweet. The á la carte is an extensive menu offering 10 starters, 10 regional curries and 8 sweets.

Mango lassi and sweet lassi are enjoyable traditional yogurt drinks that most diners go for, although the Cobra lager is popular too. Pre-meal snacks consist of pickles and chutney's, papadoms, crunchy sticks and achappam. The Mysore Bonda starter of gingery potato balls dipped in coconut chutney is tasty as is the Banana Boli. The fried aubergine Kathrikka, served with tomato chutney is however a little too bland.

The curries here are right on the money. Particularly likeable is the aubergine main, Bagar Baingan, in a roasted nutty paste, whilst the Moru Kachiathu, Rasa Kayu and Stir fried Savoy Cabbage dishes went well with tangy lemon rice and were mopped up with a good paratha bread and appam. Pal Paysam, a rice pudding with raisin and cashew nuts, was a great way to finish the meal.

Rasa means 'taste' and lives up to all expectations. It's popular and by 9pm the two dining rooms are full with some customers waiting at front of house for their tables. The owner, Das Sreedharan, has a great many restaurants in London (listed opposite) but this is the only purely vegetarian eatery in the group.

The other Rasa's are veg/non-veg combinations and can be found at: Rasa W1, 6 Dering Street W1(veg & meat), Rasa Samudra, 5 Charlotte St W1 (veg & seafood), Rasa Travancore (mixed), 56 Stoke Newington N16, Rasa Maricham (veg & meat), Holiday Inn Hotel, 1 King's Cross Road WC1. Also there are takeouts at Rasa Express, 5 Rathbone St near Oxford Street. (tel 020 7637 0222,) and Rasa Express, 327 Euston Road offer a lunch time only snack and meal takeaway.

Tasti Pizza
Pizza, Mediterranean, Kosher,

Vegetarian ★★★★
Taste ★★
Price £

⊞ 23 Amhurst Parade, N16

☎ 020 8802 0018

🚌 Seven Sisters LU then bus to Stamford Hill

🕐 Sun-Thurs 11am-10pm

👶 Child friendly

i   Eat-in counter service & Takeaway service

A small kosher vegetarian pizza parlour with traditional Jewish/ Mediterranean snacks and soft drinks repertoire. Opened in 1994, inside it looks, well, just like a place that makes pizzas. It is mainly takeout although there is seating for up to eleven eat-ins. I took out, drove off and gobbled down my attractive cheese and tomato, topped with mushroom regular-sized pizza at nearby Clapton Common. The pizza base was crispy, a little burnt but overall tasted very good. The Latkes here are good and they also do hummus, tahini, falafel, jacket potato and chips. Whilst Tasti Pizza in Golders Green has closed, a new branch in North London is due to open soon.

Whole Foods Market
Organic, vegetarian, international

Vegetarian ★★★★
Organic ★★★★★
Taste ★★★★
Price £

⊞ 32-40 Stoke Newington Church St, N16

☎ 020 7254 2332

🖰 www.wholefoodsmarket.com

🚌 Stoke Newington BR 10 min walk

🕐 Mon-Sat 8am-6.30pm, Sun 9am–6.30pm
     shop closes 9pm

🥕 Vegan options

☀ Outside seating only

They've upped the taste stakes at this very popular organic supermarket and eaterie – simply perfect for a sunny day. A new menu of raw and slow foods was introduced in February 2008 and the high quality really shows. On the 'cold case', as they call cold dishes here, was a delicious Tumeric Cous Cous with an excellent feta and mint, a good three bean salad, wild rice salad and a very enjoyable spicy Chinese salad. All the dishes tasted delicious and were served on a proper plate – although the thin disposable wooden knife and fork had trouble coping with the long stems of the broccoli accompanied by quality sun dried tomatoes. Also on cold case, and looking delectable, is a very good wild mushroom soba salad and a handsome traditional Greek Salad of kalamata olives, sweet cherry tomatoes and red onions.

The menu changes every two weeks but some firm favourites are retained. On the hot case an inspired Tibetan recipe of Spinach and Tofu with sprouting purple broccoli in rice is recommended, whilst Red Kidney Bean and white butter bean casserole is also very good. The ratatouille of mixed roasted yellow red and yellow peppers, carrot, courgettes and the roasted potato with rosemary and garlic turned out to be substantial and tasted great. As with all Whole Foods Market Stores, food is sold by the weight with hot £1.30/100g and cold £1.50/100g, which works out a bargain at roughly £3–£5 a plate .

The hot case foods are served lightly warmed to retain maximum nutrients, however they will heat the foods up further if that is your preference. In the chiller unit are many vegetarian soups that they will warm up for you and there is a snack counter including a veggie breakfasts such as muesli, fresh fruit salad and soya yoghurt. Two vegan beers are available, one vegan cheesecake and a big choice of delicious vegetarian cakes.

Whole Foods Market focus on supporting their community and here they include Indian and Rastafarian dishes. All the eateries at Whole Foods Market operate independently although there are some recipe swops between branches.

If there is one criticism that can be made it is that only outside eating is available. When it starts to rain people gobble up their food pretty quickly or huddle under the awning thankfully holding a piping hot organic coffee. Despite this drawback the food here is very good and on fine days this is a great place to get a veggie meal or snack.

The organic shop review is on page 265.

Finsbury Park

Expressorganic
International, Classic

⌨ *Platform 5&6 , Finsbury Park Station, N4*

☎ *020 7281 8983*

🕐 *Mon-Fri 7am-9pm, Sat 10am-8pm, Sun 10am-6*

🏃 *Vegan options*

i *Takeaway*

Vegetarian ★★★★
Organic ★★★★★
Price £

Omnivorous train station kiosk specialising in organic takeout food, snacks and drinks for discerning commuters and eco-warrior Arsenal supporters.

Opened in July 2003, it's located on the northbound over ground platform of Finsbury Park Station. This is snack attack central serving vegetarian wraps and sarnies and three types of vegetarian soups. Drinks include organic coffee, organic milk and soya milk, organic bio-yoghurt, while hunger busting snacks include vegetarian Bombay Mix and vegetarian organic cakes of which the vegan date slice is recommended. Prices are reasonably competitive and organic vending machines serving nuts, crisps and flavoured water are there when the kiosk is closed.

Expressorganic stays open late for football matches and other big local events. Some people eat seated on the platform benches others take their food on the train. 'We tried salads and pastas but these didn't go down to well' says Amanda Fletcher of Expressorganic. 'What we have now is highly manageable foods for a busy train'.

Further Expressorganic kiosks and vending machines are at Highbury & Islington overground station, Eastbound (Mon-Sat, 7am-8pm),
Seven Sisters, overground station, Northbound (Mon-Fri, 7am-8pm, Sat 12.15pm-8pm).

Jai Krishna
Vegetarian Restaurant
Indian, classic

Vegetarian ★★★★★
Taste ★★★
Price £

- 161 Stroud Green Road, N4
- 020 7272 1680
- Finsbury Park LU, 10min walk
  Crouch Hill BR, 2min walk
- Mon-Sat 12noon-2pm, 5.30pm-11pm
- Vegan options
- Child friendly
- Eat in &Takeaway
- BYO

Popular budget-priced neighbourhood all-vegetarian Indian restaurant serving extensive range of North and South Indian food. Situated close to Tesco's along the Stroud Green Road dining strip, from the outside it has smart modern Venetian blinds while inside it is packed every night of the week. This is not surprising because it's inexpensive for what you get and the bring your own wine policy with only £1.25 corkage per bottle or 30p per can of beer also keeps the prices down. Most of the youthful t-shirted diners are wine drinkers and bring in bottles from Jack's Off Licence opposite.

There is, however, one odd thing about Jai Krishna, at the table you get a menu and a pen and paper to write down what you want to order. Then you have to take it to the counter and they then deliver the plates to your table. Why they do this is anybody's guess but it's a tradition they've continued in their new more modern veggie restaurant on Turnpike Lane, Jai Shri Kristna (see page 160 for details).

The menu features all the Gujarati signature dishes among which the Patra, their speciality of Advi leaves with a tamarind sauce, stands out as an enjoyable starter. Looking around the tables, the dosas, samosas and Indian pizzas were going down a treat. The atmosphere was buzzy, chatty and some tables were celebratory. New additions to the menu include the Papri Chaat starter and the Mix Platter, both of which have proved popular. The curry dish list is long and mains of Okra Curry, Mixed Vegetable Curry and Brown Rice with vegetable come packed with flavour and quality ingredients and are big enough for two. Most people, however, whilst seemingly knowledgeable about ordering veggie Indian food order twice the volume they can eat. If you want low-priced value for money veggie in the Finsbury Park, Crouch End areas this is the restaurant of choice. Lunchtimes are, however, quiet.

New Southgate

Jaaneman Vegetarian Restaurant
Vegetarian Indian, classic

Vegetarian ★★★★★
Taste ★★★
Price £

- 170 Bowes Road, N11
- 020 8888 1226
- Arnos Grove or Bounds Green LU, 5 min walk
- Fri-Sun 6pm-10pm
- Vegan options
- Children-friendly
- BYO wine (no corkage charge)

A small neighbourhood Gujarati/South Indian pure veggie eaterie bang on the North Circular with bags of free off street parking space. The menu now includes North Indian choices and has a good selection of popular starters and main dishes with a real strength in the sweet department – it has it's very own sweet centre next door (see page 289 for more details).

The Special Thali comes highly recommended and consists of two curries, four purées or three chapattis, dal, boiled rice, one pappadom and one sweet as well as salad and pickle.

Hendon

Carluccio's Caffé
Italian, classic

Vegetarian ★★★
Taste ★★★★
Price ££

    ▢ *Fenwick, Brent Cross, Hendon, NW4*
    ☎ *020 8203 6844*
    ✍ *www.carluccios.com*
    🕐 *Mon-Fri 10am-8pm, Sat 9.30am-6.30pm, Sun 11am-5pm*
    🥕 *Vegan options*
    🍼 *Child friendly, high chairs*

The place to go when braving Brent Cross shopping centre.
For review see Carluccio's Caffé, St Christopher's Place, W1 (page 35).

Isola Bella
Kosher, Thai, Italian

Vegetarian ★★★★
Taste ★★★
Price £££

    ▢ *63 Brent Street, NW3*
    ☎ *020 8203 2000*
    ✍ *www.isolabellacafe.com*
    🚌 *Hendon Central LU, 5 min walk*
    🕐 *Sun-Thurs 8am-11pm, Fri 8am-4pm*
       Closed Sat (summer), Open Sat evenings (winter)
    🥕 *Vegan options*
    i *Takeaway Service, Booking required*
    🍼 *Child friendly, high chair*
    ☀ *Outside seating for 20*
    🍷 *BYO Kosher Wine (they supply glasses)*

This cheerfully noisy, predominantly Jewish family–style neighbourhood restaurant serves a huge number of Thai and Italian vegetarian choices. Spacious, rich in personality, Isola Bella is a bit like the TV series 'Cheers', if you go there long enough it's a place 'where everyone knows your name.'

Set along a Hendon Jewish shopping parade, outside it looks just like a typical modern café. Inside, there's an incessant din of chat, gossip and birthday party celebrations with the odd indoor firework going off. The front of house is the main socialising zone for orthodox Jewish clientele and although most men's heads are covered, it's not mandatory. Staff are friendly and efficient with a good sense of humour.

The large menu is 80% veggie and the portions are enough for two or even three. We skipped the starters and dived straight for the mains.

Sida Loui Fay is a superb Thai crunchy medley of mushroom, cauliflower, broccoli, green bean, carrot, onion, potato and cornichons, stirfried in soya sauce and garnished with cashew nuts. The Salsa Baby Potato, a house speciality topped with salsa and béchamel sauce, was delicious, but far too large for my petite companion to finish. Other dishes I saw being enjoyed at other tables included noodles, soup casseroles, omelettes, pizzas and pastas and all looked appetising. A recent innovation to the menu that is proving popular is the Hot Plate consisting of Falafel, Fried Cauliflower, mushroom, potato nuggets and Won Ton which is served with dips and is enough for two and a great deal for only £12.

Of the Oriental desserts, Wimala is reasonably good, a thick crêpe filled with banana and maple syrup and served with ice cream and whipped cream. However, the pièce de resistance is the Israeli-imported Chocolate Trio of three layers of meringues and dark, milk and white chocolate. Simply divine!

Jays Restaurant
Indian, International, Classic

Vegetarian ★★★★★
Price £

- 🖃 547 Kingsbury Road, NW9
- ☎ 020 8204 1555
- 🚅 Kingsbury LU, 2min walk
- 🕓 Daily 12.30pm-11pm
- 🥕 Vegan options
- 🍼 Child friendly
- i Takeaway Service

Established for over 10 years, this small, modern restaurant is very popular with locals and gets quite busy. Focusing mainly on South Indian dosas, curries, snacks and tandooris, they also strive to give a great selection of veggie choices from around the world including Singapore noodles (£5.75), Thai Red and Green Curry (£5.50), Italian pasta dishes (£6), Mexican enchiladas (£6.50) and Burritos (£5.50) and a variety of Chinese soups. To the purist this kind of international menu will be a little off putting as it is hard to see how one kitchen can produce so many different dishes. The food may not be entirely authentic, but their use of sunflower oil in cooking does make many of the dishes suitable for vegans.

Those with doubts about this kind of menu should stick to the Indian selection which is well priced with lots of snacks and starters and mains such as Maysore Masala Dosa (£5.75), Chilli Paneer (£5.75) and Indian curries for around the £5.50 mark.

A lunchtime buffet is available week days 12 noon-3.30pm except bank holidays. Jays is fully licensed and has an extensive juice bar and a good selection of other soft drinks.

Rajen's Thali Restaurant
Indian, Classic

Vegetarian ★★★★★
Taste ★★★★
Price £

- 🖃 195-197 The Broadway, West Hendon, NW9
- ☎ 020 8203 8522
- 🚅 Hendon BR, 1 min walk, Hendon Central LU 15min
- 🕓 Wed-Mon 12noon-3pm, 6pm-10pm
- 🥕 Vegan options
- 🍼 Child-friendly
- ⅄ Licensed Bar
-   Free car park in the evenings
- i Takeaway Service 10am-7pm (except Tuesdays).

There's great value for money in this classic Indian grand-style restaurant serving good quality traditional dishes. Outside, it may look a bit cheesey with its red neon 'Open' sign, but inside it is well decorated with gracious dark wooden furnishings, a smart material draped ceiling, some intriguing Indian wall pictures and a specially commissioned bar transported from India itself.

Every day of the week there is a different regional thali menu. The Thursday night I went the region was Kutchi-Kathyavadi, Western India, part of Gujarat. Traditionally a relatively simple thali, I discovered the Rajen's offering a satisfying constellation of flavours.

Starters began with small yellow squares of Patra Dohkla, an excellent Bhel Puri that included peanuts and peas, a speciality Dabeli which had a smooth potato filling, a small samosa and a bowl of tamarind and chutney accompanied by a fresh salad. A glass of cooling sweet lassi worked well with the meal, although I can say the passion fruit juice here is good too.

The Kathyavadi Sabji (vegetables) accompanied by chappatti without butter was enjoyable. The black beans were of good flavour and the cabbage very enjoyable. Kadhi, a savoury yellow curry made with yoghurt, was served with a deliciously fluffy white rice and went well with the accompanying Dahl. All the Thalis come with salad and delicious Indian pickles and relishes. To finish there was a rather nice fragrant bulghar wheat dessert called Lapsi.

On Saturday night things liven up with their karaoke 50 party sit downs (karaoke-phobics, you've been warned). The rest of the time it's good Bollywood background music.

Overall, the service was impeccable and knowledgeable and excellent value at £7.50 a head with children for only £5 over the weekend and only £5.99 on other days. At lunch a free lassi or coke is included in the price – not bad considering the food is so well served and presented. Rajens is well worth a visit.

Rose Vegetarian
Indian, Chinese, Classic

Vegetarian ★★★★★
Taste ★★★
Price £

⌑ 532-534 Kingsbury Road, Kingsbury, NW9
☎ 020 8905 0025
✍ www.rosevegetarian.co.uk
🚌 Kingsbury LU , 2min walk
🕓 Mon-Thurs 12noon-10pm, Fri-Sun 12noon-10.30pm
🥕 Vegan options
i Takeaway Service
◊ Child friendly

This family run canteen-style eaterie is committed to promoting vegetarianism with everything cooked on the premises. The place is quite big already seating about 70, but a new extension is planned in response to its growing popularity. The décor is pleasant enough with glass topped tables displaying an inviting desserts menu underneath and a few pretty Asian pictures on the walls.

At the lunchtime when I visited, it was busy and chatty with a mix of Indian and non-Indian locals, although weekends are the busiest sometimes with parties. The eat-as-much-like lunchtime buffet (12-3pm Monday to Friday) is good value at £5.99 (children up to six years old £3.00) and all the food was served at the correct temperature. To begin, Chinese Hot and Sour soup was quite good whilst the Chinese Vegetable noodles with hot Schezuan sauce was okay too. Bombay Aaloo was good rich and tasty but the red curry marinated baby potatoes with herbs and spices were a little too hot for my liking. The very mild Vegetable Korma was enjoyable with a fairly good aromatic flavoured Pulao Rice, although plain rice is also available. The buffet also included a reasonable Punjabi Kahdi, a Tandoori Roti, I had mine topped with a little butter. Other buffet choices were Tandoori Naan, Green Salad, Yoghurt Raita, Roasted Papad and to finish three pieces of Julab Jamun dessert.

This was excellent value and it is unfortunate they do not do an evening version. None of the food on the buffet is labelled so do ask the staff and they will serve you.

The menu choice here is massive and comes in a book about the size of an Argos catalogue – two hundred and fifty-one food and drink choices. Well presented with some pictures, it covers many favourite North and South Indian, Tandoori and Tawa specialites as well as Chinese, Jain and even Vegetable Burger and Chips! Crispy Bhajia and Vegetable Samosa are the most popular Bombay Chaat – on ordering you can specify mild, medium and hot.

I also tried on a separate occasion from the menu, Tandoori Panner Tikka (£4.99) that comes up inviting and substantial on a sizzling hot metal platter resting on wooden block and tastes quite good. Next time I plan to go for the mixed grill version with mushrooms, mogo, bell peppers, tomatoes offering a wider variety of flavour. The Vegetable fried rice I had was also very tasty.

Service here is reasonable and Rose Vegetarian is a place I will go back to again for great value for money and the sheer variety of tastes.

Mill Hill

Good Earth
Chinese, classic

🖽	141 The Broadway, Mill Hill, NW7
☎	020 8959 7011
🚌	Mill Hill BR, 5-10 min walk
🕐	Mon-Sat 12noon-2pm, 6pm-11pm
	Sun 12.30-2.30pm, 6pm-10.30pm
i	Booking required
	Takeaway service also available

Vegetarian ★★★★
Taste ★★★★★
Price £££

This restaurant runs along the same lines as Good Earth, Knightsbridge although at Mill Hill the vegetarian choice is more limited but still good. *For food review see Good Earth, Knightsbridge (page 165).*

St John's Wood

Sofra St John's Wood
Turkish, classic,

🖽	11 Circus Road, NW8
☎	020 7586 9889
🖉	www.sofra.co.uk
🚌	St Johns Wood LU
🕐	Daily 12noon-11pm

Vegetarian ★★★
Taste ★★★
Price ££

See Ozer, Oxford Circus for food review (page 44).

Willesden

Saravanas
Indian, classic

Vegetarian ★★★★★
Organic ★★★
Price ££

📇 77-81 Dudden Hill Lane, Willesden, NW10
☎ 020 8459 4900
🖱 www.saravanas.co.uk
🚋 Dollis Hill LU, 2 min walk
🕐 Daily 12noon-10.30pm
🥕 Vegan options
i Eat in (table service) & Takeaway available

Popular South Indian vegetarian restaurant serving all the Indian favourites and offering a full-on menu of 121 choices. Regulars here often start with Methu Vadai, two fried urid dhall doughnuts and the Chilli Panneer, home-made cottage cheese fried with spices. Portions here are mega and those with a penchant for conspicuous consumption should opt for the Masala Dosai, a gigantic pancake packed with spicy potatoes. Of the three thalis on offer the Bombay Thali – pilau rice, chapati, vadai, four veggie curries, raita, rasam, pappadom, butter chilli and dessert – represents good value at only £6.99. Another good deal is the lunchtime buffet with drink for only £4.25. This is a popular restaurant and well worth a visit for good value classic Indian cuisine.

Crouch End

Jai Shri Krishna Vegetarian Restaurant
Indian, classic

📇 10 Turnpike Lane, N8
☎ 020 8888 7200
🚋 Turnpike Lane LU, 1min walk
🕐 Daily 12noon-2pm, 5.30pm-11pm
🥕 Vegan options
🍼 Child friendly but no high chairs
🍴 BYO
i Eat in & Takeaway

Vegetarian ★★★★★
Taste ★★★
Price £

This is the sister restaurant to the ever popular Jai Krishna restaurant in Stroud Green Road. The place is smartly decorated but also offers good quality bargain Indian food with plenty of vegan options.
For the food review see Jai Krishna (page 152).

West London

Le Pain Quotidien

KENSINGTON
GARDENS

KENSINGTON GORE

KNIGHTSBRIDGE

KNIGHTSBRIDGE

HIGH STREET
KENSINGTON

GLOUCESTER ROAD

QUEEN'S GATE

EXHIBITION ROAD

BROMPTON ROAD

BASIL ST

PONT STREET

WALTON STREET

CROMWELL ROAD

GLOUCESTER
ROAD

HARRINGTON GDNS

QUEEN'S GATE

THURLOE ST

SOUTH
KENSINGTON

DRAYCOTT AVENUE

SLOANE AVENUE

SLOANE
SQUARE

OLD BROMPTON ROAD

CRANLEY GRNS

FULHAM ROAD

SYDNEY STREET

KING'S ROAD

SMITH STREET

FLOOD STREET

KING'S ROAD

OAKLEY STREET

OLD CHURCH ST

BEAUFORT ST

Restaurants

1) Carluccio's Caffé p.163
2) Carluccio's Caffé p.163
3) Daquise p.164
4) Good Earth p.165
5) Hugo's p.167
6) Leon p.169
7) Luscious Organic Café p.170
8) Ottolenghi p.171
9) Le Pain Quotidien p.172
10) Le Pain Quotidien p.172
12) Thai Square p.173
12) Whole Foods Market
    Kensington p.175
13) Zaika p.175
14) Zuma p.177

Shops

a) Bamford p.262
b) Bamford and Sons p.262
c) Chelsea Health Store p.262
d) Here p.263
e) The Organic Pharmacy p.263
f) The Organic Pharmacy p.264
g) Planet Organic p.264
h) Space NK p.264
i) Whole Foods Market
   Kensington p.265

Knightsbridge, Kensington and Chelsea

Cash to splash? Head for sensational innovative Indian at Zaika, hip-mod Japanese at Zuma, or maybe try great mock carnivore Chinese at the remarkable Good Earth. Eco-conscious South Kensington has the great organic Restaurant, Hugo's and something quite different with Polish vegetarian dishes at Daquise. Load up with organic at Here in Chelsea Farmer's Market or Planet Organic in Fulham, or the vast Whole Foods Market Kensington – the biggest natural and organic food store in the world with a huge choice of veggie eats. This is also a great area for organic cosmetics with Space NK and the Organic Pharmacy among the outlets (see The Shopping section for further details). Further afield is the wonderful Luscious Organic Café, near Holland Park.

Carluccio's Caffè
Italian, classic

Vegetarian ★★★
Taste ★★★★
Price ££

▢ 1 Old Brompton Road, SW7
☎ 020 7581 8101
✎ www.carluccios.com
🚍 South Kensington LU, 0.5 min walk
🕔 Mon-Fri 8am-11pm, Sat 9-11pm, Sun 9am-10.30pm
🥕 Vegan choices
🍼 Child friendly

This Carluccio's is very popular with tourists especially those visiting the very nearby museums and the 'South Ken' ladies who lunch.
For food review see Carluccio's Caffè, St Christopher's Place (page 35).

Carluccio's Caffè
Italian, classic

Vegetarian ★★★
Taste ★★★★
Price ££

▢ 236 Fulham Road, SW10
☎ 020 7376 5960
✎ www.carluccios.com
🚍 Fulham Broadway LU, 10 min walk
🕔 Mon-Fri 8am-11pm, Sat 9-11pm, Sun 9am-10.30pm
🥕 Vegan options
🍼 Child friendly

Modern, bright and airy. Grab a window seat, relax, enjoy the food and watch the world go by, although it does get very busy in the evenings.

Daquise
Polish, traditional,

🖾 *20 Thurloe St, SW7*
☎ *020 7589 6117*
🚌 *South Kensington LU, 2 min walk*
🕐 *Daily 11.30am-11pm*
i *Evening bookings advised*

Vegetarian ★★★
Taste ★★★★
Price *££*

Daquise

Step back to Poland c.1947 at this historic restaurant which serves some very enjoyable classic Polish vegetarian dishes. Located on a busy South Ken street corner, it somehow exudes an air of mystery from a bygone age and indeed it is said that cold war spies would meet here. Today, it's a popular haunt for Polish writers, artists and sculptors, and lanky East European models grazing away from the catwalks of London Fashion week but alas no sinister secret agents in long raincoats and sunglasses.

At 7.30pm it's as busy as ever with a mix of young couples, single diners drinking Polish lager or one of the speciality vodkas or a carafe of the quite acceptable house wine. Daquise is on two levels and diners are advise to opt for the ground floor with its large Elizabeth II Coronation mural, a military painting by Fabian and some figurines, rather than the downstairs bar which is more of an overflow or venue for private parties.

I must have been the diner from hell going into a Polish omnivore restaurant seeking vegetarian and hating beetroot, the country's most celebrated ingredient. For starters there are three beetroot soups. Flummoxed at first, the waitress suggests the house speciality main of warm Crispy Potato Cakes served with sour cream and apple sauce and indeed they were delicious. To re-enforce my beetroot phobia I taste the Barszcz with Ushka, clear beetroot soup with mini mushroom ravioli. To my horror, it was fabulous and next time I'll definitely order it.

The vegetarian Polish Platter is an appetising selection of Mushroom Golabki (cabbage leaves stuffed with mushroom and rice), Pierogi (pasta shells stuffed with cabbage and mushroom), Potato Pancake and cooked cabbage, (sauerkraut). Vegetable Stroganoff is a big plate of courgettes, aubergine, peppers, mushrooms and onions all mildly spiced and served with a small mountain of rice and cream. It was substantial and tasty.

Pancake à la Daquise is enough for two and is a delicious hot pancake folded round ice cream topped with a refreshing orange caramel sauce and sprinkled almond flakes. If only to try such delicious desserts, Daquise is well worth a visit.

Good Earth
Chinese, classic

Vegetarian ★★★★
Taste ★★★★★
Price £££

- 233 Brompton Road, Knightsbridge, SW3
- 020 7584 3658
- Knightsbridge LU, 5 min walk
- Mon-Sat 12noon-11pm, Sun 12.30-10.30pm
- Vegan options tables available

Classy Chinese restaurant serving a superb selection of vegetarian dishes. If it's atmosphere you're after ask to be seated in the voluminous basement which has a more animated ambience and flamboyant traditional Chinese décor. The street level dining room does, however, house a busy pre-meal drinks bar.

The dining here is upscale, service precise and formal, with the chances of a member of staff breaking into a smile 100-1. Good Earth attracts a monied clientele smartly dressed in jacket and tie or open shirts and women in designer clothes.

The Vegetarian Menu is a highly inviting with a generous choice of four starters, three soups and ten or so mains. The tofu and mock-meat dishes made from soya are a big speciality here and the Vegetarian 'Chicken' Szechuan that comes in a delicious hot sweet sauce is particularly enjoyable and well-presented. Egg Noodles with Bean sprouts is top notch and went well with the Spicy Crunchy Tofu, a mega serving of mange tout, tofu and spicy sauce. These three dishes are sufficient for two. However, most diners order twice as much which is not surprising as the food here looks very good.

Restaurants also at:
143-145 The Broadway, Mill Hill, London NW7 (Tel 020 8959 7011)
14-18 High Street, Esher, Surrey (Tel 01372 462489)
Express Good Earths are takeaway only and are at:
Wimbledon, 81 Ridgeway, SW19 (Tel 020 8994 8883)
Richmond, 6 Friars Road, Surrey (Tel 020 8948 3399)
West Hampstead, 335 West End Lane, NW6 (Tel 020 7433 3111)
Wandsworth, 116 St Johns Hill, SW11 (Tel 020 7228 3140)

Hugo's
International, modern organic

Vegetarian ★★★
Organic ★★★★
Taste ★★★★
Price £££

- 🖽 *51 Princes Gate, Exhibition Road, SW7*
- ☎ *020 7596 4006*
- 🚌 *South Kensington LU, 5 min walk*
- 🕐 *Mon-Sat 9.30am-11pm, Sun 9.30-7pm*
- ◊ *Child friendly*
- ☀ *Summer terrace with outside seating for 40*
- *i* *Takeaway service*

Buzzy, family-run organic restaurant, café and bar serving quality recipes created by Carol Charlton, author of the *Organic Café Cookbook*. Often around, Carol's delighted to indulge in mealtime conversation about organic food happenings, sustainable farming and fairtrade issues whilst husband Bryn, a former chairman of Greenpeace, is equally happy for a chat.

Students are the predominant clientele (Imperial College is nearby and Hugo's shares a building with the Goethe-Institut) but Hugo's is also popular with visitors to the Albert Hall and South Ken locals.

Hugo's wears its organic heart on it's sleeve and its menu comes complete with a mission statement supporting organic farming and fair trade practices as well as their list of organic ingredients. Knowledgeable waiting staff have a black belt in answering any organic queries you might have and provide good service.

Organic Eggs Florentine (eggs with spinach) is a popular dish on the brunch menu, served until 5pm. Although largely an omnivore menu, vegetarian choices are marked and the meal gets off to a good start with complimentary green and black olives. Organic Celeriac and Chive Soup is a delicious recipe with a good spicy tasty and comes with olive bread with dashes of olive oil. The Vegetarian Tart of spinach, broccoli and asparagus was pepped up with added pine nuts and the mixed leaf salad with cherry tomatoes, balsamic vinegar and Parmesan shavings and was well above average. Of the three main vegetarian choices the Mushroom Feuilletée with Stroganoff Sauce on fragrant rice is to be recommended and features both fresh wild and domestic mushrooms. The Pasta of the Day, tasted fine but was not of the same high standard. The organic Chocolate Tart Dessert was devilishly delicious. A non-organic creme brûlée with a raspberry side sauce is also enjoyable.

The house organic wine, Domaine Millas, made with chardonnay and grenache grapes, is refreshing but Hugo's really scores with its list of organic beers and ciders that include Bücher Pilsner, Golden Promise Ale, Weston's Strong Cider. Coffees and teas are organic and fair trade.

Hugo's makes an excellent port of call when round Kensington and is made even better by it's enthusiasm for organic food.

Their sister restaurant is in Queens Park (tel 020 7372 1232), see page 137 for the review.

Leon Brompton Road
Mediterranean and English, fast food

Vegetarian ★★★
Organic ★★★
Taste ★★★
Price £

⌨ 136 Brompton Road, SW3
☎ 020 7589 7330
✍ www.leonrestaurants.co.uk
🚌 Knightsbridge LU, 5 min walk
🕐 Mon-Fri 8am-11pm, Sat 9am-11pm, Sun 10am-6pm
i Takeaway and eat in
🥕 Vegan options
🍼 Child friendly

One of the many Leon eateries that have sprung up around London in recent years.

For food review see Leon Spitalfields (page 222).

Other branches at: 75 Marylebone High Street W1, 9 Young Street W8, 201-203 King's Road SW3, Upper Festival Walk SE1, 18 Great Marlborough Street W1, Exhibition Road SW7, St Pancras NW1.

Planet Organic
Organic Vegetarian, International

Vegetarian ★★★★
Organic ★★★★★
Taste ★★★
Price £

▢   25 Effie Road, W6
☎   020 7731 7222
✎   www.planetorganic.com
🚌   Fulham Broadway LU, 1 min walk
🕐   Mon-Sat 9.30am-8.30pm, Sun 12noon-6pm
🥕   Vegan options
🍼   Child friendly
✉   Mail order
i   Counter Service and takeaway

A welcome addition to Fulham, this branch opened in June 2004, and is similar in layout but slightly smaller than the flagship store on Westbourne Grove. The meal choices are the same and reviewed on page 182.

Luscious Organic Café
International, Organic, Macrobiotic

Vegetarian ★★★★
Organic ★★★★★
Taste ★★★
Price ££

▢   40-42 Kensington High Street, SW8
☎   020 7371 6987
✎   www.lusciousorganic.co.uk
🚌   High Street Kensington LU, 10 min walk
🕐   Mon-Fri 8.30am-8.30pm, Sat-Sun 9.30am-9pm
🥕   Vegan options
☀   Outside tables
i   Eat-in and takeaway, counter and table service

This organic eaterie is rapidly establishing itself as a magnet for vegetarians, vegans and macrobiotic enthusiasts. Situated just opposite the Odeon Cinema on Kensington High Street and next door to Holland Park, it looks a bit like a bank from the outside but inside it's a fantastic organic food store and Soil Association approved café. The café is small and has four white wooden tables of various sizes. The atmosphere is friendly and the music moody and modern.

The short blackboard menu offers a variety of soups including lentil, Tomato & Basil and Barley & Vegetable all at £4.49. The four hot mains were all priced at £5.99 and included Moroccan Spinach & Chick Pea Casserole with rice & salad which was suitable for vegans and very enjoyable. The Vegetable Chilli was mild, but flavoursome and came with brown rice & a surprisingly good side salad of celery, cucumber, sprouting beans and white cabbage that really showed how great organic veg can taste. Also available was Spinach & Goat's Cheese Lasagne and three other vegetable stews all of which looked good and were obviously made with some care.

Luscious has a great juice selection of which Pretty In Pink (beetroot, apple & carrot) and the Ginger & Spice (carrot, apple & ginger) are the most popular. On the smoothie front the Strawberry & Blueberry concoction (£2.79) is to be recommended.

The only criticisms to be made was that the shop seemed to infringe on the café a little, which was not uncomfortable or cramped, but did detract from the atmosphere of the place. Luscious Organic could easily be mistaken for being totally 100% vegetarian but one soup contained fish stock and the store does sell a small amount of non-veggie food products. It's a good idea to ask if you have any doubts, but the store and café are very veggie conscious and all the products and dishes are well marked. Of particular note is the chiller cabinet which is choc full of pre-packed sandwiches and salads and sandwiches can be heated up and eaten in at no extra charge. Bargain hunters should also look out for some to the great value veggie specials such as the Vegan Breakfast of Seaweed Salad, Spinach Tortilla, Tofu Spinach Pancake and the Calzone with a tofu and vegetable filling, each for around £3.

Those with special dietary needs will also find themselves well catered for here with plenty of wheat, gluten or dairy free products from which to choose. If you're just after a snack the vegan date & walnut cake or apricot and almond cake are both good, as is the organic coffee.

Ottolenghi (Kensington)
Mediterranean, Classic Modern and Pastries

Vegetarian ★★★★
Organic ★★★★
Taste ★★★★★
Price £££

🖵 *1 Holland Street, W8*

☎ *020 7937 0003*

🖰 *www.ottolenghi.co.uk*

🚌 *Kensington LU, 5 min walk*

🕓 *Mon-Fri 8am-8pm, Sat 8am-7pm, Sun 9am-6pm*

🥕 *Vegan options*

i *Takeaway only*

The smallest of the Ottolenghi's it offers only a takeaway service and a catering service.

For food review see Ottolenghi Notting Hill (page 181).

Le Pain Quotidien
French, classic

Vegetarian ★★★★
Organic ★★★★★
Taste ★★★★
Price ££

▢ 9 Young Street, Kensington, W8
☎ 020 7486 6154
🖰 www.lepainquotidien.co.uk
🚌 High Street Kensington LU, 2min walk
🕐 Mon-Fri 7.30am-7pm, Sat 8am-7pm, Sun and holidays 8am-7pm
🥕 Vegan options
i Table service & Takeaway
No bookings Sat-Sun 9.30am-7pm

One of the smaller Le Pain Quotidiens and situated very close to Whole Foods Market, Kensington.

For food review see Marylebone (page 41).

Le Pain Quotidien
French, classic

Vegetarian ★★★★
Organic ★★★★★
Taste ★★★★
Price ££

▢ 15-17 Exhibition Road, SW7
☎ 020 7486 6154
🖰 www.lepainquotidien.co.uk
🚌 South Kensington LU, 2min walk
🕐 Mon-Fri 7am-10pm, Sat 8am -10pm, Sun and holidays 8am-7pm
🥕 Vegan options
☀ Outside seating
i Table service & Takeaway
Limited booking policy at this café

One of the smaller branches of Le Pain Quotidiens.

For food review see Marylebone (page 41).
Other branches at: 75 Marylebone High Street W1, 9 Young Street W8,
201-203 King's Road SW3, Upper Festival Walk SE1,
18 Great Marlborough Street W1, Exhibition Road SW7, St Pancras NW1.

Thai Square South Kensington
Thai, Classic

Vegetarian ★★★
Taste ★★
Price £££

▢ 19 Exhibition Road, SW7
☎ 020 7584 8359
🖰 www.thaisq.com
🚌 South Kensington LU opposite
🕐 Mon-Sat 12noon-3pm, 6pm-11pm, Sun 12noon-3pm, 6pm-10.30pm

An attractive intimate venue.

For the food review see Thai Square Trafalgar Square (page 31).

Le Pain Quotidien

Whole Foods Market Kensington
Organic Vegetarian, International

Vegetarian ★★★
Organic ★★★★★
Taste ★★★
Price £

🏠 *The Barkers Building,*
   63-97 Kensington High Street, W8
☎ *020 7368 4500*
🖰 *www.wholefoodsmarket.com*
🚌 *Kensington LU, 5 min walk*
🕐 *Mon-Sat 8am-10pm (Store), Sun Upstairs at Market 10am-6pm,*
   Sun Market Hall 12noon-6pm

This is the largest natural and organic food store in the world where vegetarians are well catered for. Set on three gigantic floors, like great museums and art galleries, don't expect to take it all in on one visit. WMK is a place to re-visit time and again where you'll discover more and more intriguing delights.

For sit-down eating, head to the top floor that is cleverly divided into several dining sections. Depending on your preference they have a casual dining area that is always busy, a more private environment and an area that is a lot smarter. The main dining area, surrounded by umpteen serving stations, is a unique blend of communal bench style combined with a canteen feel, that's much loved by young families with children and neighbourhood regulars. Busy at lunchtimes, the atmosphere is friendly, recorded pop music plays and some savvy folk bring their cardboard takeaway boxes from the ground floor to eat here. In the adjacent section, there are several banquettes for quieter privacy where more sophisticated diners chow down and elsewhere there are other tables dotted around with coffee drinkers perusing laptops .

WMK is a very fast moving catering environment where menu concepts change frequently. On one visit there was a dedicated vegan section that included tofu sesame, tofu kebab, tofu curry and numerous jacket potatoes only for it to be removed a few months later for something else. Many of these vegan choices are still available but you do need to get to know on which stations to look. One very interesting option from WMK that seems to have stood the test of time is the 'build your own Veggie Burrito' for £5.29. Ordering the crispy version, the server fills the larger crisp burrito with a choice of guacamole, two types of beans, brown rice, mozzarella, chopped jalapeno pepper, lime and lettuce. Ask for it to be served on a large plate as unfortunately mine was served on such a tiny one lots fell onto the table. That said, it was of good flavour and a change from the soft wrap versions that are more commonplace. A 'build your own pasta bowl' for £5.99 is also available.

On the Mezzes Station, virtually all the choices are veggie and there's a nice platter deal of six choices plus pitta bread for £6.99. The aubergine mutabel, veg moussaka, chickpea salad, potato and roasted pepper salad all tasted good, whilst the butternut squash mutabel was very good indeed. Geared up for mass-dining, service is quick with some servers more knowledgeable than others. As with all establishments catering for huge numbers, quality can vary but WMK does a consistently good job. The new Gelato section of vegetarian sorbets looks amazing and one I'll definitely return to. The juice bar with organic drinks is also one to try.

For takeaways hit the groundfloor that has a multitude of vegan and vegetarian choices that you purchase by weight for £1.79/100g. The vegetable biryani of potato, onion, ginger, green chilli and garam masala is very popular and other Indian dishes included aloo baigan, okra masala, vegetable samosa, garlic naans and the attractive small cut corn cobs in coconut sauce. At the salad station, favourites are the purple potato salsa, the roasted buttersquash, a bean ragout for vegans and the vegetarian Caesar salad. An additional 30 different individual salad ingredients are displayed to help you customise your own salads for as little as £1.53 per carton. On organic soups there's also a huge choice from tomato & basil to a deliciouisly fragrant mushroom & fennel for £2.25 (small) or £3.50 (large).

Zaika
Indian, Modern

Vegetarian ★★★★
Taste ★★★★★
Price ££££

🖼 *No1 Kensington High Street, W8*
☎ *020 7937 8834*
🖋 *www.zaika-restaurant.co.uk*
🚌 *High Street Kensington LU (3min walk)*
🕐 *Lunch daily 12noon-2.45pm,*
    Dinner Mon-Sat 6pm-10.45pm, Sun 6pm-9.45pm
🌶 *Vegan options*
🍼 *Child friendly*

Chef Patron, Sanjay Dwivedi, continues to dazzle with simply the best Indian Vegetarian Tasting Menu in London. Zaika is a voluminous dining room, opulent with a careful balance of modern design and Indian sculptural classicism, coupled with an inviting bar at its entrance. The place is filled with well-heeled local residents, tourists from swanky hotels and couples out for a romantic evening.

The Tasting Menu has six courses with matching wines all managed under the watchful eye of General Manager, Luigi Gaudino. My meal began with a pre-starter of a small cup of crème mushroom soup, topped with a tiny mushroom. The Paneer Platter consists of three recipes: Tandoori Paneer with mint, tiny potato dumplings and paneer poached in coconut milk and served with chilli mash. All this tasted good and went well with a glass of Champagne. The Aloo Chat/Samosa course of Potato and cabbage 'tikki', chickpeas laced with tamarind chutney alongside an inspired tiny goats cheese samosa with pear and clove chutney matched well with the South African Chardonnay. Utta Pam, Lentil pancake with 'dosa' potatoes and 'sambhar' sauce provided one of the really high flavour points of the meal. The alternative option of a dosa is also good here and came with a fine Chateau Kefraya Rose from the Lebanon.

One of the highlights of the menu is the Khumbi Tamatri Khichidi, a culinary art piece of Truffle, Spiced wild mushroom rice and mini papadum & tomato 'makhni' ice cream. It's one of those molecular gastronomy dishes that you either love or hate. Personally I loved the dish, particularly when served with a glass of Sicilian Cerasoulo di Vittoria.

The next course, Subzi Ki Thali, is a superbly flavoursome selection of garlic and cumin tempered spinach, roast baby aubergines finished with a tamarind coconut masala, black lentils, served with saffron rice and baby nan and raita. The Malma Malbec Reserve 2004 from Patagonia accompanying turned out to be a good choice.

To finish, excellent is the Reshmi Mithai dessert of pine kernal, cashew and pistachio brittle with chocolate mousse and refreshing masala icecream coupled with a smooth drop of Ramos Pinto Collector, Porto Reserva from Portugal.

The Tasting Menu is tremendous value at £38 and a further £20 buys you the five matched glasses of wine – all of which are suitable for vegetarians. The Chef Patron's interest in healthy vegetarian cuisine informs the cooking at Zaika which avoids traditional ghee in preference for healthier monounsaturate olive oils. Sanjay Dwivedi, who has been highly commended in the last edition of this book, has excelled himself again and made Zaika one of the places in London to enjoy an exceptional vegetarian meal.

Zuma
Japanese, modern

🏠 5 Raphael St, SW7

☎ 020 7584 1010

🖥 www.zumarestaurant.com

🚌 Knightsbridge LU, 5min walk

🕐 Lunch served Mon-Fri 12noon-2.30pm, Sat-Sun 12.30-3.30pm;
   Dinner served Mon-Sat 6pm-11pm, Sun 6pm-10.30pm

🖋 Vegan options

i Booking essential

Vegetarian ★★★★
Organic ★★★
Taste ★★★★★
Price £££££

Tucked away down a side street minutes away from Harvey Nichols and Harrods, Zuma is where the rich and famous and exquisite Japanese vegetarian intersect. This is the peachiest of places where meals will devour your bank account. Expect £160 for two and dress down as if it's where you eat all the time although the suited and booted are in evidence at some tables.

As you go in there's a great bar and lounge, followed by an open kitchen surrounded by seats and good dining tables. At the far back are two private excellent dining areas.

The menu is extensive and a nightmare to navigate. Those new to Zuma should call the manager; declare their vegetarianism and let him unlock the door to gastronomic paradise.

Dishes are small, beautifully presented, designed for sharing and mostly organic. To begin with Steamed Edamame, a traditional Japanese green bean dish is excellent. Kaiso Salad Goma Renkon Zoe, is one of the most scrumptious seaweed salads one will ever find and comes with sesame and lotus root. Home-made tofu with intensely flavoured condiments, Zara Dofu, is good whilst the spicy tofu with avocado salad and herbs is also delicious and flavoursome. The Veggie Rolls of avocado, asparagus, ginger, hiso, cabbage, cucumber and carrot are wonderful. Also well worth a try are the seasonal vegetables such as sweet potato with teriyaki and sesame which, along with the asparagus with wafu sauce and sesame, come from the Robata Grill.

Desserts are of a high standard and the Green Tea and Banana cake with coconut ice cream and peanut toffee sauce is to be recommended. For sake lovers, the selection is enormous and well worth a try if your bank balance can take it.

Notting Hill

Notting Hill is one of the most expensive parts of London and also one of the most fashionable. If you want to get a veggie snack in the company of the rich and famous you could try E&O. This area also has a branch of Ottolenghi for fine Mediterranean cuisine in a stylish environment. To combine shopping and eating you can also find a branch of Planet Organic and the unique Books For Cooks.

Restaurants

1) Books for Cooks p.179
2) Carluccio's Caffé p.180
3) E&O p.180
4) Ottolenghi p.181
5) Planet Organic p.182

Shops

a) Bamford and Sons p.266
b) Urban Bliss p.266
c) Books for Cooks p.266
d) Green Baby p.267
e) Natural Mat p.267
f) Planet Organic p.267
g) Notting Hill Farmers' Market p.286
h) Portobello Wholefoods p.268
i) The Tea and Coffee Plant p.268

Books for Cooks
International, classic and modern

Vegetarian ★★★★
Organic ★★★★
Taste ★★★★★
Price £

📖 *4 Blenheim Crescent, W11*
☎ *020 7221 1992*
🖚 *www.booksforcooks.com*
🚌 *Ladbroke Grove LU, 5 min walk, Notting Hill Gate LU, 10 min walk*
🕐 *Lunch served Tue-Sat 12noon-2pm (or when food runs out)*
i *Coffee and cakes served Tue-Sat 10am-6pm*
🌶 *Vegan options*

At this shop dedicated to cookbooks you can eat veggie recipes straight from the latest cookbooks. It's an absolute bargain and a definite must for all London foodies.

The formula is simple. They take a new book and cook some recipes from it and offer the results to customers at a ridiculously low price. If it goes down well they order more books for the shop.

I struck gold the lunchtime I dropped in as the featured book was The Gate Vegetarian Book (from the much loved Gate restaurant in Hammersmith, see page 184 for eats review) by Adrian and Michael Daniel, published by Mitchell Beazley, £25.

The Hot and Sour soup, Thom Yam was a delicious starter and came with a quantity of egg noodles making it unavoidably slurpy with some lunchers resorting to spoon and fork to get it down. Accompanied by freshly baked foccacia bread, for some it was a meal in itself. The main, Japanese Vegetable Terrine with Barley Miso dressing dazzled with some exquisite flavours. Four vegetarian desserts are on offer and the Citrus Almond Polenta cake was superb and the Torta Te La Nonna even better. All three courses came to just £7. So what's the catch? Well there isn't one except that there are only five tables.

The food is all prepared at the back of the bookshop by an excellent chef, (that day Sarah Benjamin) in what is not so much a restaurant but more a test kitchen of restaurant standard.

The atmosphere is friendly, formal and of course stuffed with foodies, both local and from afar. The menu changes every day with either a veggie starter or main and once a week there is both. Phone in the morning to see what's on offer and then make sure you are there well before noon as the food sometimes runs out by 12.15pm. On my visit, however, you could still get a table at 1.30pm. Books for Cooks now they serves its own organic wine and they also publish a wonderful cookbook once every couple of years.

Carluccio's Caffé
Italian, classic

Vegetarian ★★★
Taste ★★★★
Price ££

⌧ *Westbourne Corner, 108 Westbourne Grove, W2*
☏ *020 7243 8164*
⌨ *www.carluccios.com*
🚇 *Notting Hill Gate or Bayswater LU, 7 min walk*
🕐 *Mon-Fri 8am-11pm, Sat 9-11pm, Sun 9am-10.30pm*
🥕 *Vegan options*
⌀ *Child friendly, high chairs*

Located in the heart of Notting Hill, this Carluccio's Caffé is a short walk from the famous Portobello Road Market.
See Carluccio's Caffé, St Christopher's Place for food review (page 35).

E&O
Vietnamese, modern

Vegetarian ★★★
Taste ★★★★
Price £££££

⌧ *14 Blenheim Crescent, W11*
☏ *020 7229 5454*
⌨ *www.rickerrestaurants.com*
🚇 *Ladbroke Grove LU, 5 min walk, Notting Hill Gate LU, 10 min walk*
🕐 *Daily 12noon-12midnight*
🥕 *Vegan options*
☀ *Outside seating*
i Booking essential in evenings

Although it continues to looks like a bog standard black-painted corner pub on the outside, E&O remains a supremely hip restaurant and bar catering for the Notting Hill set. Here, savvy and attentive waitering staff serve modern Pan Asian cuisine with a twist, mostly on small plates tasting menu-style but with some big dish numbers too. Lunch will set you back north of £30 and dinner £50.

Inside, there's a small strip of a bar whilst the dining room is a spacious, white tableclothed affair where movers and shakers like celebrity vegetarian Stella McCartney book a booth. Lunchtimes are okay for walk-ins, evenings require a reservation and allow two days to park if a non-resident. The short menu is Vietnamese with Thai, Malaysian, Japanese and Chinese influences, mainly veggie with some omnivore appeal. On the veggie dimsum, there is edame, soy and mirin or mushroom and waterchestnut green tea dumplings or roasted coconut and pomegranate betel leaf. The special Vegetable Phad Thai (£10.50) main is a biggie, delicious and sufficient without starter or dessert. Garam masala curry with tomato and aubergine makes another tempting choice.

Ottolenghi
Mediterranean, classic food & pastries

Vegetarian ★★★★
Organic ★★★★
Taste ★★★★★
Price £££

⌨ *63 Ledbury Road, W11*
☎ *020 7727 1121*
✎ *www.ottolenghi.co.uk*
🚌 *Notting Hill Gate LU, 7 min walk*
🕐 *Mon-Fri 8am-8pm, Sat 8am-7pm, Sun 9.30am-6pm*
⌀ *Child friendly*
🍸 *No alcohol licence*
i *Takeaways/counter service*

Thumbs up to this stylish eaterie serving well-made vegetarian salads to eat in or out. The fixed price menu is a selection of four salads (£12), three salads (£9.50) or three salads with a main (£14.50) which isn't cheap, but the high quality and venue make it worth the expense.

It's a split level affair with an inviting front of house buffet and patisserie counter. The small downstairs dining area is decorated in ultra chic white with futuristic white chairs surrounding a single huge plastic table. Affluent mums and kids people the mornings here, followed later by designer-dressed ladies-who-lunch and solitary grazers keen for a chat or just a quiet read.

Everything is made on the premises, about 60% is organic and the menu changes every day with 10 vegetarian choices including two soups, salads and a main course such as quiche.

The top salad for regulars is the Organic Chickpeas with Jerusalem Artichokes, tumeric, caraway seeds, tomato and rocket which is great! Organic Couscous, beautifully yellow with saffron and herbs, comes with cucumber, roast plum tomatoes and lemon and is good too. The organic lentils with capers arrives well balanced with memorably flavoured balsamic vinegar and herbs. The Organic Butternut Squash comes with sweet potato, red endive spring onion and a dash of pomegranate dressing and is wonderfully tasty. All the salads work well together and when eaten in, come served on decent plates. Among the warm mains, the Broccoli quiche is heavenly.

Breakfast tea is organic and, surprisingly for a place of this calibre, comes delivered with tea bag. Bottled Luscombe organic raspberry lemonade is good and there's a selection of Innocent Smoothies too. The vegetarian pastries and cakes at the shop front are enticing. The best looking was the Passion Fruit & Meringue (£2.80), which was a real treat and the seasonal mixed berry and semolina tart was a also something of a triumph.

If any criticism could be made, it is the very small number of warm vegetarian dishes to choose from and at it's busiest time (around 1pm), it can get a bit cramped with people waiting to get a seat. Despite these drawbacks I couldn't keep away, on my second visit the Roast Aubergine with saffron yoghurt salad was gorgeous, whilst the Polenta with Roast Pumpkin, chestnuts and gorgonzola was substantial and delicious. I finished off by sharing a Lemon and Mascopone tart and a White Chocolate cheesecake both of which were wonderful. Ottolenghi is one of those places where it's hard to resist temptation!

The Ottolenghi restaurant in Islington serves evening meals also, (see page 115), whilst the one in Kensington is takeaway only (see page 171). The latest opening is in Belgravia at 13 Motcombe Street, Belgravia, SW1 (see page 79) which is a similar set up as Notting Hill.

Planet Organic
Organic Vegetarian, International

Vegetarian ★★★★
Organic ★★★★★
Taste ★★★
Price £

🖻   *42 Westbourne Grove, W2*
☎   *020 7727 2227*
✍   *www.planetorganic.com*
🚌   *Bayswater or Queensway LU 5 min*
🕐   *Mon-Sat 8.30am-9pm, Sun 12noon-6pm*
🥕   *Vegan options*
🍼   *Child friendly*
i   *Counter Service, eat in or takeaway*

Modern organic cafeteria at the back of the first of the really famous organic supermarkets in London. A big space with comfortable wooden tables, this is real in-store dining with shoppers queuing near by.

Vegetarian salad choices have increased dramatically from eight to seventeen and there's a better choice of hot dishes – all made on-site from seasonal produce. Dishes include Stir Fry Tofu, vegetarian lasagne or ratatoullie. The hot Peanut Butter Curry and the Veggie Shepherds Pie are two other flavoursome choices. The Celeriac Salad is one of their best dishes and the Kumquat salad makes an interesting change. Firm favourites include the Greek salad with feta and the Vegetable Stir Fry.

The cafeteria is also a good organic tea-time venue. The vegan Pear and Pecan nut cake is delicious and other sweet treats include polenta cake and Date and Walnut cake. The coffee is quite acceptable, but those paper cups and plates for eat-in get the thumbs down. Planet Organic has a good juice bar and continues to pull in many a wheatgrass fanatic from around London.

For the shop review see page 267.

Planet Organic

Hammersmith & Shepherd's Bush

The wealth of Portobello and Notting Hill has had its affect on the nearby neighbourhoods of Hammersmith and Shepherd's Bush, both of which have gone through a process of gentrification in recent years. There are some great vegetarian restaurants in this part of London among the best being Blah, Blah, Blah, The Gate, and 222. For delicious Indian vegetarian cuisines there is the very smart Sagar and further west the renowned Woodlands.

Hammersmith

The Gate
Modern International

🖽   *51 Queen Caroline Street, W6*

☎   *020 8748 6932*

🖂   *www.thegate.tv*

🚌   *Hammersmith LU, 5 min walk*

🕓   *Lunch Mon-Fri 12noon-3pm, Dinner Mon-Sat 6pm-11pm*

🥄   *Vegan options*

🍼   *Children-friendly*

i   *Booking advised*

Vegetarian ★★★★★
Taste ★★★★★
Price £££

Outstanding modern vegetarian dishes so moderately priced they are worth beating a path to. The path in this case is from a conventional restaurant street entrance on a residential back street, through a courtyard and upstairs to a former art studio.

Modern art is set high up on the yellow walls whilst a diverse low volume mix of pop and jazz re-enforces the atmosphere. Dubbed the 'Disney canteen', lunchtimes are busy with nearby film studio folk and execs from Universal Pictures, Sony Ericsson and Harper Collins. Evenings attract a relaxed talkative eco-intelligent crowd of casually dressed thirty somethings. Service is friendly and attentive.

The short and informative menu is inviting and comprises of eight starters, five mains and six desserts, which change every two months.

Complimentary olive bread and oil gets the meal off to an agreeable start and is followed by a delectable starter of Plantain Fritters, three deep fried green banana balls loaded with sultanas, carrot and pine nuts on a well-matched cream chilli sauce with a small side-salad. The Warm Root Vegetable Salad is a big starter, a tasty, well arranged mix of roast swede, parsnip and carrot, rocket leaves, crispy toasted pumpkin seeds and a mustard dressing. Haloumi Kibis, a tandoori-marinated cheese number served on a skewer deserves a mention as it's a firm favourite with regulars. The signature main dish however is the beautifully presented vegan Cashew Nut Roast with dried wild mushrooms and comes with roast veg and a marvellous cranberry compote. Aubergine Schnitzel, a successful modern twist on moussaka arrives as two large tender grilled aubergine slices layered with smoked mozzarella and French-styled creamy baked potato, fried kale and rounded off with horseradish sauce and tastes voluptuous.

Desserts make a big showing here and are generally large enough to be split. Pecan and Plum Crumble comes with crème anglais and is recommended. Cranberry Sponge Pudding is likeable, and comes with Drambuie ice cream. The vegan ice cream and sorbet is made on the premises.

The Gate, now has an increased choice of red and white vegetarian and vegan wines of which about half are organic including a recommendable Touchstone Chardonnay that's relatively inexpensive. Vegan dessert wine and port are also available. The Gate is one of the great vegetarian restaurants of London.

Queen's Head
British and Mediterranean, classic

Vegetarian ★★
Taste ★★★
Price ££

🖥 *13 Brook Green, Brook Green, W6*
☎ *020 7603 3174*
🚌 *Hammersmith LU, 3 min walk*
🕓 *Mon-Sat 12noon-11pm, Sun 12noon-9pm*
🥕 *Vegan options*
☀ *Outdoor seats*
i *Counter Service*

This comfy traditional pub, that was packed out the Friday evening we visited, is not quite what it was for vegetarians. It still offers a reasonable choice of four vegetarian snacks, two starters and a very popular main.

The snack choices include Mature Cheddar Ploughmans, Free Range Mayonnaise with watercress, Jacket Potato with Somerset Brie, mushrooms and pesto. Portions are generous, but for more substantial appetites, Bread and Brie Wedges with raspberry coulis and salad garnish is not bad for under a fiver. The Penne pasta, sautéed mushrooms, peppers, spinach with tomato and basil sauce is their most popular veggie dish. Each pub in the Chef & Brewers national chain, does veggie options and some blackboard specials that change weekly.

See also another Chef & Brewers pub, The Bull's Head, Chiswick (page 189).

Sagar
South Indian, traditional

Vegetarian ★★★★★
Taste ★★★★
Price £

🖥 *132 King Street, W6*
☎ *020 8741 8563*
🚌 *Hammersmith LU, 3 min walk*
🕓 *Daily 12noon-11pm*
🥕 *Vegan options*
🍼 *Child friendly*
i *Booking advised at weekends*

Sagar opened in February 2003 and serves inexpensive home style South Indian vegetarian cuisine. One of the new wave of informal, modern designed vegetarian Indian restaurants, it's welcome addition to Hammersmith's main street and gets busy from early evening with young couples and families building up to out-on-the-town good timers later on. Service, however, is efficient and the turn around on tables quick.

Inside, the décor is pleasant: coloured wooden walls with sections of panelling filled with dried flowers and South Indian paraphernalia set in lit wall recesses.

The menu is very well explained and offers great value for money. My wife and I split three starters: Idli (two sweet white steamed rice cakes served with sambar and coconut chutney) and Sev Puri, a Bombay Chowpati speciality which was superb. These crispy poori are topped with chopped onion, tamarind, coriander, garlic chutney and sev and are delicious with the other chutneys. However, the Bhajia were disappointingly uncrunchy.

For the main course, we split the Rajdani Thali, and opted for mild sauces. The Veg Kurma, a creamy curry with cashew nuts tastes good as did the Channa Masala, a tomato curry with chick peas and the Mattar Paneer, a curry with cheese and peas. Chappathi, Aloo Gobi, Raita and Pilau rice were other enjoyable, well-executed dishes. To top up, we ordered spiced spinach with home made cheese, Saag Paneer that went down well. Full, I tried the Thali's Vermicelli and Nut Sweet but didn't think much of it.

The Lunch Special is a real bargain for £4.95 and includes Masala Dosa, a whacking big fried pancake filled with mild flavoured potato and onions, rice of the day, veg curry, raitha, salad, sambar and chutney.

Sagar is definitely one of the best of the new wave of more modern Indian vegetarian restaurants, and is definitely worth a visit if you are in the area.

Branches also at:
17a Percy Street, London W1, Tel 020 7631 3319
& 27 York Street Twickenham, Middlesex, Tel 020 8744 3868

Shepherd's Bush

Blah Blah Blah
International, modern

Vegetarian ★★★★★
Organic ★★
Taste ★★★★
Price ££

🖃 *78 Goldhawk Road, W12*
☎ *020 746 1337*
🚌 *Goldhawk Road LU, 1 min walk*
Lunch Mon-Sat 12.30pm-2.30pm,
Dinner Mon-Sat 6.30pm-10.45pm
🥕 *Vegan options*
🍼 *Child friendly*
🍸 *BYO drink, corkage £1.45 per person*
Bookings advised Thurs, Fri, Sat evenings

With a name like Blah Blah Blah you know you're in for something very different in vegetarian dining. Forget the décor, it's the food that matters at this rough-round-the-edges neighbourhood restaurant – modern, well-crafted, carefully presented and good value.

Outside, above the burgundy painted entrance are two bulls' head sculptures – just the thing for a veggie eaterie. Inside, it's retro, wooden flooring, a chunky old Viennese styled wall mirror, enormous TV studio lights hanging from the ceiling, odd chairs and long backed vinyl seating. Towards the back is the open kitchen that's clean and professional.

Set on two floors, the more private downstairs dining area is Moorish in feel. I prefer the ground floor just for it's sheer design nonchalance which grows on you the more you drink.

The short menu changes every four to six weeks and typically has just six starters, five mains and four desserts. The Plaintain Fritter starter consists of three small balls filled with raisins, ginger, sweet potato and coriander and comes on an attractive chilli and pineapple sauce, finished with a coconut lime coulis. Mushroom Polenta with cap, oyster and button mushrooms is even more delicious. The Baked Tostada main is a gorgeous layered tower of Mexican tortillas filled with refried beans, sweet potato gratin served with a jalepeno sauce and is recommended. Other choices might include Leek & Mushroom Pie, Moussaka and veggie Indonesian recipes. The Rhubarb and Apple Crumble dessert can come up with a rather tough pasty casing and bit heavy. The Roast Plum Crumble with vanilla custard, however, is delicious. Mains at dinner are around £10.95 with a 10% discount at lunchtime.

A much loved dining spot of West Londoners, Blah Blah Blah, is a great vegetarian venue for partying. I love it!

Chiswick

The Bull's Head

Vegetarian ★★
Taste ★★★
Price ££

⌨ *15, Strand on the Green, W4*
☎ *020 8994 1204*

This pub does some good vegetarian choices.
See review for Queen's Head on page 186.

Carluccio's Caffé
Italian, modern

Vegetarian ★★★
Taste ★★★★
Price ££

⌨ *342-344 Chiswick High Road, W4*
☎ *020 8995 8073*
✍ *www.carluccios.com*
🚇 *Chiswick Park LU, 5min walk*
🕐 *Mon-Fri 8am-11pm, Sat 9-11pm, Sun 9am-10.30pm*
✴ *Vegan options*
☐ *Child friendly, high chairs*
☀ *Excellent outside tables*
i *Booking advised in evenings*

See Carluccio's Caffé, St Christopher's Place for review (page 35).

Eco Chiswick
Italian, Fast Food

Vegetarian ★★★★
Taste ★★★★
Price ££

⌨ *144 Chiswick High Road, W4*
☎ *020 8747 4922*
✍ *www.ecorestaurants.com*
🚇 *Turnham Green LU, 5min walk*
🕐 *Sun-Thurs 12noon-11pm, Fri-Sat 12noon-11.30pm*
✴ *Vegan options*
i *Eat-in (table service) and Takeaway*
☐ *Child friendly*

Eco have now opened a branch in Chiswick, having established a great reputation for their delicious pizzas and pastas in Clapham. The new restaurant retains the same vibrant spirit of the original restaurant but also has some unique features such as the curved wooden ceiling that ripples like a wave. The menu is the same as the original Eco but there are plans to add extra nutritious wholewheat pizzas to the menu.
For a food review see Eco, Clapham (page 197).

Woodlands
South Indian, Classic

Vegetarian ★★★★★
Taste ★★★★
Price £££

⊞ *12-14 Chiswick High Road, W4*
☏ *020 7994 9333*
🚈 *Stamford Brook LU, 2 min walk*
🕓 *Daily 12noon-3pm, 6pm-11pm*
🌱 *Vegan options*
i   *Table Service and takeaway*
    Booking advised
🍼 *Child friendly*

Fine gracious Indian vegetarian dining at one of the largest Indian restaurant chains in the world that specialises in dosas and uthappams. This particular Woodlands opened in late 2002 and sports a relaxing medley of modern décor and vintage artifacts on the walls. The best tables to reserve for comfort and social posturings are the banquettes around the perimeter.

Service is more perfunctory than friendly, but despite this people really do seem to enjoy themselves here. An Indian family of ten get finger licking as they dip the puris into the sauces and chat, while a young couple romance the night away on a dimly lit banquette. Most diners are locals with about two thirds of the diners being true vegetarians.

The menu is extensive and all the food and drink is well-presented. To start, Aloo Papdi Chaat, a snacky Mumbai street food, is wonderfully delicious with chopped potatoes on crushed pastry discs, green chillie and chutney immersed in yogurt with mixed spice. The London Royal Thali is a good way of trying a wide range of specialities in small amounts. It begins with two excellent steamed hot Idli (rice cakes) with sambar and coconut chutney. The Thali set comes with a good Masala Dosa, a small pancake filled with mild spiced potato, onions and snow peas and Uthappam (lentil pizza) topped with chilli. In the serving dishes a thick lentil souped Sambar, a Vegetable Korma, a tasty north Indian–styled Pilau rice, and Raita. I was too full to finish the small Sheera dessert of cream of wheat with nuts and ghee. The house red Syrah turned out to be a good choice. Woodland Chiswick may be out of the way for some but is worth the trek.

Other branches at:
Marylebone Lane, W1 (page 49), 37 Panton Street, Piccadilly, SW1 (page 32) and Wembley, North London.

Ealing

Carluccio's Caffé
Italian, modern

Vegetarian ★★★
Taste ★★★★
Price ££

⊞ 5-6 The Green, Ealing, W5
☎ 020 8566 4458
✐ www.carluccios.com
🚌 Ealing Broadway LU, 5 min walk
🕐 Mon-Fri 8am-11pm, Sat 9-11pm, Sun 10am-10pm
🥕 Vegan options
🍼 Child friendly, high chairs
☀ Outside seating
i Booking advised in evenings

This branch has been refurbished to a high standard.
See Carluccio's Caffé, St Christopher's Place for food review (page 35).

FarmW5
Mediterranean, classic

Vegetarian ★★★★
Organic ★★★★
Price £

⊞ 19 The Green, W5
☎ 020 8566 1965
✐ www.farmw5.com
🚌 Ealing Broadway LU, 5 min walk
🕐 Mon-Sat 8am-7pm, Sun 10am-6pm
🥕 Vegan options
i Eat-in (counter service) or takeaway

This is a bijou dining space at back of organic fine food store offering Cypriot/Lebanese veggie specialities. Seating just 12 people, the organic veggie salad platter is a bargain for £5.95. Fill your plate up from a choice of four salads including Baked Aubergine with chickpeas and onions and Wholewheat Pasta with grilled courgettes and sundried tomatoes. Other salads include Green Broad Beans cooked in a good olive oil and topped with pomegranate. Another delicious option is homemade hummus, tahini and chilli sauce with avocado and falafels, served with pitta bread. For those looking for comfort food there's also a warm fresh spinach, olive and lemon juice and chickpea casserole.

FarmW5 is run by Bilal, who calls it his 'little veggie heaven' and is passionate about locally sourced organic produce. About 90% of the produce is organic, all the soups are vegetarian and there's usually a few veggie quiches. Sandwiches are made from a range of ten organic breads and the organic cookies are handmade as is the vegan chocolate cake.

Fresh organic juices are a speciality and organic coffee, hot chocolate and teas are served with organic milk. A couple of options are available for non-vegetarians. For high quality organic dishes at affordable prices FarmW5 is well worth a visit.
See page 271 for the shop review.

Organic Pizza House
Italian, Fast Food

- 100 Pitshanger Lane, W5
- ☎ 020 8998 6878
- 🚌 Ealing Broadway LU (15min walk)
- 🕓 Mon-Sun 11am- 12midnight

Vegetarian ★★★★
Organic ★★★★★
Price £

Located on the former Pizza Organic site, this veggie organic fast food eaterie opened on 15th December 2008. The place has been completely redecorated with a modern emphasis and sports a completely new menu that is 95% organic ingredients. On starters, worth a try is the lentil soup or and there is also falafels with hot spicy tomato and garlic sauce. Some of the staff are former Pizza Organic so you can be confident that their pizzas and pastas will be of a very high standard. There's a whopping good range of desserts to choose from including carrot cake and a banoffie pie. Of note is the very attractive set menu at lunchtimes for £8.95 or £10.95 in the evenings.

West Kensington

222 Veggie Vegan Restaurant
International, modern

- 222, North End Road, W14
- ☎ 020 7381 2322
- 🖰 www.222veggievegan.com
- 🚌 West Kensington LU, 1 min walk
- 🕓 Buffet Lunch Mon-Sun 12.30pm-3.30pm, Dinner 5.30pm-10.30pm
- 🥕 Vegan and wheat-free options
- 🍼 Child friendly
- i Eat-in (table service) & Takeaway

Vegetarian ★★★★★
Organic ★★★★
Taste ★★★
Price ££

In an unpromising part of town, 222 is a promising vegetarian restaurant that draws vegan foodies from all over London, including visitors from the nearby Earls Court Exhibition Centre and the surrounding conference hotels. Opened in November 2004, the restaurant is run by Ben Asanami, previously head chef at Plant.

Located at the intersection of North End Road and Lillie Road, outside is a welcoming façade of orange lighting while inside there's a good small informal dining room with pale beechwood tables and chairs, pine flooring and sunken ceiling lighting. The nostalgic Marvin Gaye and other R&B playlist sets this informal eatery somehow in the 1960's/70's era.

The fairly short menu is a world food mix of Mediterranean, Afro-Caribbean, West Indian cuisine. Avocado Pomodoro starter is halved avocado with tomato sauce topped with a vegan cream that tastes quite good and comes attractively presented on a plate warmed from the oven. Baked Champignons although enough mushrooms for two is served with a rather mundane lettuce salad and a cocktail sauce. The main of Chickpea Curry, in contrast, is right on the money with a delicious spicy flavour, lots of tasty chickpeas and fresh seasoned vegetables and a fine brown basmati rice. Broccolini Di Parma is a milder event, consisting of pancakes filled with a tofu cottage cheese, broccoli and pimento that arrives as a big portion with some very enjoyable sauteéd potatoes.

Some old favourites from Plant can still be enjoyed here. Seitan Stroganoff, a highly satisfying main, is big on mushrooms and also features an enjoyable herb cashew cream sauce, caramelised onions, red peppers and seitan, a processed type of wheat gluten that imparts a deliciously smoky flavour.

The best dessert is the Home Tofu cheesecake that varies daily and is generous enough for two. Although not a cheesecake in the traditional sense the one I tried was beautifully flavoured with pineapple juice, orange zest and came accompanied with a mocha ice cream. The Fresh Fruit Salad is also superb with a great choice of fresh fruit.

Service at 222 fluctuates from attentively rapid to slow depending on how busy they are. Many customers are regulars and are prepared to put up with the wait as long as the food is good, particularly when they serve a good organic wine for only £2.50 a glass. The red Côtes de Thongue is pretty reasonable and there's also organic Freedom beer and a wide choice of juices and smoothies.

The buffet lunch at 222 is a selection of salads such as pasta, tomato, cucumber and a choice of baked potato, carrot tart, sweetcorn tart, veggie stirfry and wholemeal organic bread and costs £7.50 to eat in or £5.50 for a take-away box.

222 is a destination vegan restaurant that ticks almost all the boxes for a good, inexpensive night out. For drivers it also has the added bonus that one can park directly outside in the evening.

South London

Brixton

Honest Foods
International, Classic

Vegetarian ★★★
Price £

⌨ *424 Coldharbour Lane , SW9*
☎ *020 7738 6161*
🚍 *Brixton LU and BR, 2 min walk*
🕐 *Mon-Wed 9am-4pm, Thurs-Fri 9am-10pm*
   Sat 10am-10pm, Sun 11am-4pm

Located on the former site of vegetarian eaterie Café Pushka, Honest Foods offers a friendly service, inexpensive veggie bites and a substantial vegetarian breakfast including veggie sausages, eggs, mushrooms, tomatoes and potato pancakes. Whilst only about half the menu is vegetarian, they continue to attract a rather lot of veggies especially for their vegetarian Indian Thali that is very well prepared. Honest Foods also does outside catering and can put together a vegetarian menu on request.

Franco Manca
Italian, traditional

Vegetarian ★★
Organic ★★★★★
Price £

⌨ *4 Market Row, Electric Lane, SW9*
☎ *020 7738 3021*
🖎 *www.francomanca.com*
🚍 *Brixton LU, 5min walk*
🕐 *Mon-Sat 12noon-5pm*

Organic pizzeria Franco Manca has achieved, in a very short space of time, quite a reputation amongst pizza aficionados for great tasting pizzas. A comparatively small restaurant, it is situated on what used to be the successful Eco pizza restaurant that now has branches in Clapham and Chiswick. Franca Manca has completely transformed the interior into a very basic rustic décor with old wooden benches and a vast wood burning oven.

The menu is short and the choice for vegetarians is very limited, but the quality is very high. The Tomato, Mozzarella, Oregano and Garlic Pizza, is an absolute bargain at £4.60 with other toppings such as mushrooms and olives also available. All the pizzas are made from organic Italian flour and follow the Neopolitan tradition of being prepared from slow rising sourdough for a minimum of twenty-four hours before being baked. The result is a beautiful looking soft crust that is a joy to eat. This is a definite must for all veggies who love good pizza.

Clapham, Streatham and Tooting

For one of the best vegetarian restaurants in London and well worth beating a path to in Tooting is the Indian vegetarian restaurant, Kastoor. At Clapham High Street, Eco offers top notch pizza and pasta, Esca next door has exquisite salads and virtually opposite is Breads Etcetera – makers of superb sourdough organic bread. Enjoy one-stop organic shopping at either the Whole Foods Market store at Clapham Junction or for a quality veggie takeout there's the smaller neighbourhood shop, Dandelion. Further on at Streatham and worth a veggie whirl is the Whole Meal Café.

Clapham

Breads Etcetera
Organic sandwiches, veggie brunch

Vegetarian ★★★
Organic ★★★
Price £

- 127 Clapham High Street, SW4
- www.breadsetcetera.com
- Clapham Common LU, 5 min walk
- Tue-Sat 10am-6pm, Sun 10am-4pm, Mon bread sales only 2pm-7pm
- Outside seating
- i Eat-in and Takeaway

Specialises in producing 'no added yeast' organic sourdough breads since 2001, this comfortable relaxing café is perfect for light snacks and brunch. Take your choice between organic Danish Rye, Light Rye, Six Seed, Fruit, Walnut, Ciabatta and many others. The muffins and cookies are delicious but not organic as yet. Fillings include goat's cheese, roasted pepper & pesto, buffalo mozzarella & basil, mushroom, leek & cheddar. On the brunch menu there's a 'Strictly Vegan' seasonal vegetable Pyttipana with tomato, baby spinach & carrot salad, as well as a homemade veggie burger, tomato, baked beans, spinach and free range egg.

You can also get DIY Toast with as many spreads as you like. The quality of their breads is top notch, especially the Six Seed. If you can't get down to Clapham, why not try them at Planet Organic or one of the Apostrophe cafés dotted around London who they supply. All the cheeses here are suitable for vegetarians and you can widen your choice by letting them know you are veggie as they do convert some non-veggie dishes. This is a really nice, friendly place with the added appeal of organic Monmouth coffee.

They also have a bread shop in Northcote Road (see page 272).

Eco
Italian, fast food

🏠 162 Clapham High Street, SW4

☎ 020 7978 1108

✎ www.ecorestaurants.com

🚌 Clapham Common LU, 2 min walk

🕐 Mon-Thurs 12noon-4pm and 6.30pm-11pm,
   Fri 12noon-4pm and 6pm-11.30pm,
   Sat 12noon-11.30pm, Sun 12noon-11.30pm

🥕 Vegan options

🍼 Child friendly

i Table service & Takeaway

Vegetarian ★★★★
Taste ★★★★
Price ££

South

Clapham, Steatham & Tooting

Contemporary, vibrantly designed pizza–pasta paradise serving ten vegetarian pizzas, four pizza bread sandwiches, pastas, calzones, and a big range of salads. Eco has a modern décor with wavy plywood, asymmetric tables and bendy metal lighting. The atmosphere is upbeat and the staff alert and friendly. Eco was designed fourteen years ago by Anana Zenz who did Belgo in Chalk Farm. In the evenings there are often queues waiting for tables with lunchtimes are much less manic.

Eco serves amongst the best pizzas in London. All the pizzas are made from scratch so they can build one just as you like it. I can vouch for the Amore, a delicious array of chunky fresh artichoke, long roasted red peppers, green beans, aubergine, tomato sauce, garlic and olive oil. Take a spritz of their olive oil condiment –it's good. A mixed side salad here is real fine.

The Eco team also own Esca, next door. Esca is a relaxed eaterie and deli with some organic fare. It's worth a visit if you're in the area – see review on page 198.

Eco also has a branch in Chiswick (see page 197).

Esca

Mediterranean, classic

Vegetarian ★★★★
Taste ★★★★
Price ££

⌧ 160 Clapham High Street, SW4

☎ 020 7622 2288

✐ www.escauk.com

🚌 Clapham Common LU, 2 min walk

🕐 Mon-Fri 8am-9pm, Sat 9am-9pm

🌶 Vegan options

⌂ Child friendly

i Eat in (table service) & Takeaway

This is a high quality, great value, deli counter with 17 vegetarian dish choices that can be eaten at informal large tables at the back. Esca means 'bait' in Italian and its food certainly looks tempting enough to draw people off the street. The place has a wonderfull high ceiling, making it light and airy with subtle lighting that is romantically dimmed in the evenings.

The lunchtime I visited it was busy with couples taking a long lazy grazing two hour lunch, and office workers in and out in a thirty minutes. There's super-friendly service here and the manageress is a vegetarian herself and is helpful on menu selections. Each day there's a vegetarian soup, in this case Sweetcorn Chowder which came as a huge bowl of golden soup (enough for a light lunch) that was delicious and came with a couple of thick slices of organic olive bread for only £3.75. The bread here is too good to miss, so even if you are having a main, order a bread basket (£2.25) that has great selection and is accompanied by balsamic vinegar and olive oil.

There is a choice of three vegetarian dishes for mains which cost just £7.90. Of particular note was the artichoke, okra, asparagus and lentils with garlic salad, whilst another delicious option was the goat's cheese, courgette and onion. Both dishes went well with the Doricum Catarrato Sicilian 2006, a floral aromatic dry white wine. For a warm main, the Sweet Potato Gratin arrives as a large attractive square slab, with a green leaf and lettuce salad at a bargain £4.75. For those on the move there are some ready made sandwiches at about £3 as well as packs of organic dried fruit.

At the front of the shop there is a magnificent display of vegetarian cakes and desserts. The Date and Walnut Slice looked so tempting, but in the end I succumbed to the Apple Riccotta Crumble with vanilla ice cream that looked delightfully home made with it's roughly cut fruits and was just delicious.

Esca has now expanded its operation with a new branch in the City of London at New Street which opened in August 2008. The new outlet has approximately 50 covers and is similar in décor to the Clapham Common eaterie.

For the shop review see page 273.

Esca

Good Earth Express
Chinese, classic

Vegetarian ★★★★
Taste ★★★★★
Price £££

🖃 116 St Johns Hill, SW11
☎ 020 7228 3140
🖉 www.goodearthgroup.co.uk
🚇 Wimbledon LU/BR
i Takeaway and delivery service only

See Good Earth Knightsbridge (page 165) for food review.

Whole Foods Market
Organic, Vegetarian, International

Vegetarian ★★★★
Organic ★★★★★
Taste ★★★★
Price £

🖃 305–311 Lavender Hill, SW11
☎ 020 7585 1488
🖉 www.wholefoodsmarket.com
🚇 Clapham Junction BR, 2 min walk
🕐 Mon-Fri 8.30am-8.30pm, Sat 8.30am-7.30pm, Sun 11am-6pm
🗡 Vegan options

Whole Foods Market has good inside seating looking out onto the street and is really vibrant at the weekend, although on weekday afternoons it's still pretty busy with affluent, casually dressed, Wandsworth and Clapham folk chilling out.

This south west London institution has a similar array of hot and cold dishes to the Stoke Newington branch (see page 150 for food review) but also has a few dishes unique to the store made by chef Minh. Specialities include Brown Rice with Arame (Japanese seaweed) and soy sauce that tasted good, as was the Tofu with Brocolli and a Tamari sauce. Other attractive dishes were the Roast Fennel with vegetarian parmesan, pinenuts and garlic, Cous Cous with roast vegetables and the Spicy Aubergine salad. The desserts are very good and include F&W's own organic vegetarian ice-cream and sorbet range. It's great to see a large chain allow chef's autonomy and this is reflected in the quality of the food being served here.

Vauxhall

Bonnington Café
Japanese, French, German
East European Medieval and Raw, Classic

Vegetarian ★★★★★
Organic ★★★★★
Taste ★★★
Price £

⊞ *11 Vauxhall Grove, SW8*
☎ *020 7820 7466,*
🚌 *Vauxhall LU/BR, 2 min walk*
🕐 *Daily 12noon-2pm, 6.30pm-10.30pm*
🖋 *www.bonningtoncafe.co.uk*
🥕 *Vegan options*
☀ *Outside tables in summer*
i *Advanced booking recommended*
Ⴘ *BYO, no corkage charge*

Communally, co-operative run vegetarian restaurant with different chefs cooking on different nights, an arrangement which accounts for the eclectic range of cuisines on offer. The second, fourth and fifth Sunday night is Raw Food Night and that's the night I visited.

The café is on a residential backstreet and outside looks completely unappealing and derelict. The area is gradually going through the process of gentrification and in the last twenty five years considerable improvements have been made. The community spirit is still strong and the café is near Bonnington Square and its delightful community gardens where diners relax in summer before going to the café.

The diners are predominantly socially and eco-aware vegetarians. Anja Ladra, the enthusiastic young chef who also runs the specialist vegan raw food catering company, Raw Fairies (see page 290), says 'Eighty-per cent come on Raw Sunday's specifically for the raw food rather than just because it's vegan. There's a growing interest in raw plant-based foods that enable people to achieve greater energy and vitality'.

Inside the café the décor is not quite as down at heel as it used to be. Nevertheless, my chair was old and rickety and about to break but was replaced by a better one immediately without fuss. The knives and forks were new, but cheap and the glassware, a hotch potch of styles. The tables were wooden and solid and the walls quite reasonable in white and plum, whilst the ceiling at the back curiously had maps of the area on it and newspaper sheets. Noticeably, the type of diner has become more affluent here than in past years. A young couple brought their own bottle of vegetarian organic wine from Waitrose to drink, whilst another from the neighbourhood said they ate here regularly and supported the ideals of the place. Candlelit, the atmosphere is intimate, everybody seems to know each other, one could be forgiven for feeling a bit of an outsider, but any fears are allayed by our cordial waitress.

Most diners opt for two courses from the menu blackboard as they are very filling. The starter of Beetroot Paté is a small neat design in the centre of the plate and comes with flaxseed crackers and the Thai Cabbage Salad also looked very good. I had a main of Courgette Quiche on Hazelnut Crust which tasted good and came with a heaped salad of two types of raw cabbage, red pepper, broccoli, ginger, parsnip and carrot together with spinach leaves and a reasonable dressing. Another main, Sprouted Buckwheat Pizza, was a very tasty small pizza topped with sun dried tomato, marinated mushroom, carrot, pepper and courgette, with a rather good herbed buckwheat crust which came with a fresh salad, as do all the mains.

I was quite content with the friendly, lively atmosphere, made more pleasant with a cheap bottle of vegetarian Malbec that I'd bought from Tesco. Other diners were opting for 'The Green Juice' – of celery, cucumber, broccoli, fennel and green leaves – which looked very healthy. Among the desserts, the Pecan Banana slice is nicely presented and quite tasty, whilst the chocolate mousse cake with vanilla frosting and berry coulis would be one for next time. Overall, Raw Sunday whose all organic menu changes every time, is an interesting experience and relatively inexpensive.

Also on the blackboard is the vegan menu, available every day, that includes such choices as Cauliflower and Broccoli soup and mains of Chickpea Courgette and Squash Korma curry or Adzuki beans, Mushroom and Barley stew. Not all the chefs at Bonnington Café are completely organic, but Draeyk – an amiable vegan chef who runs the Thursday Night Vegan Night – has an organic allotment on nearby Vauxhall City Farm, where he grows his veg. He says 'most vegetarians here are now eating it for health reasons. This has become a more important reason than animal welfare that was the principle concern several years ago. There's an interest in how our community has evolved. We get artists from all over London and visiting architects interested in the set-up here'.

The café's low prices are enshrined in it's constitution and the place can get busy – proof the community eateries can really work.

Bonnington Café

Streatham

Whole Meal Café
International

Vegetarian ★★★★★
Organic ★★★
Taste ★★
Price £

⌨ *1 Shrubbery Road, SW16*
☎ *020 8769 2423*
✍ *www.wholemealcafe.com*
🚌 *Streatham BR or Streatham Hill BR, 5 min walk*
🕐 *Daily 12noon-10pm*
✎ *Vegan options*
🍼 *Child friendly*
i *Counter service/takeaway*

This relaxed, neighbourhood, 100% vegetarian café has a menu that is one third vegan and now bakes it's own organic bread. A stone's throw from Streatham High Street, the outside is welcoming and the inside bright and airy with white walls and polished tables. Lunchtime is busy with casually-dressed local workers, shoppers and a few bookworms and laptop users.

The Homity Pie (£6.75) is a big slab of mashed potato, onion and garlic which comes with a large mixed salad and is substantial if a bit bland. Proving a lot more popular is the 'Special Salad', a big plate of cottage and cheddar cheese with garlic, mushrooms and hummus for£7.20. For less hungry bods, there are the usual baked jacket potato choices, hummus salads, vegan soups and quiches. The vegeburgers made with breadcrumbs, nuts and veg are also a popular choice here. Dessert lovers should leave room for the Banoffee Pie with cream and a dusting of chocolate that's good for those who like their desserts sweet and goey.

Evenings are candlelit. There's a short organic wine list of house Merlot and Touchstone Chardonnay as well as Pinot Grigio, Pinot Noir,a white Bordeaux and some organic beers. Drivers should try the non-alcoholic Red Grape Juice which is delicious. Whole Meal is a good little place if you're in the Streatham area and looking for a low priced meal that's value for money.

Tooting

Kastoori
Indian and East African

	Vegetarian ★★★★★
	Taste ★★★★
	Price £££

🏠 *188 Upper Tooting Road, SW17*
☎ *020 8767 7027*
🚇 *Tooting Broadway LU or Tooting Bec LU, 5 min walk*
🕐 *Lunch Wed-Sun 12.30pm-2.30pm, Dinner Daily 6pm-10.30pm*
🍼 *Children-friendly*
🌶 *Vegan Choices*
i Table service & Takeaway service

With a Michelin Bib Gourmand Award in 2008 for moderately priced dining (three courses for less than £28), it's well worth the trip to Tooting to try this family-run restaurant offering vegetarian Gujarati/East African cuisine. Set along a predominantly non-descript shopping High Street, Kastoori's interior is contrastingly, elegant and roomy with white walls adorned with white sculptures, comfortable yellow and blue chairs and bright yellow clothed tables. Evenings and weekend lunchtimes get very busy, while weekday lunchtimes are much more relaxed. The menu is Indian home-style, so there aren't that many Indian customers as they want a change from what they get at home.

The restaurant is run by the amiable Thanki family, dedicated vegetarians who themselves are Gujarati Jains who had previously lived in East Africa. The menu has clear descriptions, service is good and waiters offer helpful advice.

The spicy papadams with a hot mix of coriander, ginger and peanut chutney, a carrot and tomato pickle and a cooling raita was enjoyable. The Dahi Puri starters, a Thanki family creation, are attractively looking crispy shells the size of table tennis balls filled with diced potato with onion, puffed rice, chickpea and mildly flavoured sweet tamarind sauce and yoghurt. The trick is to bite into them and eat them in one gulp – it takes a bit of practice to avoid the sauce running down the chin. The signature Samosa starter is absolutely sensational - richly filled with vegetables and accented with cinnamon, whilst the Onion Bhajia is good but not memorable.

There's a good selection of 13 curry mains and the Bhatura Bread, fried with fennu (fennel and sesame), is recommended as an accompaniment, as are the chapati. The Tomato Curry is novel, tasty and not as hot and spicy as the menu made out. The Kastoori Kofta, a spicy curry sauce with chunky vegetable balls, went down a treat. A handsome Panir Passanda of cheese pockets stuffed with coriander and mint in a nut and melon seed sauce is a good dish and large enough to split. There are 12 special mains, one of which is available each day. Kasodi (Swahili sweetcorn), comes in coconut milk and peanut sauce and is delicious, whilst the Green Banana Curry is well worth a whirl.

The usual dessert treats are here, such as the sweetish Gulab Jambu, Khir (aromatic rice pud) and Kulfi (mango or pistachio ice cream). Recommended is the Shrikland – a spicy, sweet curd cheese sprinkled with nutmeg, with flavours of cardamom and saffron.

Much effort has been made to make the wine list match the cuisine. Echeverra Sauvignon Blanc turned out to be a good choice across our meal, although now a new Cuma Tarrontes, Argentinian white has been added to the list for those wanting organic. Masala Tea, a spicy traditional tea, completes the Kastoori dining experience.

Wimbledon

Good Earth Express
Chinese, classic

Vegetarian ★★★★
Taste ★★★★★
Price £££

- 81 Ridgeway, SW19
- 020 8944 8883
- www.goodearthgroup.co.uk
- Wimbledon LU/BR
- i   Takeaway and delivery service only

For food review See Good Earth, Knightsbridge (page 165).

Le Pain Quotidien
French, classic

Vegetarian ★★★★
Organic ★★★★★
Taste ★★★★
Price ££

- 4/5 High Street, SW19
- www.lepainquotidien.co.uk
- Wimbledon LU, 5min walk
- i   Table service & Takeaway
- Vegan options
- i   Limited booking policy at this café
- No bookings Sat-Sun 9.30am-7pm

Opened in July 2008, this is a welcome addition to the local café culture. *For food review see Le Pain Quotidien, Marylebone (page 41).*

Blackheath

Provender Blackheath
International, Classic, Organic

Vegetarian ★★★★
Organic ★★★★★
Taste ★★★★
Price £

- 🏠 *50, Tranquil Vale, SE3*
- 🚌 *Blackheath BR, 5min walk*
- 🕐 *Mon-Sat 8am-6.30pm, Sun 10.30am-4pm*
- 🥕 *Vegan Options*
- 🍼 *Child friendly*
- ☀ *Outside seating*

Having moved from its long established location on Dartmouth Road, this new café is still a wonderful place to sample organic café foods at their freshest. With comfortable seating, one can feast ones eyes on the trays of snack foods in the window and the organic brown scones, carrot cake, fruit strudel slices on the wall-to-ceiling shelves. The Spinach and Paneer baked pasty are an absolute gift for two quid, a deliciously light construction with a perfect touch of spiciness. The vegetable lasagne and the mixed beans and short grain rice dish and falafel look good too. The organic coffee here is delicious and herbal teas are available. With an eco-aware policy, Provender has won several accolades including a Best Of Lewisham 2007 award in connection with 'its huge selection of vegetarian and organic food with the tastiest hot buffets'. The café may have moved but the quality of food and service remains very high.

Crystal Palace

Domali Café
English and mediterranean, classic

Vegetarian ★★★★
Taste ★★★
Price £

- 🏠 *38 Westow Street, SE19*
- ☎ *020 8768 0096*
- 🚌 *Crystal Palace BR, 10 min walk, Gypsy Hill BR, 5min*
- 🕐 *Mon-Sat 9.30am-11.50pm (last orders 11pm), Sun, 9.30am-10.30pm*
- 🍼 *Child friendly*
- 🥕 *Vegan options*
- ☀ *Good outside seating*

Domali has had a major refurb in recent years and is now brighter with attractive modern bar lighting. Complimenting the décor is a new blackboard menu format that changes every few days. Domali is named after its vegetarian owners Dominic and Alison and is pretty well established on this main dining strip since opening its doors in 1996.

The vibe here remains laid-back, with veggie breakfasts served until 6pm. The blackboard menu features a tempting array of upscale sandwiches and salads as well as more substantial hot mains such as Tuscan Bean Casserole with chargrilled bread, Chickpea Burgers, and Penne with butternut squash. Comfy leather sofas, good wooden tables and chairs, vibrant contemporary artwork combine to create a bohemian and hip ambience. The service is both relaxed and attentive.

Evenings are candlelit and more intimate. Domali attracts a pleasant, casually dressed twenty-thirtysomething crowd of juice, wine and designer-lager drinkers not out to get smashed. At the back is a very popular garden with outdoor heaters.

Reputed for it's music, Domali has a good play list of jazz and new folk. Weekday morning's it's a different kind of sound – that of mums and kids enjoying a spot of breakfast. Children portions and high chairs are available and there is a good range of options including their homemade muesli and fresh fruit salad. Recommended at lunch/ early evening are the Weekday Deals (9.30am-6pm) at £6.90 for any Vegetarian Blackboard Special plus a free non-alcoholic drink. There are eight specials from which to choose, although many of the mains are heavily bread-based. S.L.T (Veggie Sausage, tomato, lettuce and mayo) comes up huge and enough for two. The sausage is fairly good and a better option than the veggie bacon.

With its relaxed atmosphere Domali is a great place for a drink and there are several vegetarian and vegan wines, plus a good range of juices and smoothies for kids. Both the vegan white Inzolia and the red Primitivo wines are organic and available by the glass but only a few food items are organic as they want to keep their prices affordable for the price-conscious Crystal Palace clientele. 'Hopefully' says Alison 'if organic prices go down we'll make the switch. However, we do buy locally and use smaller suppliers that are in need of support.'

Domali has some tempting vegetarian cakes including Chocolate and Raspberry Fudge and Carrot. A really likeable hangout.

The Spirited Palace
Caribbean, classic, organic vegan

⌨ *105 Church Road, SE19*
☎ *020 8768 0609 or 07939 474 507*
🚌 *Crystal Palace BR, 5 min walk, Gypsy Hill BR, 10min walk*
🕐 *Tue-Fri 11am-10pm, Sat-Sun 2pm-10pm*
🍼 *Child friendly*
☀ *Outside seating*
i *Eat in(table service) and Takaway*
🍸 *BYO (£1 corkage per table)*

Vegetarian ★★★★★
Organic ★★★★★
Taste ★★★
Price £

Putting the healthy vegan spirit into Crystal Palace, The Spirited Palace offers it's own unique twist of Caribbean cuisine in this quirky informal café. If arriving for lunch, don't be shocked by the 'closed' sign, it's open and you'll be let in. Matanah, who runs the place, does so as a security precaution when things are a bit quiet. Much busier are evenings and pre-booking is advisable at weekends as food events are sometimes on.

Although the outside is green and grotty looking, inside there's an inviting serving counter with small vegan pizzas, savoury pasties, raw salads and shelves well stocked with ingredients for sale that are used in the café's recipes – should you want to have a crack at making them at home. Skip the lone table and the few stools and head downstairs through the labyrinth of doorways to the main dining space that's decorated with wall to wall palm tree scenes with soul music playing. Folksy wooden tables and benches, red plastic chairs and comfy armchairs, complete this peculiarly surreal Caribbean experience.

The lunchtime we visited, the menu was verbal. The menus we were told were being printed up and the food being labelled. Best in taste was the Wheat 'Meat' made from gluten, black-eyed beans, plantain, brown rice and seasonal bean curd. The Macaroni & Soya Cheese, Dumplings, Bulghar and Yam were quite good also and altogether very reasonable value for a fixed £7.00 per plate. To it's credit food miles are kept to a minimum with some produce sourced from local farmers' markets and from the nearby Spa Hill Allotments (see page 300).

Of interest to veggie live foodies is the Raw Plate that includes raw plantain, sweet potato, wakame and cashew nuts, together with a whole medley of nutritional goodies. There's also raw and cooked cakes from £2.50 such as sweet potato pie, strawberry jam cake and fruit buns.

Ginger fanatics will be delighted with The Spirited Palace as they make the strongest ginger drinks in London. The ginger, apple and carrot juice tastes quite good, whilst the homemade ginger beer was delicious and nearly knocked my socks off. 'I make it a bit stronger than normal for a bigger kick' said Matanah 'A lot of the cooking and baking is done from my home in Sydenham from where it is brought in. And I'm always experimenting.' That's exactly the impression one gets, of a place in experiment, whose menu changes daily, but at it's core it is firmly organic and vegan and one worth supporting.

Greenwich

Mulberry Tea Rooms
English, classic, light meals

Vegetarian ★★★★
Price £

- 🖼 *Charlton House, Charlton Road, SE7*
- ☎ *020 8856 3951*
- 🚌 *Charlton BR (15min walk)*
- 🕐 *Mon-Fri 9am-3pm*
- 🥕 *Vegan options*
- 🍼 *Child friendly*
- ☀ *Outside seating*

This forty seater tearoom is located in the central foyer of a magnificent Jacobean mansion built in 1607. Although the rest of the house is not open to the general public except for private hire, it is possible to have an enjoyable walk around the grounds and the charming surrounding parkland. Inside this Vegetarian Society approved tearoom, sliced quiches, wraps, baguettes, jacket potatoes and vegan samosa are served. On Fridays a curry casserole is also available. 'About seventy percent of the dishes are vegetarian and great care is taken in making the food to ensure things are exactly right for vegetarians' says Viv Hammond, herself a vegetarian.

Selhurst

Pepperton
European, Eastern, African, Classic

Vegetarian ★★★★★
Organic ★★★
Taste ★★★
Price £

🖼   25 Selhurst Rd, SE25
☎   020 8683 4462
🖱   www.peppertonuk.co.uk
🚌   Selhurst BR, 5min
🕓   Tue-Sat 12noon-10pm
☀   Outside tables in Secret Garden
🌱   Vegan options
i   Table service & Takeaway

A small but bright neighbourhood vegetarian restaurant with a contemporary art gallery and alternative therapy rooms. Opened August 2003, Pepperton is more than a veggie restaurant, it's a lifestyle venue. Décor wise the place has the feeling of relaxed cool karma. The ground floor has immaculately new polished wooden tables, stripped wooden floor, a comfortable sofa and the walls are always lined with interesting modern art or photographic images. This is a restaurant concerned about local community welfare, healthy and nutrition via vegetarian and vegan eating. Upstairs there are various new age alternative regimes available. Not to be missed on a sunny day is the Secret Garden, an oak tree garden with seating for twenty people

Pepperton is run by African vegetarian and former social worker Celestine Agbo who also gives talks on vegetarian food and art to local schools and has a facility in the Secret Garden for children to participate in art projects. Celestine Agbo also gives psycho–counselling sessions when the restaurant is closed and is a friendly smiling face always ready for a chat with customers.

The menu is an eclectic mix of salads, side dishes and mains. Stew of Pepperton looks good and is an enjoyable recipe of yam, plantain, black–eyed bean and Scotch Bonnet pepper and well worth £6.75 – the average price for mains here. Brazilian Stuffed Peppers are filled with a reasonably flavoursome mix of aubergine, herbs, tomatoes and goats cheese and comes with a good wild rice. Other choices include two penne pastas, a ricotta and spinach filo dish, a Mexican chilli and bean recipe and jacket potatoes with cheese or beans (£5.50).

Juices here are only £1.10 for a large glass and there is organic white and red wines, Utkins vodka, gin and beer. There's a good selection of desserts and all the cakes are vegan.

Pepperton is set on a small shopping parade – a bit out of the way from things, although it's opposite a pub much favoured by Crystal Palace Football supporters. Fans of Pepperton include the surrounding multi-ethnic community of East and West African, Chinese, Polish and English vegetarians. The place is also popular with the Croydon Vegan Society. Pepperton is well worth a visit for local South East London vegetarians.

Putney

Carluccio's Caffè
Italian, modern

Vegetarian ★★★	
Taste ★★★★	
Price ££	

🏠 Putney Wharf, SW15
☎ 020 8789 0591
🖱 www.carluccios.com
🚌 Putney Bridge LU, 5 min walk
🕐 Mon-Fri 8am-11pm, Sat 9-11pm, Sun 10am-10pm
🗲 Vegan options
🍼 Child friendly, high chairs
☀ Outside seating
i Booking advised in evenings

By the river, near Putney Bridge and lovely in the Summer.
See Carluccio's Caffè, St Christopher's Place for food review (page 35).

Thai Square Putney Bridge
Thai, classic

Vegetarian ★★★	
Taste ★★	
Price £££	

🏠 2-4 Lower Richmond Road
Embankment, Putney, SW15
☎ 020 8780 1811
🖱 www.thaisq.com
🚌 Putney Bridge LU, 5min walk
🕐 Mon-Thurs 12noon-3pm and 5.30pm-11pm
Fri-Sat 5.30pm-11.30pm (bar 5.30pm-2am)
Sun 12noon-3pm and 5.30pm-10.30pm

Magnificently designed, award winning building, with excellent River Thames views and a wide selection of veggie Thai dishes. Take your pick of six starters, three soups, four salads and ten mains. Reserve your table in advance for the best tables with a marvellous view of Putney Bridge.

East London

Rootmaster
www.ro... ster.co.u

Rootmaster Bustaurant

Brick Lane & Spitalfields

Restaurants

1) Bengal Cuisine p.215
2) Preem p.216
3) Rootmaster Bustaurant p.217
4) Shampan p.218
5) Sunday Up Market p.220
6) Café Mediterraneo p.221
7) Carluccio's Caffé Spitalfields p.221
8) Leon Spitalfields p.222
9) Spitalfields Food Market p.124
10) Spitalfields New Market p.225
11) Spitalfields Organics p.225
12) Story Deli p.219
13) Wagamama p.225

Shops

a) Ambala p.279
b) Spitalfields Organics p.279

Brick Lane

First and foremost renowned for Indian restaurants, Brick Lane has seen the arrival of an array of fascinating new eateries. For gastro-adventure, head straight to Story Deli that has perhaps the best organic pizzas in London or try the Sunday Up Market stalls for Ethiopian and Mediterranean fast food. Alternatively, take your taste buds on a gastronomic journey aboard the Rootmaster vegan restaurant, a Routemaster bus albeit stationary in Ely's Yard.

Brick Lane has a reputation for being London's No.1 Indian dining strip and a hip cool place to gravitate towards, and yet there isn't a single pure veggie Indian eaterie to be found here. Most it seems are run by Moslem (meat-eating) Bangladeshis who nevertheless recognise the need to give a good vegetarian food selection. Competition for your wallet or purse is rife with restaurant touts trying to get passing business on the street with 25% discount meal deals and a lager pint thrown in! The area is often swamped with tourists, students, foodies and locals. For those looking for good vegetarian food here should try Shampan, Bengal Cuisine and Preem.

Bengal Cuisine
Indian, Classic

Vegetarian ★★★
Price £

🖃 *12 Brick Lane, E1*
☏ *020 7377 8405*
🚌 *Shoreditch LU or Liverpool St LU & Rail (10min walk)*
🕐 *Daily 12noon-12midnight*
👶 *Child friendly*

A menu of classic vegetarian Indian dishes mixed vegetable balti, vegetable dhansak, biryani, korma and vegetable sizzler dishes. They also offer classic Indian snacks, some of which are suitable as mains as well as a good rice and vegetable selection.

Want to cook curry like the experts? Bengal Cuisine does 'Cook Your Own Curry' every Tuesday 6pm-9pm, where the chef takes you to the kitchen and shows you how to do it. You choose starter, main, side, rice and bread. You get two drinks and the deal costs £25 per person. The cookery course gets 2-8 persons per session. The vegetarian business lunch of starter and main course is £6.95, while the Sunday buffet (from 12noon-7.30pm) offers 10 dishes £5.95 (adults), or £3.95 (kids).

Preem Restaurant and Balti House
Indian, Classic

Vegetarian ★★★
Price £

- 🏠 *120 Brick Lane, E1*
- ☎ *020 7247 0397*
- 🖥 *www.preembricklane.co.uk*
- 🚌 *Shoreditch LU or Liverpool St LU & Rail (10min walk)*
- 🕐 *Mon-Sat 12noon-2am, Sun 12noon-1am*
- 👶 *Child friendly*

Veggie are well catered for here with a choice of seven veggie starters, twenty-four veggie side dishes and main courses such as masala dosa, biryani, vegetable balti and vegetable masala balti. Budget for £8 per head excluding drinks and tip.

Rootmaster Bustaurant
International, Modern Vegan

Vegetarian ★★★★★
Organic ★★★★★
Taste ★★★★
Price £

- 🏠 *The Routemaster bus, Ely's Yard*
  The Old Truman Brewery car park,
  Hanbury Street, E1
- ☎ *07912 389314*
- 🖥 *www.root-master.co.uk*
- 🕐 *Mon-Sun 11am-10pm – booking advised in the evenings*
- 🚌 *Shoreditch LU or Liverpool St LU & Rail (10min walk)*
- i *Table service evenings*
  Takeaway
- 🥕 *Vegan options*
- ☀ *Outside tables*

Just like a London bus at rush hour, this stationary Routemaster that has been converted into an alternative restaurant, can sometimes be full to capacity. We had booked for our evening meal, but David (the conductor/maitre'd) was turning people away as he escorted us to our seat on the top deck, 'Take the large communal table at the far end of the deck, others will join you round it as the night continues'. Candlelit at 7.30pm, some couples on side tables were already sipping organic wine aperitifs and nibbling on what turned out to be good flavoured green olives and delicious sun dried tomatoes.

With most of the windows already steamed up, one could just about discern the art installations made from crushed cars that are scatted around Ely's Yard car park. The combination of heat from the kitchen below and the vibration of the bus generated by diners and waiters going

Rootmaster Bustaurant

up and down the stairs could bring on an acute bout of travel sickness. Unwinding a few of the old bus's windows definitely helped. With all the original bus seats removed, David sauntered past the solid tables with a short but enticing all vegan and organic menu. 'The Winter Squash is still off the menu, but I'm making this fabulous chocolate cake that you must try'.

Portions tend to come up large here so we skippedstarters and headed straight for the mains. Purple Sprouted Broccoli with maple wild rice and tofu came as a mountainous feast, laced with a ginger cream sauce and was delicious. Teriyaki stir fry with edame beans, tofu, peppers, mushrooms and cashew nuts was very good with lots of different flavours. By now we had been joined on our table by a lively amiable Argentinian/New York crowd. Maximillian, a new vegetarian, kindly offered me some of his starter – lightly fried tempura in a sweet chilli dip – that was very good indeed, whilst the spicy miso soup also looked worth a try. The conversation was interesting about veggie restos, Facebook and the vibrant East End and it was made easier with a good organic Rosé from the all organic vegan wine list – our end of the upper deck was spontaneously turning into a party. David the maitre d' had sat down and joined us with some eccentric theatrics about the finer nuances of the menu and then announced that people had to get up so he could get to the chilli sauces that were stored in a compartment underneath the seats where we were sitting. After the musical chairs, the Triple Chocolate Fudge cake was worth waiting for and came with a thick icing. The Gyoza, a dish of small wanton wraps filled with fruit, was also very good. Both desserts came with quality Swiss Glace ice cream.

At the other tables, there was a mixed crowd of casually dressed 25–35 year olds – the kind of people that have made Brick Lane and its markets such a success. The mood was buoyant and the retro rock and roll created an upbeat atmosphere. The only major inconvenience to the experience was the lack of a toilet, customers had to cross the yard to a dance club diner.

Owner, Sylvia Garcia, herself a passionate vegan, runs a tight bus here. The result is an intriguing series of menus that change according to the seasonality of produce. It's her first venture into the restaurant world and with her capable team on board it has proved the perfect vehicle for her culinary vegan ambitions.

On Sundays, with Brick Lane in full swing, the bus is very popular serving light snacks like vegeburgers with potato wedges (£6.50) and Mexican bean wraps (£5). On fine days there is a lot more space with outside seating. For me, however, an evening on the Rootmaster Bustaurant is definitely London's liveliest organic vegetarian experience.

The Shampan Restaurant
Indian, Classic

Vegetarian ★★★
Price £

🖃   *79 Brick Lane, E1*

☎   *020 7375 0475*

🖉   *www.shampan.co.uk*

🚌   *Shoreditch LU or Liverpool St LU & Rail (10min walk)*

🕓   *Sun-Wed 12noon-1am, Thur-Sat 12noon-2am*

🍼   *Child friendly*

i   *Table service, Takeaway*

Traditional, upscale Bangladeshi and Indian restaurant that avoids the use of food colourings and artificial additives. The menu features six vegetarian starters, eleven vegetarian speciality mains including Vegetable Tikka Masala and several Bangladeshi specials of which Sag Uribessi Gatta (a dish with spinach and seeds of Bangladeshi runner beans) makes an excellent choice for veggie diners. The Shobji Kufta Bujon, lightly spiced vegetable balls in a spicy sauce of tomatoes and mushrooms is very popular too. Vegetable biriani and a vegetarian Thali is also on the menu and there is a good selection of veggie side dishes for those wanting to mix and match.

Story Deli
Italian, Fast food

⊞ 3 Dray Walk, E1

☎ 020 7247 3137

🚇 Liverpool St LU 7min walk

🕐 Daily 12noon-8pm

◊ Child friendly

🌶 Vegan options

☀ Outside tables

i   Table service, Takeaway

Vegetarian ★★★★
Organic ★★★★
Taste ★★★★
Price ££

Story Deli stands proud as a charming recycled rustic décored pizzeria with eight dedicated vegetarian pizzas and a willingness to convert to veggie or vegan all the other pizzas on their gigantic pizza list. Located in the heart of Brick Lane, it's packed out on Sundays with the New East End hip crowd. Snag a window seat and watch the throngs of shoppers pass by or sit on one of the curious recycled cardboard boxes by the massive wooden communal table, a former dressmaker's table complete with drawers. With large framed mirrors, voluminous white globe lights dangling from the ceiling and candles around the place, there's a very pleasing old world atmosphere here.

Large and square, stone baked and hand-rolled, all the pizza bases are yeast-free and made from organically grown flour. A little harder to cut than normal pizza bases despite being thinner, the downside is that they are not so easy for sharing as the toppings come in discrete areas on the pizza rather than uniformly across it. That said, where there's a will there's a way. Picking at it ad lib with forks as one contented couple did, knocked that one on the head.

The favourite veggie pizza is the Roast Vegetable although the Chanterelle Pizza is hard to resist and the best organic pizza I've tasted. Arriving with delicious chanterelle and button mushrooms, veggie mozzarella and mascarpone, it came laden with roasted sweet onion, porcini pesto and garnished with a touch of rocket and toasted pine nuts – delicious! Also looking swell was the Mushroom Rocket that comes with vegetarian parmesan, tomato, roasted mushrooms and this time a heap of rocket. Vegetarian cakes and flapjacks with organic coffee are available, as are organic beers, wine and lemonade.

Owners Lee and Ann, the day to day driving force behind Story Deli are both totally passionate about organic, run a tight ship coupled with friendly helpful service. I Loved it.

The Sunday Up Market

Eley's Yard, Corner of Bricklane and Hanbury Street
The Old Truman Brewery, E1

www.sundayupmarket.co.uk

Sunday 9am-5pm

Entering from Brick Lane, **Planet Falafel's** miniscule stall offers nicely packed veggie falafel wraps at £3.80 and falafel and salad for £2.80. Nearby is the vivacious **Red Tent Ethiopian Food**, renowned for its hand-roasted organic coffee (£1.50) which is made in a traditional way using a clay pot and served in a tiny cup. They also offer three Ethiopian veggie dishes served with a flat bread called Enjera. At £3.50 a plate, the spicy mixed vegetable casserole was carefully prepared and cooked using vegetable oil, making it a substantial vegan meal. If you fancy trying to create the flavour of Ethiopia at home, they sell the coffee beans and organic tea. The friendly service and conversation are all provided free of charge and make this one of the real treats of the Upmarket.

East · Brick Lane

Spitalfields

Spitalfields is within five minutes walk of Brick Lane and has a great selection of international food bars at lunchtime as well as some established restaurants with veggie fare. Spitalfields Market has been redeveloped in recent years and now has a modern shopping and market complex adjoined to the traditional Victorian structure. Good mezzes are still to found at Café Mediterraneo, while upmarket diners such as Leon, Carluccio's and Wagamama are new arrivals to the area.

Café Mediterraneo
Mediterranean, organic vegetarian

Vegetarian ★★★★
Organic ★★★★
Taste ★★
Price £

- ▢ *Old Spitalfield Organic Market, Honer Square, E1*
- ☏ *020 7377 8552*
- 🚌 *Liverpool St BR/LU, 5 min walk*
- 🕐 *Mon-Fri 8am-4pm, Sun 8am-5pm*
- ⬦ *Child friendly*
- ☀ *Outside tables*
- *i* *Counter/takeaway service*

For atmosphere it's best to catch this on Sunday, organic market day at Spitalfields, although on weekdays it's popular with city workers. The décor not much to write home about – think indoor market basic. Go to counter to admire the inviting Lebanese and Syrian mezzes, order then grab a table outside. The house special, the Pumpkin and Sesame salad, is the best pick. They also do a reasonable Okra Salad and a Broad Bean dish that comes with a delicious garlic mayo dip and their own recipe hummus is top notch. It's a good pit stop also for organic coffee and soft drinks and has just a few meat dishes for carnivorous companions.

Carluccio's Caffé Spitalfields
Italian, classic

Vegetarian ★★★★
Taste ★★★★
Price ££

- ▢ *27 Spital Square, E1*
- ☏ *020 7392 7602*
- ✎ *www.carluccios.com*
- 🚌 *Liverpool St LU, 5 min walk*
- 🕐 *Mon-Fri 8am-11pm, Sat 9am-11pm, Sun 9am-10.30pm*
- ☀ *Outside tables*

For full restaurant review see Carluccio's, St Christopher's Place, W1 (page 35).

Leon Spitalfields
Mediterranean and English fast food

Vegetarian ★★★
Organic ★★★
Taste ★★★
Price £

🖃 *3 Crispin Place. E1*
☎ *020 7247 4369*
✎ *www.leonrestaurants.co.uk*
🚌 *Liverpool St BR/LU, 5 min walk*
🕐 *Mon-Wed 8am-10pm, Thurs-Sat 8am-11.30pm, Sun 10am-10pm*
🥕 *Vegan Options*
🍼 *Child friendly*
☀ *Outside tables*
i *Counter/takeaway service*

This huge Leon serves the usual Leon formula of natural fast food in a stylish modern environment. It can get very busy here and the Sunday afternoon I visited the place was packed with a relaxed market crowd. Outside there's a mixed assortment of tables and chairs with lots of hungry people tucking into Leon's famous brown takeaway boxes. Inside it's a contrast of hard edged metal ceiling plumbing, giant industrial lamp lighting and soft comfy chairs.

Usually the queue to order food and drink moves quickly, but on a busy Sunday things can get much more hectic and there is sometimes a twenty minute wait for coffee – although they do tell you that when you order. In the evenings things are a lot more relaxed with dinner served on plates at your table and a quick and easy takeaway service. I tried their Roasted Sweet Potato Falafel with aioli that came with basmati rice that was very good indeed for £5.80. For vegans they can make it without the aioli and substitute a chilli sauce. The Leon Gobi also came with basmati rice and had a good sweet flavour for a reasonable £5.80.

The mains here are substantial with Grilled Haloumi and an assortment of spice vegetables and rice or Roasted Sweet Potato falafel with a chilli sauce each for only £3.50. The Superfood Salad is stacked with antioxidant and vitamin-rich veg and comes with extra virgin oil for only £4.65. A large carafe, enough for two, of organic house red is excellent value for £7. All the wines here are organic.

Each day there's a veggie soup (£2.80), served with flatbread and three veggie starters which tend to be potato-based. The most enterprising is Patatas Bravas, a dish of roast potatoes with a spicy plum tomato and oregano sauce.

In the evening, it's fairly busy with city types. The best seats for a view of the restaurant are at the back with red leather seating and shelves of cookery books. Larger parties are catered for at the big tables where there is often a party atmosphere with retro jazz and a good deal of laughter – it's a great place to enjoy a party.

The six desserts are vegetarian and include a chocolate tart and a pecan pie. There are also some refreshing fruit combinations such as melon, mint and pomegranate, and pineapple with basil (£2.50).

Leon Spitalfields

Spitalfields Food Market

⌖ *Commercial St, E1*

✎ *www.spitalfields.co.uk*

🚌 *Liverpool St BR/LU, 5 min walk*

🕐 *Main Market Sun 8am-5pm, food stalls open daily 11am-5pm*

With the big refurbishment completed in June 2008 encompassing a brand new roof and modern lighting, mercifully some of the grand old market character has been retained. For hungry market moochers there's no better place than Spitalfields with its multitude of international cuisine food stalls. Try one of their meal deals as you stroll around the organic purveyors or chow down in the communal seating area – if you can find a place.

Popular and with the longest queue is **Indonesian Food** that does tofu satay, veg noodle and spring rolls. For less of a wait, hotfoot it to **Rainforest Creations** for organic, raw, vegetarian food. Their dishes include Caribbean Roti Wrap and some delicious salads for about a fiver. Another good place to get salads is **Rainforest Box** with a selection of exotic ingredients such as Red Quinoa, Wild Rice and Mung beans. They also serve some interesting flans which come with salad for around a fiver. Rainforest have an additional small stall at the Bishopsgate part of Spitalfields Old Market.

For a full-on organic drink, **Jumpin' Juice** whisks a wicked smoothie of strawberry, raspberry, apple, orange, banana with cherry for £3.75 and a range of energy smoothies. Jumpin Juice is amongst the organic food stalls on Sunday.

Estro is a busy organic fruit and veg stall that also purveys a line of Clean Bean Organic Tofu. Try a free samples of smokey organic tofu, 5 spice or sesame and ginger – all delicious and made nearby. Quite enjoyable is their dipping sauce that's a tamari soya sauce, cider vinegar, sesame, garlic and vinegar combo.

Cranberry is a dried fruit and nut specialist with a selection that's half organic and that also runs a stall at Borough Market. They offer a delicious range of figs, mangoes, pineapples and apricots that are well worth a try and much better than the stuff you get a supermarket.

Celtic Breads have an awesome stall of organic breads. Based in Cricklewood, they bake all their own produce and now sell at 20 markets and many London organic food shops. One of the most popular breads is the Sour Dough Rye that is yeast and wheat-free, for those worried about allergies. There's also a good selection of gluten-free breads.

Spitalfields New Market,

⌨ *Crispin Place, E1*

Artisan Foods does very brisk trade with a good selection of vegetarian mini-quiches including spinach, broccoli, mushroom and leek each for only £2. There are also plenty of veggie tartlets to choose from including Mushroom & Stilton and Cherry tomato and Pesto. All the cakes are vegan as are nearly all the muffins. However, if you really want to spoil yourself try the Chocolate Brownie with Walnuts (£2), a whopping big slice – enough for two. Nearby is **Flour Power City** the accomplished artisan organic bakers who have a large bread stall here.

Al Leone Organics started in October 2007 with this stall offering a good selection of organic fruit and veg – all from suppliers certified by the UK Soil Association. You won't believe your eyes at their purple carrots – great for kids who need a wee nudge of encouragement to eat up all their veg! They also own an adjacent cake stall which as yet is not organic, but is still very tasty.

Vegetarianism goes spectacular at **DeMec,** a truly innovative jewellery stall specialising in vegetable ivory. To the uninitiated, vegetable ivory is made from Amazonian palm seeds (Phytelephas macrocarpa) whose colour, hardness and density are uncannily similar to ivory. Understated earrings begin at £8.99, with bracelets from £29 and some very intricate necklaces for a great deal more. They are only at Spitalfields on Sundays can also be found at Greenwich Market at the weekends and Piccadilly Market on Tuesdays and Wednesday – for further information telephone 020 8579 9206.

Spitalfields Organics
Organic foods, supplements and home provisions

⌨ *92 Commercial Street, E1*

☎ *020 7377 8909*

🚇 *Liverpool St BR/LU, 5 min walk*

🕐 *Daily 9am-7pm*

Their shop is worth a visit. See review on page 279.

Wagamama

⌨ *Old Spitalfield Organic Market, Honer Square, E1*

✎ *www.wagamama.com*

Vegetarian ★★★
Taste ★★★★
Price £

Fans of the Wagamama chain will love this new venue.
See page 48 for the food review.

East
Spitalfields

Bethnal Green

Three to try: Wild Cherry, The Gallery Café and The Thai Garden. The first has Buddhist affiliations although you would never guess it, the second is community charity run although you would never guess it and the third has established a reputation for the quality of its food. Also in the area is an organic shop, Friends Organic and down Columbia Road is the enterprisingly named Flea Pit which has a great vibe and offers tasty veggie, organic light meals.

The FleaPit
International, classic

   49 Columbia Road, E2

   020 7033 9986

   www.thefleapit.com

   Liverpool St LU

   Tue-Fri 5pm-11pm, Sat 12noon-11pm, Sunday 9.30am-2pm

Vegetarian ★★★★★
Taste ★★★
Price £

Simple but well made light veggie dishes are served on retro crockery in this laid back café and organic drinks bar. Located on the corner of Columbia and Ravenscroft Road, it's pleasant enough with comfy sofas and chairs, local art work on the walls and a bar stocking eighteen organic beers, four organic spirits and two organic liqueurs.

The FleaPit is split into the Lounge and the Pit. The latter has film screenings, live gigs, workshops and poetry readings. To avoid disappointment it's best to phone or check their website for events, as on some nights the lounge gets booked out.

Our night began with a glass Organic Freedom Beer from the pump and the organic house Merlot that was quite reasonable – the small complimentary bowl of nuts was a nice touch. The blackboard menu in the Lounge is very simple with a choice of just a few dishes and a couple of desserts. The small plate of four warm falafels and tahini with pickles and cucumber (£3.95) was delicious. A more substantial dish of warm grilled aubergine, new potatoes, chickpea salad, cherry tomatoes, courgette and green leaf salad with a good dressing was wonderful for only £6.50. Quiet full we passed on the Chocolate Brownie served with crème fraiche.

On Sunday's famous Columbia Road Flower Market, the place is packed with coffee and juice drinkers whilst the normal menu is replaced by cakes and biscuits with a few snacks if you get luck.

The Gallery Café
International, Classic

Vegetarian ★★★★★
Organic ★★★★
Taste ★★★★
Price £

⌨ 21 Old Ford Road, E2
☎ 020 8983 3624
🚌 Bethnal Green LU, 2 min walk
🕐 Mon-Fri 9am-8pm, Sat-Sun 10am -6pm
🥕 Vegan options
🍼 Child friendly
☀ Outside Seating
i   Eat-in (counter service)/takeaway service
♫ Last Friday of the Month 9am-10pm with live music

Still one of East London's best kept veggie secrets for daytime eating and drinking, chatting and chilling out. Things have got even better here in recent years with an improved menu, a wider choice of dishes and much more attentive service. The one thing that hasn't changed around here are the prices, which remain very reasonable.

Outside, there's a small charming Georgian terrace area, inside it's an airy, spacious, long room with windows at both ends letting in plenty of natural light. On the walls is work by local artists and there are comfy armchairs and two sofas at the front.

The blackboard menu has light meals such as organic soup and bread, bagels with a variety fillings and a choice of butter or vegan spread, flans, quiches, toasted ciabattas, filled jacket potatoes, falafels and green salads. Among the larger daily specialities, Vegetable Supreme (£4.90) with peas, tomato, mushroom and sweetcorn was tasty and came on a bed of white fluffy rice with a choice of salad. The Chilli without carne, was one of the best I have tasted, with plenty of heat but also more complex flavours. Other favourites here include veggie Spag Bol, Pesto Linguine, veggie sausage and mash and organic veggie burgers, all of which prove popular with the local mum's with pushchairs, office workers and teachers who keep this place busy.

For desserts and cakes you will be spoilt for choice. The decadent Toffee Apple and Pecan Pie (£2.50) will slay you, whilst the Torte Au Citron is also well worth a try. Vegans are also well catered for with plenty of cakes and cookies to choose from.

At the weekends there are three kinds of wrap (£3.50) as well as a bean burger with mushy peas and potato wedges (£4.75). A breakfast menu is served 9.30am–11am, which includes vegan organic porridge and scrambled egg on taste with tomato and mushrooms and at the weekends a homemade muesli option is available.

Help yourself to tap water but the bottled Belvoir Organic Lemonade and the Organic Blood Orange and Mandarin Pressé are a bargain at £1.60, as is the very good organic cappuccino. On live music evenings organic wine and organic beer is available.

This is a place on the up and well worth a visit, particularly in the evenings when it is candle-lit and relaxing ambient music is played. The Chef, Fitzroy Thomas, also runs the Wholsum vegetarian organic store along Dalston Lane.

For a review of Wholsum see page 282.

The Thai Garden
Thai

| | Vegetarian ★★★ |
| Taste ★★★★ |
| Price £ |

- 📖 *249 Globe Road, E2*
- ☎ *020 8981 5748*
- 🚇 *Bethnal Green LU, 5 min walk*
- 🕐 *Lunch Mon-Fri 12noon-3pm, Dinner Mon-Sat 6pm-11pm*
- 🥕 *Vegan options*
- 🍼 *Child friendly*
- i *Table/takeaway service*

Award-winning neighbourhood traditional Thai restaurant with an extensive menu of forty vegetarian dishes, many of which are vegan. The Thai Garden actually calls itself 'meat-free' as the rest of the menu is seafood and it prides itself with being MSG-free and GM-free. Evenings are busy, lunchtimes quiet.

The place is filled with classic Thai ornaments and is properly tableclothed. Service is formal and attentive and although the downstairs dining area is small it has a good atmosphere and there's also a private dining room upstairs.

Worth trying is the Tom Khar soup, a coconut soup with cauliflower and galanga flavour or the Gang Jerd Sar Lie, a seaweed soup with babycorns, carrots and onions. The noodle choice is huge and they only use Thai fragrant rice in their dishes. The veggie mock duck dish Gang Phed Ped Yang Jay comes with Thai aubergines, pineapples and beanshoots in red curry with coconut cream and is excellent.

A glorious dessert for those watching their weight is the Tropical Fruit Salad and for dietbreakers, Thai Custard, a yellow bean, egg and coconut cake.

Wild Cherry
International, Classic

⌨ *241 Globe Road, E2*
☎ *020 8980 6678*
🚋 *Bethnal Green LU, 5 min walk*
🕐 *Tue-Sat 10.30am-4pm*
🥕 *Vegan options*
🍼 *Child friendly*
☀ *Outdoor garden seating in Summer*
i *Counter/takeaway service*

Vegetarian ★★★★★
Organic ★★
Taste ★★★
Price £

A busy bright, modern-looking canteen-style eaterie, associated with the London Buddhist Centre next door. Surprisingly, inside there's no in your face Buddhism at all, apart from a discreet mission statement referring to commitment to spiritual growth and a few leaflets by the entrance. Instead, dotted around the walls are pictures exhibited by local artists, whilst the eating area is decked out with spic and span modern chairs and tables. Formerly called The Cherry Orchard, it's run by friendly Western Buddhist women with the aim to promote vegetarianism and provide home cooked veggie meals to the local community.

At 1.30pm it's packed with chatty office types, social workers and student bookworms munching a choice of salads, jacket potatoes and wraps. Servings here are generous, especially the made-on-the premises bakes and casseroles that change daily. The Spinach and Chick Pea Curry with brown rice is massive on spinach and tasty but rather monotonous. The Thai Noodle Salad is a better choice as it gets progressively tastier the more one eats it and the Chicory and Butter Bean Bake with potato and chilli is another good option. Desserts include vegan cakes with some sugar and wheat-free options – the lemon poppy seed cake was delicious. The drinks include organic juices and teas, GM-free soya milk and herbals.

On Saturdays they offer a traditional veggie breakfast of scrambled egg, veggie sausage, tomato, mushroom and potato as well as muesli, fruit salad and pancakes with organic maple syrup. A selection of cold wraps are on offer throughout the day.

In Summer, their outside garden, adorned with small trees and pretty flowers is a pleasant place to enjoy your meal. A short walking distance away and connected with the Buddhist Centre are Friends Organic (page 279) and The Gallery Cafe (page 227).

Victoria Park, Homerton & Broadway Market

The closure of The Crown was a real loss to this part of town, but the arrival of The Pavillion Café has filled the vacuum. For a real laid back, chilled out Hackney caff experience, Pogo offers inexpensive all-vegetarian offerings that'll suit all pockets. Over at up and coming Broadway Market is all the talk about the terrific bijou veggie café aptly called Gossip.

Gossip
International, classic

	64 Broadway Market, E8
☎	07834 357 076
🚌	London Fields BR, 7min walk, Bethnal Green LU 20min walk
⏰	Daily 8am-7pm
🥕	Vegan options
☀	Outside tables
i	Eat-in (table service) and takeaway

Vegetarian ★★★★★
Organic ★★★★
Taste ★★★
Price £

Higgledy-piggledy vegetarian, vegan café that's going down a storm in fashionable Broadway Market. Order at the tiny counter at the front and grab a seat at the back, preferably one that isn't wobbly. Tables are small and the place a little cramped but no one was grumbling the lunchtime I visited. It's very popular with mum's with kids at tea time and whilst being relaxed during the week, on Saturdays it's jam packed with visitors to the market – a great place to get organic produce.

Owner, Magdalena, creates an organic soup daily – the recently tried vegan Courgette, Mushroom and Broccoli soup (£3.20) was very good and came with a chunk of organic bread. Vegetarian Quiche is one of the best tasting warm options and comes with a good mixed salad with top drawer olives for just £5. Other tasty options include the Roasted Red Pepper and Goat's cheese tartlet and the falafel served with salad and bread for just £4.70. The sandwiches here are also very good with the vegan 'ham' option with gherkins, tomato and lettuce being well worth a try. Gossip also offers a great range of organic teas, coffees and juices and some very tasty cakes for a sweet treat – I can vouch for the vegan chocolate cake.

Service here is friendly and Magdalena definitely stamps her individuality around this unique place – good luck to her.

The Pavilion Café
Organic, International, Café

Vegetarian ★★
Organic ★★★★
Taste ★★
Price ££

- ⊞ *Victoria Park Pavilion, (next to the boating lake)*
  Corner of Old Ford Road and Grove Road, E9
- ☏ *020 8980 0030*
- ✎ *www.the-pavilion-cafe.com*
- 🚌 *Bethnal Green or Mile End LU, 10 min walk*
- ◷ *Daily 9am-6pm (times vary depending on the season)*
- ✦ *Vegan options*
- ◊ *Children-friendly*
- *i* *Counter orders, then they bring to table*

The Pavilion Café is probably the best thing to happen to Victoria Park since they rocked against racism here in the 80s. This place was always a good location for a café, right next to the boating lake, but was badly run for years and never really enjoyed much success. All this changed when organic foodies and entrepreneurs Rob Green and Brett Redman took over the place, transforming it into a stylish organic café offering great food and delicious hot and cold drinks.

The emphasis here is upon simple, well cooked food made from quality ingredients with Cotswold eggs, Jersey Milk and organic fruit and veg all used in their daily menu. There is plenty of quality organic meat on the menu for the carnivores, but veggies will also find themselves well catered for with warm pancakes and wholemeal toast options on the breakfast menu and plenty of wholesome veggie soups, sandwiches and salads for those looking for something more substantial.

The cappuccino here is very good and there is a good selection of cakes and pastries that do run out when the place gets packed. But do check at the counter as to what cakes are vegetarian. This place is at its best on fine days with plenty of outside seating, but is busy every weekend come rain or shine. Those wanting to cook organic at home should take not of the organic box scheme which the café now runs.

Broadway Market

Of particular note is **Ash Green Organic Foods** grocery stand (tel 01892 730738) which trades on Saturdays 10am–5pm. They have a colourful spread of fruit and veg from their 16 acres of orchards in Kent. They also work a free home delivery service throughout Kent. For further details see page 144 in the Farmer's Market section.

Pogo Café
International, Café

🖼 *76a Clarence Road, Hackney E5*

☎ *020 8533 1214*

✎ *www.pogocafe.co.uk*

🚌 *Hackney Central BR, 5 min walk*

🕐 *Wed-Sat 12.30pm-9pm, Sun 11am-9pm,*

🌱 *Vegan options*

⚲ *Children-friendly*

i Counter/takeaway service

🍸 *BYO (£1 corkage per person)*

Vegetarian ★★★★★
Organic ★★★★
Taste ★★★
Price £

Pogo is a neighbourhood hang-out offering value for money, home-made vegan café-style eats with good vegan cake and a selection of organic coffee. Organic fans will be particularly pleased as now more than 90% of the food is organic and the quality of coffee has much improved. The café is located in a run-down enclave of Hackney and is situated opposite the Pembury Estate, but inside the atmosphere is friendly and welcoming.

Opened in August 2004, this non-profit making worker's cooperative still has their legendary old sofas, wooden dining tables, comfy chairs and books and games for children to play, but it now also offers free wi-fi access for your laptop or you can use their own desktop computer. The décor remains pretty simple, but the work of local photographers helps keep things interesting, while the play list is a mixed bag of Morrissey, Motown and chill out music. Evenings are busier than lunchtimes and attracts an 18-40 casually dressed crowd, although weekday lunchtimes get a few straight dressed Town Hall folk. The best buzz is Sunday lunchtimes when the place is busy with local veggies enjoying a veggie Sunday lunch.

The menu is pretty much organic fast food with a choice of four burgers made with smoked organic tofu and a range of fillings for around £3.50, which are very tasty. If a burger is not sufficient you can add a salad and crunchy potato wedges for an extra £2. The made-to-order milkshakes include a Raspberry Shake, made with soya ice cream, which is substantial and delicious. Cakes here look good and the Chocolate Blueberry cake is definitely one to try if you fancy something sweet.

This is a great café which is a little rough around the edges but has won a place in the affections of the local community. Definitely a place to try if you're in the area.

East

Victoria Park, Homerton & Broadway Market

Dalston

Wholsum
International and Caribbean, vegetarian and organic

🖾 *16 Dalston Lane , Dalston, E8*
☎ *020 7249 9601*
🕐 *Mon-Fri 8am-5pm*
🍴 *Vegan options*
☀ *Outside seating*

Vegetarian ★★★★★
Organic ★★★★
Taste ★★★★
Price £

High quality, mostly organic vegetarian lunch meals are served in this informal café in the heart the regenerating Dalston district. In January 2008 the place was completely refurbished and now looks much smarter. Focussing on the lunchtime trade the Caribbean light meals at £6 a plate are good value. Available too are jacket potatoes, ciabatta, panninis, bagels with organic fillings, salad boxes and soups. Run by Fitzroy Thomas, also chef at The Gallery Café (Bethnal Green), who uses several of the same successful recipes here. On fine days there is seating outside.

Wapping

Lilly's
American Diner, Classic

🖾 *75 Wapping High Street, E1*
☎ *020 7702 2040*
🚍 *Wapping LU, 2 min walk*
🕐 *Daily 11am-11pm, Sat&Sun Brunch 12noon-5pm*
☀ *Outside tables for 12 people*
🍼 *Child friendly*

Vegetarian ★★★
Organic ★★
Taste ★★★★
Price ££

This laid back New York Style diner offers a ray of hope in an area without much in the way of veggie cuisine. It is decked out in burgundy and cream, nice leather banquettes and cosy tables with some big lights creating a bright modern atmosphere.

The Vegetarian Breakfast is a real feast consisting of three cooked veggie sausages, tomato, mushrooms, beans and toast which will satisfy the hungriest of appetites. For something lighter, check the pancake stacks with blueberries, banana and maple syrup. For dessert, the locally made Organic Full Dairy Vanilla Ice Cream is great. As well as good food, the service here is friendly and attentive.

Forest Gate

Forest Gate has a large and active Indian population and nowhere is this more evident than on Green Street with numerous Indian jewellery and sari outlets and, of course, lots of very good Indian eateries. Among the best is Amitas for exquisite Dosas, Baburchi that does good Chinese options too, Vijay's Chawalla with its busy bakery, Eastern Foods, Mishtidesh and Ambala for snacks and confectionery. On nearby Romford Road there's City Sweet Centre and Ju'aram.

Amitas
Indian, classic

Vegetarian ★★★★★
Taste ★★★★
Price £

🖾　*124-126 Green Street, E7*
☎　*020 8472 1839,*
🚌　*Upton Park LU, 5min walk*
🕐　*Tue-Thurs 12noon-10pm,*
　　Fri-Sun 12noon-10.30pm (Last orders 10.15pm)
i　*Eat-in (table service)*

Amitas's large modern canteen style eaterie with it's menu of Gujarati stalwarts offers surprisingly good food at very low prices. It gives the better known Indian restaurants of Drummond Street and Brick Lane a run for their money. Located on the corner of Kitchener Road the place really gets busy around 8pm with a mixed Anglo-Indian crowd enjoying themselves. There are comfortable burgundy leather seats and wall banquettes. If there is room grab a window view and watch the varied street culture and crowded streets as you tuck in to delicious Indian food.

The usual classic snacks, South Indian dosas, Chinese noodle dishes and a choice of four thalis are priced for £5.95-£7.95. The Mix Bhajia snack starter for two of potato, methi, lentil bhajias, fried aubergine pieces and two very hot green chilli bhajias was exceptionally good. Well executed too was the Vegetable Biryani main with a mixed vegetable rice accompanied by a top notch cucumber Raita yogurt. Gazing around, the dosas seemed in big demand and the Masala version I chose is up there with the best in London.

To drink, there are bottled beers and spirits and wine is served by the glass for only £2.50. The sweetened lassi and mango juice are both good. A separate dessert menu offers flavoured ice creams and fruit sundaes (£2.50-£3.25), Pistaccio Kulfi, Gulab Jaman and Rasmalai at £1.95. This is definitely a place worth going out of your way to visit.

Baburchi
North and South Indian, classic

⌂ *149-153 Green Street, E7*

☎ *020 8472 8887*

🚌 *Upton Park LU, 5min walk*

🕓 *Tue-Sun 12noon-9.30pm*

◔ *Children-friendly*

i *Eat-in (table service) and takeaway*

Great value Indian and Chinese buffet in this large canteen restaurant. Formerly called Sakonis, Baburchi continues to offer the same good food and has improved its buffet. On arrival be sure to let them know you are vegetarian as eight choices on the buffet have been introduced for non-vegetarian diners. We were the only English diners but were made to feel totally at ease with the most amiable and helpful staff and genuine friendliness from the other diners. These are westernised Indians with kids that drink Coke and Fanta and put Heinz tomato ketchup on their uttapa! Mobile phones ring constantly as dad does a bit more business whilst the kids play on Gameboys and mum's pleased to have a night off. Some of the women have saris but otherwise its all denims, baseball caps and trainers. The restaurant gets busier as the evening wares on with the place busiest between 7 and 9pm.

Baburchi does an á la carte menu menu but everyone goes for the mighty eat-as-much-as-you like buffet, that changes daily. The dinner buffet in only £7.99 and is recommended, while lunch is a simpler version of the same and is only £5.99. Among the tasty dishes to look out for are Aloo Papadi Chat, Crispy Bhajia, Sev Puri and Masala Dosa – all of which are served at a good temperature. After a break try the four chinese options. Don't miss the Paneer Chilli which is excellent and the Szechuan spicy noodles are good – especially when the waiter has refreshed the station with it piping hot.

For drinks the sweet Mango Lassi is good but even better is the Fresh Lime Juice (Limbu Sharbat). You could also do a lot worse than the Rose *Faluda*, a rose flavoured shake drink which comes with a straw so you can spoon up the vanilla ice-cream. I was too full to even consider any of the desserts on offer but my partner soldiered bravely on with a delicious Gulab Jambu dessert.

City Sweet Centre
Indian, classic

Vegetarian ★★★★★
Taste ★★★★
Price £

⌨ 510-512 Romford Road, E7
☎ 020 8472 5459
🖱 www. citysweetcentre.com
🚌 Woodgrange Park LU, 7min walk
🕐 Daily (except Tues) 10am-8pm
🥕 Vegan options
🍼 Children-friendly
i Eat-in (table service) and takeaway

Busy 100% veggie eaterie with all food made on the premises in their kitchen. The big event here is the freshly made sweets (see shop review on page 280) although there is a fair size dining area. Among the veggie dishes I can vouch for the Bhel Puri, Pani Puri, Special Puri, Patis Chaat, Dahiwada, Samosas and Dhoharia – all of which are fresh and tasty.

Vijay's Chawalla
Indian, Classic

Vegetarian ★★★★★
Taste ★★★
Price £

⌨ 268-270 Green Street, E7
☎ 020 8470 3535
🚌 Upton Park LU, 3min walk
🕐 Daily 11am-9pm
🥕 Vegan options
🍼 Children-friendly
i Eat-in (table service) and takeaway

Popular Indian fast food vegetarian canteen with separate shop counter selling Indian sweets, breads and snack takeaways. It gets particularly busy on Friday, Saturday, and Sunday evenings. Inside, two TV sets blare Bollywood music while near the entrance are three relaxing fish tanks.

Most people start with a couple of vegetarian snacks and a main or go for one of the three thalis for £7.50. Mixed Bhajia is an enjoyable spicy pakora selection and the Aloo Papadi Chaat and the large samosa here are also tasty. The menu has useful illustrations and the Chana Masala, three big pooris with delicious spicy chick peas and a petite salad is just what you see in the pictures. The Passion Fruit juice is well worth a whirl. Save room for the desserts of which I can vouch for the New Mango Delight (£2.50) a colourful mango sorbet served in a half mango skin. This is a great place to go for an Indian veggie meal on a budget.

Wanstead

The Larder
Mediterranean, classic

Vegetarian ★★★
Organic ★★★
Taste ★★★★
Price £

🖃 *32 High Street, E11*
☎ *020 8989 7181*
🚇 *Wanstead LU, 2min walk*
🕐 *Mon-Fri 9am-7pm, Sat 9am-5pm, Sun 10am-4pm*
🍼 *Child Friendly (Play pen at back)*
☀ *Outside seating*

The Larder has developed quite a following of East London vegetarians for its good quality light meals and snacks, relaxing informal atmosphere and a thoughtfully provided children's play area. Bare brick walls, olive paint, wooden floors and shelves of food and drink – this place keeps things simple. By 1pm the many tables are packed with locals – mum's with kids, foodies and local professionals. In the Summer the small outside tables which overlook the pleasant park are snapped up quickly.

There are a lot more veggie options here than appear on the blackboard with an inconspicuous menu poster on the wall and a mini-menu with additional choices on the central large wooden table. If menu games aren't your bag, ask a member of staff – they will also convert some dishes to veggie versions on request.

The vegetarian soup changes daily and the carrot, celeriac and cumin soup (£3.75) I had was good and came with wholemeal bread. Chosen from the mini-menu and confidently recommended is the Moroccan Spinach and Feta Flatbread with a very good side salad (£4.75), which was excellent. Also of interest is the Vegetable Bastilla, consisting of potatoes and carrots blended with a mixture of almonds, coriander and spices. The Vegetarian Quiche had a good strong cheese flavour and is one of the best I've tasted, whilst the Vegetarian Nachos (£5.95) with guacamole, salsa, jalapeno, peppers and sour cream is enough for two.

Being a stockist of fine foods, the sandwiches are of a high stanadard too and include toasted mozzarella, sun dried tomatoes & pesto (£3.75), while hummus, olives, tomatoes, seeds and salad are served in brown, ciabatta or baguette for £3.50.

All the cakes are vegetarian and the Black Magic Chocolate cake topped with a sparkling topping is particularly good. Organic Green & Black Hot Chocolate and Luscombes organic lemonades are available although surprisingly the coffee here is not yet organic.

For shop review see page 283.

Canary Wharf

Carluccio's Caffé
Italian, classic

Vegetarian ★★★
Taste ★★★★
Price ££

⌗ *2 Nash Court, E14*
☎ *020 7719 1749*
🚌 *Canary Wharf LU*
🖱 *www.carluccios.com*
🕓 *Mon-Fri 8am-11pm, Sat 9-11pm, Sun 10am-10pm*
🥕 *Vegan options*
🍼 *Child friendly, high chairs*
i *Excellent outside tables*

A great place to head for when in Canary Wharf. It has a prime position in Dockland's financial district with good outside seating to soak up the high-tech architectural atmosphere and Carluccio's Italian food.
See Carluccio's Caffé, St Christopher's Place for food review (page 35).

Leon Canary Wharf
Mediterranean and English fast food

Vegetarian ★★★
Organic ★★★
Taste ★★★
Price £

⌗ *Promenade Level, Cabot Place West, E14*
☎ *020 7719 6201*
🚌 *Canary Wharf LU, 2 min walk*
🖱 *www.leonrestaurants.co.uk*
🕓 *Mon-Fri 7am-10pm, Sat 11am-6pm, Sun 12noon-6pm*
🥕 *Vegan options*

This is one of the more smaller branches of Leon.
See Leon, Spitalfields for food review (page 222).

Wagamama
Japanese, Modern

Vegetarian ★★★
Taste ★★★★
Price £

⌗ *Jubilee Place, E14*
☎ *020 7516 9009*
🚌 *Canary Wharf LU, 2 min walk*
🖱 *www.wagamama.com*
🕓 *Mon-Sat 11.30am-10pm, Sun 12noon-9pm*

The largest branch of this famous noodle bar chain. Popular with student and budget conscious diners.
For food review see Wagamama, Wigmore Street (page 48).

Shops

SHOPS

The first organic food shop, 'Wholefood' in Baker Street was conceived in 1965 by Mary Langman, one of the first organic farmers in Britain and a founder member of the Soil Association. It was filled with organic produce from suppliers throughout the country and was the prototype for the entire British organic food market.

Organic produce was made available to a wider market in the 1980's on the suggestion of younger members of the Soil Association. At present regulations for organic produce are strictly controlled by the Advisory Committee on Organic Standards (ACOS) and European Union (EU) legislation. ACOS authorises nine organic UK certification bodies that monitor the proper maintenance of organic food production. Genuine organic products have packaging that displays the registration number of an ACOS (eg UK2, UK5 etc) or an EU approved certifier. In the European Union overseas products comply with EU legislation. However, with different levels of control procedure in different countries what is and what isn't organic can be confusing for the consumer.

Availability of organic produce

Globally, levels of organic production are small-fry. Just 4% of EU agricultural land is certified organic farmland. Consequently, when there's a run on a particular item at your local wholefood shop, demand can overwhelm supply especially outside the local growing seasons. If you have trouble sourcing a particular item the stores reviewed in this section should be able to help.

Organic Perceptions

Certainly people see organic food in a very good light. According to Professor Carlo Leifert of The Tesco Centre of Agriculture at the University of Newcastle 'Consumers do perceive organic food as healthier, more sustainable, better for the soil and tastier.' There has been some support for this in a study in the well respected scientific journal, Nature (Nature 410, 926-930, 2001) where organic apple production was found to be more sustainable and produced better tasting apples than similarly conventionally grown apples. Subsequently, in Spring 2007, three independent EU studies showed higher nutritional values in organic apple puree, tomatoes and peaches, whilst in the US researchers found higher levels of important nutritional constituents in organic kiwis compared with non-organic. More recently, a study published in the Journal of the Science of Food and Agriculture, showed that drinking organic milk has greater health benefits than normal milk. Preliminary results of the £12m Four-Year Quality Low Input Food Study has shown organic fruit and vegetables contain 40% more antioxidants compared to non-organics and higher levels of beneficial minerals such as iron zinc.

Veggie and Organic shopping trends

In London, a wholefood or organic shop is never far away. Many are small stores catering for neighbourhood need and invariably provide a more personal service than the big retail chains. The organic wholefood chains have also flourished in recent years with Whole Foods Market, Planet Organic, Natural Kitchen and As Nature Intended all doing well in a tough market. In the event you need delivery there are several specialist firms listed in this chapter. Demand for such organic box schemes and mail order has increased dramatically the last few years.

In this chapter, organic shops and wholefood shops have been grouped together. Also, of note are the many Indian vegetarian sweet shops often overlooked by veggies that offer delicious arrays of traditional confectioneries and snacks.

Many of the hottest things on the organic and vegetarian retail scene have been at expensive end of the spectrum. Stella McCartney's store in Bruton Street, Bamford and Sons and Equa are all featured here. Katherine E Hamnett was one of the first designers to source organic, fairtrade cotton and her range of sloganised T-shirts and sweatshirts are stocked in Selfridges and Liberty's.

Cheap organic fashion is available at H&M stores around London, whilst Marks and Spencers also has an increasing range. Aveda offers hairdressing with organic products and on site there's a great organic cafe, whilst Green Baby has everything for a baby's organic needs. Organic health and beauty has been increasing in popularity for several years and the Organic Pharmacy in the King's Road is featured here.

Whether your looking for fashion or groceries, cosmetics or haircare products, consumers in London have an ever increasing choice – happy shopping!

Central London

Bloomsbury

Alara Wholefoods
Organic foods, drinks, eats, bodycare

⌧ *58-60 Marchmont Street, WC1*

☎ *020 7837 1172*

🚇 *Russell Square, 1 min walk*

🕒 *Mon-Fri 8am-7pm, Sat 10am-6pm, Sun 11am-5pm*

Large neighbourhood vegetarian, health food and alternative remedy shop that's strong on organic hot and cold foods, juices, smoothies and hot drinks. In recent years they have widened their organic beauty lines with the Dr Hauschka and Weleda ranges. For more information about their food see their restaurant review on page 13.

Established in 1979, the store is now run by vegetarians, Mehr and Parry, who are equally passionate about organic food. Parry is particularly knowledgeable and can give lots of advice about the health and nutritional benefits of their products. At Alara Wholefoods they import some quite funky food bars and Joseph's sugar-free organic cookies which are suitable for diabetics. The fresh organic fruit and veg is well displayed and delivered every day.

What is noticeable about Alara Wholefoods is the sheer range with just a few of each line that quickly gets replenished. Consequently they have a good range of tofu, honey, juices and a huge range of seeds and dried fruits.

Alara Wholefoods should not be confused with Alara Foods – a long-standing organic and gluten-free muesli manufacturer. To confuse matters further this shop stocks Alara Foods' Soil Association certified cereals and six different types of Alara Museli with a very tempting Organic Branberry including dried strawberries and blueberries.

Alara Wholefoods does great food and has the kind of atmosphere that reminds one of a local New York Deli. Its got a lot to do with the way the shop is run, but is helped by the charm of this Bloomsbury street complete with attractive students from the nearby University.

Bargain tip: check out the back of the shop that runs special promotions.

Planet Organic
Organic vegetarian, international

🏛 *22 Torrington Place, WC1*

☎ *020 7436 1929*

✎ *www.planetorganic.com*

🚌 *Goodge Street LU, 5 min walk*

🕐 *Mon-Fri 8am-9pm, Sat 10am-8pm*
   Sun 12noon-6pm

Popular with nearby London University students and affluent Fitzrovians, this is a large and vibrant branch of Planet Organic with a particularly busy café.

See Planet Organic, Westbourne Grove for detailed review (page 267).

Covent Garden & Holborn

Aveda Institute
Hairdressers, beauty therapy, environmental store

🏛 *174 High Holborn , WC1*

☎ *020 7759 7355*

🚌 *Tottenham Court or Holborn LU,*

🕐 *Mon-Wed 9am-7pm, Thurs-Fri 8am-8pm,*
   Sat 9am-6pm, Sun 11am-5pm

Eco-conscious Aveda are committed to certified organic ingredients and petrochemical avoidance where possible in their extensive hair, beauty and fragrance product ranges. About 97% of ingredients are organic, the remaining 3% are neccessary to preserve shelf life.

Aveda Lifestyle Salon and Spa is a cool hair and beauty salon with very well-trained staff. Here you can find the full Aveda product range including their hair and beauty products and pure flower and plant essences. Aveda also provide complimentary holistic services including stress relieving treatments, make-up applications and classes. The institute follows the principles of Ayureveda – the ancient Indian art of healing.

On the premises is a well run Pain Quotidien Café. For the food review see Pain Quotidien Café, Marylebone (page 41). There are further branches of Aveda at Westbourne Grove branch (Tel: 020 7243 6047)and Marylebone High Street (Tel: 020 7224 3157).

Monmouth Coffee House
Coffee beans, drinks, eats

- 27 Monmouth Street, WC1
- 020 7379 3516
- www.monmouthcoffee.co.uk
- Covent Garden LU
- Mon-Sat 8am-6.30pm

Coffee cognoscenti should check this place out, with five certified organic coffees from Brazil, Peru, and Uganda and their own organic blend for expresso. The tastings area at the back is a little cramped but the atmosphere and the delicious caffeine make it worth the squeeze. *They have a larger sister shop just outside Borough Market at 2 Park Street, London SE1, Mon-Sat 7.30am-6pm, Tel 020 7940 9960 and run a stall inside the market on Friday and Saturday.*

Neal's Yard Remedies
Organic beauty, skincare, gifts, herbs and therapies

- 15 Neal's Yard, WC2
- 020 7379 7222
- www.nealsyardremedies.com
- Covent Garden LU, 5min walk
- Mon-Sat 10am-7pm, Sun 11am-6pm

A vast choice of organic products to pamper yourself and a place of interest for those choosing alternatve remedies.

The Organic Pharmacy
Natural and organic medicines and beauty products

- 36 Neal Street, WC2
- 020 7836 3923
- www.theorganicpharmacy.com
- Covent Garden LU
- Mon-Sat 10am-7pm
  Sun 12.00am-6.00pm
- Mailorder

The Organic Pharmacy have made their name offering quality organic medicines to the health conscious and rich people of King's Road and they have now expanded their reach with a store in Covent Garden. *See The Organic Pharmacy, King's Road for a more detailed review of their products and services (page 264).*

Marylebone, Mayfair & Baker Street

Bateel
Gourmet Vegetarian Chocolates and Delicacies
🖳 *138 New Bond Street, W1*
☎ *020 7629 0932*
✑ *www.bateel.ae*
🚌 *Bond Street LU, 5 min walk*
🕐 *Mon-Fri 10am-7pm, Sat-Sun 12noon-6pm*

Make a date with this date and chocolate delicacy specialist. Their sparkling non-alcoholic date drink (£8) makes a great dessert drink suitable for special occasions. They also offer beautifully presented chocolates and date truffles for that extra special indulgence.

Marylebone Farmers' Market
🖳 *Cramer St car park (off Marylebone High Street) W1*
🕐 *Sun 10am-2pm*
See page 286 for more information about farmers' markets.

The Natural Kitchen
Fine English organic foods, drinks, baby products
🖳 *77-78 Marylebone High Street, W1*
☎ *020 7486 8065*
✑ *www.thenaturalkitchen.com*
🚌 *Baker Street LU, 8min walk*
🕐 *Mon-Fri 8am-8pm, Sat 9am-7pm, Sun 11am-6pm*

Magnificent upscale but friendly neighbourhood food store with lashings of vegetarian organic food. Whilst your eyes feast on the voluptuous foods on the ground floor, give your taste buds a treat with one of their freshly made juices and tour the isles. There's an excellent selection of veggie quiches including fetta and spinach or try their mushroom and Asparagus Pie (£4.95). The Natural Kitchen has a fine range of Secrets Organic produce and you can sample their kale from the deli counter or try their coleslaw and Chickpea salad which are both glorious. The organic vegetarian ice creams are big sellers here whilst on the cheese counter vegetarian cheeses include Cornish Capra, Paxton's Aged Cheddar, Single Gloucester and a Shropshire Blue, all of which will satisfy the most discerning palates. For food on the go, there are lots of attractive pre-packed organic sandwiches (£2.40) and ready made salad meals for £4.25.

At Basement level, there are silos dispensing top notch organic freshly roasted coffee beans, teas, cereals, grains, pulses and pastas. Many of the foods sold here are not easy to come by and are made by small producers. Artisan jams, biscuits, cakes and confectionery are all of the highest standards and beautifully displayed. The most decadent confectionery is the KShocolat truffle selection, whilst for the nutritionally-worried there's a large selection of health foods including spirulina and barley grass products.

In the chiller cabinets, there's a good selection of vegi deli, tofu and veggie dips of which the hummus with sundried tomato I can vouch for. The organic wine and beer selection here is also one of the largest in London.

Natural Kitchen focuses on locally sourced, seasonal produce and is community-spirited rather than an impersonal big chain supermarket. The atmosphere is relaxed, friendly with very helpful enthusiastic staff that are switched-on and knowledgeable about organic produce. The people running The Natural Kitchen have done a marvellous job of creating an attractive and stylish place to eat and shop which is also more personal and part of the broader community.

For café review on Level One, see page 42).

The Organic Pharmacy
Natural and organic medicines and beauty products

⌨ 23 Great Marlborough Street, W1

☎ 020 7287 1607

✍ www.theorganicpharmacy.com

🚋 Oxford Circus LU (5min walk)

🕐 Mon-Sat 10am-7pm, Sun 12.00am-6.00pm

Another smaller branch of The Organic Pharmacy.

For more details see The Organic Pharmacy, King's Road (page 264).

Stella McCartney
Designer clothes

🏠 30 Bruton Street, W1
☎ 020 7518 3100
🖱 www.stellamccartney.com
🚇 Bond Street LU, 5 min walk
🕐 Mon-Sat 10am-6pm (Thurs till 7pm)

Upscale designer store in four storey Georgian Townhouse opened in 2003 by Stella McCartney, leading fashion designer and a patron of the Vegetarian Society. Dress to impress when you come as there's security on the door. Once you're inside, the atmosphere is relaxed and the service slick and sophisticated.

All the clothes and shoes are suitable for vegetarians and the perfume range is organic. Through the elegant hallway is a drawing room adorned with a wall of marquetry panels. On display are accessories, sunglasses, handbags and don't forget to peruse the marquetry drawers that can be be pulled out to yield arrays of further products.

Next on is a glasshouse garden with a beautiful maple tree surrounded by works of art and furniture. At the rear of the ground floor is the Shoe Room which houses a circular display of exclusive shoes completely suitable for vegetarians.

Ready to Wear Collections are on the first floor and at the rear is an organic Lingerie Boudoir. Further upstairs is a bespoke tailoring service for men and women under the watchful eye of a Savile Row master tailor.

Strongly eco-conscious, Stella McCartney has her own organic line of women's clothes that she intends to expand as well as introducing a men's clothes range. The shop also stocks her fast growing organic unisex skin care range that's 100% organic and boasts formulae that exclude synthetic preservatives, silicone and any ingredients of animal origin. Stella McCartney designed a range of vegetarian-suitable trainer shoes for Adidas, although not available at this shop, they are available at the Adidas's main shop in Oxford Street.

Stella McCartney also has shops within Selfridges and Harvey Nichols as well in New York and Los Angeles. However, true to her British designer roots, the flagship shop is here in Bruton Street.

Central

Marylebone, Mayfair & Baker Street

Soho

Peppercorns
Food, drink, eats, health products

⌨ 2 Charlotte Place, W1

☎ 020 7631 4528

✎ www.peppercornsonline.com

🚌 Goodge Street LU, 3min walk

🕐 9am-7pm, Mon-Fri

Tucked away down an alleyway in Fitzrovia, Peppercorn is a modern natural and organic food mini-market. It sports a large stock of Solgar vitamins and mineral products, pre-packed vegetarian and vegan takeaway food including sandwiches and cakes. The shop also has a contacts and campaigns noticeboard with leaflets.

Also at 193 West End Lane, West Hampstead (see page 258).

Whole Foods Market
Foods, Drinks, Eats

⌨ 69–75 Brewer Street, Soho, W1

☎ 020 7434 3179

✎ www.wholefoodsmarket.com

🚌 Piccadilly LU, 1 minute walk

🕐 Mon 7.30am-9pm, Sat 9am-9pm, Sun 11.30am-6.30pm

Shop organic in the back streets of Soho.

See Kensington for food review (page 174) and shop review (page 265).

Central Soho

Southwark & Waterloo

Borough Market
Southwark Street, SE1

A huge food event with all manner of fine produce on offer from organic wines to farm produced cheeses. See pages 69 for details.

Coopers
Organic food and vegetarian cafe

17 Lower Marsh, Waterloo , SE1

☎ *020 7261 9314*

🚇 *Lambeth North , Waterloo LU & BR,*

🕐 *Mon-Thurs 8.30am-4.30pm, Fri 8.30am-4pm,*

Less of a wholefood shop now and more of a lunchtime eating spot, Coopers still has a selection of organic breads, nuts, beans, dried fruits, soup mixes, vitamins and organic household essentials.

Hoxton & Shoreditch

The Beer Shop
Organic online beer shop and brewery

✎ *www.pitfieldbeershop.co.uk*

☎ *0845 833 1492*

With the Beer Shop, formerly at 14 Pitfield St, closed in 2006, they now sell online and at a selection of farmers' markets listed on their website. They offer a wide selection of organic wines, ciders and beers. Their own Pitfield Brewery makes seven organic brews with all the bottled beers vegan.

The Organic Delivery Co.
Organic food delivery service

70 Rivington Street, EC2

☎ *020 7739 8181*

✎ *www.organicdelivery.co.uk*

🕐 *Mon-Fri 10am-5pm*

Registered with the Soil Association, this firm supplies a wide range of organic products from fruit and veg to organic drinks and bread. Check out their website for full product listing. There is no minimum order, with a £2.95 delivery charge for orders below £14, but all larger orders are free throughout London. They run an organic vegetable and fruit box scheme that starts from £9.95 including daytime and evening delivery in London. The Soil Association gave their organic box delivery service a high commendation award.

People Tree
Organic clothes

⬚ *91-93 Great Eastern Street, EC2*
☎ *0845 450 4595*
✎ *www.peopletree.co.uk*
✉ *Mail order – free catalogue*

A company with a conscience. People Tree campaigns for consumers to wear organic cotton to help prevent the chronic health problems and death of tens of thousands of people associated with the use of agricultural pesticides. Whilst they don't have a shop of their own they do have an office unit (five minutes walk from Old Street tube) which is their nerve centre for their mail order enterprise. People Tree clothes are modern casual urban basics, plain or simply patterned and very affordable. The quality of material feels great and they offer some fashionable designs. A selection is available at Equa (see page 251).

Also sold at:

Finesse Lifestyle, 453 Roman Road, E3 Tel:020 8983 9286
It's A Green Thing, 79 Church Road, SE19 Tel 020 87711 178
Shoon, 94 Marylebone High Street, W1 Tel: 020 7487 3001

Clerkenwell

Rye Wholefoods
Wholefood and Organic Shop

⬚ *35a Myddleton Street, EC1*
☎ *020 7278 5878*
🚌 *Angel LU, 10 min walk*
🕐 *Mon-Fri 9am-3pm, Sat 12noon-5pm*

Quaint, 80's-style vegetarian/vegan, organic provisions shop with a couple of tables for eating in.

For food review see page 101.

North London

Islington

Green Baby
Baby Clothes and products

- 345 Upper St, N1
- 020 7359 7037
- www.greenbaby.co.uk
- Angel LU, 5 min walk
- Mon-Fri 10am-5pm, Sat 10.30am-6pm
- Mail order: 0870 240 6894

Boutique store selling affordable, 100% certified organic clothes and products for babies and children up to six years. 2009 is their 10th anniversary. Products include real nappies, baby clothing, underwear, pyjamas, eco-friendly washing products, nursery furniture. An excellent mail order catalogue is also available. Green Baby's organic clothing range is designed in the UK and produced by a fair trade women's community project in South India. As an accolade to their in-house designer Nicola, Green Baby won Prima Baby's 'leading eco fashion range' award in 2009. Green Baby's organic skin care range is made in Britain. Other items are European-made in countries such as Germany where organic cotton is quite commonly used. Green Baby wholesales to 350 independent retailers. *Other branches at Notting Hill (see page 267), Greenwich (see page 276) Their outlet store is located in Richmond, 4 Duke Street, TW9 Tel: 020 8940 8255*

Equa
Organic, ethical clothes, vegan handbags & shoes

- 28 Camden Passage, N1
- 020 7359 0955
- Angel LU 5 min walk
- Mon-Wed, Fri-Sat 10am-6.30pm, Thurs 10am-7pm, Sun 12noon-5pm
- Mail order

One of the best women's organic clothes shops in London. A blue-fronted building along fashionable Camden Passage, Equa packs a fantastic range of organic clothes into an attractively pine-wooded, white and light blue decorated, small space. Fashionable organic brands include Wildlife Works, Ciel, Loomstate, Annie Greenabelle, Stewart Brown, Edun and

People Tree. Dresses, jumpers, shirts all looked very good and well displayed although I decline to comment on the 'Eat Organic Knickers'.

Of note to vegetarians is the organic Enamore capsule collection. For vegans there are well designed vegan shoes by Beyond Skin and a selection of vegan handbags made by the Canadian duo Matt and Nat. Vegan clutch handbags come in silver and bronze colours as well as vegan bags in larger sizes. Equa also stocks the Organic Kids range.

Staff are highly knowledgeable about the clothes' provenance, organic content and ethical mode of manufacture. With very friendly service, Equa is a great resource for the organic/vegetarian shopper.

Camden Town & Primrose Hill

Ambala Foods
Specialist pickles and chutneys, Indian sweets
Head Office and Shop
- 112-114 Drummond Street, NW1
- 020 7387 7886
- www.ambalafoods.com
- Daily 9am-9pm

Opened in 1965, this modern upscale store sells a stylishly packaged range of thirteen pickles and chutneys, savouries, snacks and an inviting sweet selection.

Braintree Hemp Store
Mens and Ladies hemp clothes
- Unit 9 East Yard, Camden Lock, NW1
- 020 7267 9343
- www.braintreehemp.co.uk
- Daily 10am-6pm
- Camden or Chalk Farm, LU

Nothing to do with Braintree in Essex, this is the London branch of a large Australian chain selling hemp trousers, shirts, t-shirts, blouses and skirts. About 20% of the range is completely hemp whilst the rest of the stock is about 55% hemp mix with non-organic cotton. They have now introduced a 30% organic mix of bamboo and cotton as well as a soyabean range. Hemp enthusiasts can stock up on Organic Hemp Tea, string and even a hemp hand cream!

Greens & Beans
Wholefoods, skincare products

- 131 Drummond Street, NW1
- 020 7380 0857
- Euston LU&Rail, 2min walk
- Mon-Fri 9am-5pm

A handy place to pick up wholefood essentials, organic health and beauty items and takeaway food. They do a good range of crackers and their veggie café is always worth a look (see page 123).

Gupta Confectioners (London) Ltd
Indian sweets, takeaway snacks and savouries

- 100 Drummond Street, NW1
- 020 7380 1590
- Daily 11am-7pm

Small shop with a good vegetarian sweet selection and street nosh. Enjoyed the fried aubergine snack to takeaway.

Sesame
Organic foods, drink

- 128 Regents Park Road, NW1
- 020 7586 3779
- Chalk Farm LU 5 min walk
- Vegan options
- Mon-Fri 9am-6pm, Sat 10am-6pm, Sun 12noon-5pm

There is friendly service at this smart neighbourhood store that's 90% organic and virtually all vegetarian. The fresh fruit and veg, range of breads and cheeses are in evidence, but they also offer a good choice of honeys and oils. Takeaways of hot soups, big rice stir-fry and salads are popular and it's a great stock-up for a picnic at nearby Primrose Hill.

Whole Foods Market
Foods, Drinks, Eats

- 49 Parkway, NW1
- 020 7428 7575
- www.wholefoodsmarket.com
- Camden Town LU, 2 min walk
- Mon–Fri 8am-9pm, Sat 9.30am-9pm, Sun 11am-8pm

See Whole Foods Market, Kensington for full review (page 174).

Highbury

Highbury Park Health Foods
Organic foods, baby and
household goods, supplements

🏬 *17 Highbury Park, N5*

☎ *020 7359 3623*

🚇 *Highbury or Finsbury Park LU*

🕐 *Mon-Sat 10.30am-8pm*

Unpretentious neighbourhood store selling pre-packed organic foodstuffs, supplements, and baby products. Good on general organic items but somewhat uninspiring for foodies. The recently introduced natural organic hair colour and beauty products range is proving very popular with locals.

Crouch End

Ambala Foods (Turnpike Lane)
Specialist pickles and chutneys, Indian sweets

🏬 *61 Turnpike Lane, Wood Green, N8*

☎ *020 8292 1253*

🖱 *www.ambalafoods.com*

🕐 *Daily 9am-9pm*

See Ambala Drummond Street for review (page 252).

Haelen Centre
Wholefoods, supplements and homeopathic remedies

🏬 *41 The Broadway, N8*

☎ *020 8340 4258*

🖱 *www.haelan.co.uk*

🚇 *Finsbury Park LU*

🕐 *Mon-Sat 9am-6pm, Sun 12noon-4pm*

Well established wholefood and organic provisions store with herbal dispensary and homeopathic pharmacy upstairs. The ground floor shop is crammed with breads (many gluten and wheat-free), inexpensive organic fruit and veg, takeaway eats and convenience foods as well as organic baby foods and formulas. All the food is vegetarian and free from artificial flavourings, colourings and preservatives. They also stock organic practitioner strength tinctures. Check out their website for more details.

Stoke Newington

Born
Natural, fairtrade and organic products for
mother & baby

⬒ *168 Stoke Newington Church Street, N16*

☎ *020 7249 5069*

✍ *www.borndirect.com*

🚆 *Stoke Newington BR*

🕐 *Tue-Sat 9.30am-5.30pm, Sun 12noon-5pm*

This specialist shop offers friendly and informative service selling 100%
organic cotton and wool babywear, nightwear and underwear. They have
an exclusively range of clothing designed by Kate Goldsmith and made
in India from organically grown cotton. They also have beauty products
by Green People, Weleda and lots of organic massage oils and herbal teas
suitable for pregnancy and post-pregnancy. For the home they sell organic
bedding and some furniture manufactured with organic materials.

Food For All
Organic herbs, vegetarian wholefood and snacks

⬒ *3 Cazenove Road, N16*

☎ *020 8806 4138*

✍ *Stoke Newington BR*

🕐 *Mon-Fri 9am-6pm, Sat 10am-6pm, Sun 11am-4pm*

This organic community health store has been going since 1975 and
sports a jaw-dropping 250 organic and wild harvested herbs selection all
stored in big brown paper bags crammed onto a wall display unit. They
also offer eco-friendly body care products, organic and allergy-free foods,
medicinal remedies and food supplements. Their refill service of eco-
friendly cleaning products at the back is a good money saver and they
now have a wide range of teas. It's worth a visit just to see the herbs.

Whole Foods Market

⬒ *32-40 Stoke Newington Church St, N16*

☎ *020 7254 2332*

✍ *www.wholefoodsmarket.com*

🚆 *Stoke Newington BR*

🕐 *Mon-Sat 8am-9pm, Sun 9am-8.30pm*

✉ *Mail order*

North

Stoke Newington

The best organic store in Stokey and oh how it buzzes. It now has a crackingly gorgeous organic wine selection that has replaced the inside eaterie, leaving just an outside area for eating. Of particular note is a fabulous tofu range, attractively displayed veggie-deli foods, breads and speciality cheeses. Where items are not organic the policy is to offer the highest quality alternative. There's a good kiddy section with an organic nappy range and eco-friendly washing powders and cleaning products. At the weekends it can get very crowded, but the atmosphere is always friendly and the staff helpful and enthusiastic.

For a review of the eat-in food see page 150.

Lemon Monkey
Fine foods, Drinks, Eats

   188 Stoke Newington High St, N16
   020 7241 4454
   www.lemon-monkey.co.uk
   Stoke Newington BR
   Mon-Wed 9am-6pm, Thurs-Sat 9am-9pm, Sunday 10am-6pm

With a strong emphasis on fine foods, a commitment to supporting small producers and transparency with regard to produce provenance, the shelves of this eaterie are well worth a visit. Of note are the organic teas including white and green leafed. The herbs and spices are impressive and they offer a well chosen selection of organic wines and juices. Lemon Monkey is a good place to find quality prepared organic foods with their kids' range particularly popular.

Mother Earth Organic Shop
Foods, toiletries, drinks, eats

   5 Albion Parade, N16
   020 7275 9099
   Highbury and Islington LU
   Mon-Sat 9.30am-8pm, Sun 10am-7pm

Cluttered old-style wholefood shop with about 80% of the products being organic. There's a small organic fruit and veg section, organic cakes and breads and some patisserie. At the back of the shop locals fill their own bottles with purified water for 20p a litre. They also offer takeaway organic soup and coffee as well as sandwiches, rolls and samosas made by Hare Krishna people.

Holloway & Tufnell Park

Bumble Bee Natural Foods
Organic fruit, veg, breads, takeaway eats, wine and beer

🖃 *30, 32, 33 & 35 Brecknock Road, N7*
☏ *020 7607 1936*
🚋 *Kentish Town LU & Rail or Tufnell Park LU*
🕐 *Mon-Sat 9am-6.30pm*
✉ *Mail order*

Established in 1980, Bumble Bees has grown into a collection of food stores and a natural remedy shop (at number 35, Tel: 020 7267 3884). The three food outlets are hot on veggie foods including dried fruit and nuts, herbal teas, organic coffees and for those on the tipple more than 100 organic beers and wines. They offer an excellent range of fresh fruit and veg and baked bread is delivered daily. A large range of organic gluten-free products is also available. Whilst the three stores are separate, customers can fill up at all three and pay at the end of the shop. The remedies and non-food products store is excellent.

Hampstead & Kentish Town

Earth Natural Foods
Organic wholefoods, ecological household goods

🖃 *200 Kentish Town Road, NW5*
☏ *020 7482 2211*
🚋 *Kentish Town LU, Camden Town LU*
🖯 *www.earthnaturalfoods.com*
🕐 *Mon-Sat 8.30am-7pm*

Opened in November 2006, Earth Natural Foods has enjoyed considerable success from its large site on Kentish Town Road. The founders are all formerly of Bumblebee, and have used their knowledge to create a well-designed bright and airy modern store and a unique gallery storage area made from scaffolding poles. ENF has built up quite a reputation for their organic fruit and veg and they have a good range of organic wines, artisan cheeses and a hot and cold food takeaway menu. With a 65% organic food offering, the store offers a local delivery and vegetable box scheme to a five mile radius. Notably strong on baby care ranges and baby foods, there's also plenty of skincare products for the grown-ups.

Peppercorns
Food, drinks, eats, health products

⌨ *193-195 West End Lane*

☎ *020 7328 6874*

🚇 *West Hampstead, NW6*

✎ *www.peppercornsonline.com*

🕐 *Mon-Sat 9am-7.30pm*

Natural and organic food market, smaller and busier than their sister West End Branch.

See Peppercorns, Charlotte Place for further details (page 248)

Phoenicia
Mediterranean vegetarian delicatessen

⌨ *186-192 Kentish Town Road, NW5*

☎ *020 7267 1267*

🚇 *Kentish Town LU*

🕐 *Mon-Sat 9am-8pm, Sun 10am-4pm*

This eye catching food hall specialises in veggie food, some of which is also organic from the Lebanon, Italy, Greece and Turkey. Their fruit is delivered twice daily to ensure freshness and their deli has a good range of mezzes, dips, olives, tofu and soya products. Phoenicia's coffee shop seats thirty-five with plenty of salad choices as well as Lebanese and Moroccan wraps with a choice of fillings. Also of note is their vegetarian Lebanese baklava.

Pomona
Organic food and drink

⌨ *179 Haverstock Hill, Belsize Park, NW3*

☎ *020 7916 2676*

🚇 *Belsize Park LU 2 min walk*

🕐 *Mon-Fri 8am-9pm, Sat-Sun 8am-7pm*

This slick, modern organic provisions store is just the place for stocking up gourmet organic ingredients. It also boasts an excellent selection of organic wines, some at bargain discounts with several vegetarian and vegan options. I have it on authority that Tuesday, Thursday and Friday are the very best days for grocery freshness. They also stock organic Celtic breads and a selection of gluten-free products for the those with special dietary requirements. About 70% of the shop stock is organic.

New Southgate

Jaaneman Sweet Centre
Vegetarian Indian, classic

⊡ *170 Bowes Road, N11*
☎ *020 8888 1226*
🚃 *Arnos Grove or Bounds Green LU*
🕙 *Tue-Sun 11am-6pm*
🥕 *Vegan options*

Situated on a busy north London road this store is worth braving the traffic to visit for its selection of delicious Indian veggie sweets. Local Indians have been popping in since 1986 for this great selection of sweets such as barfi, halwa and coconut ice that are milk-based and cooked with cholesterol-free vegetable oil on the premises. Other special veggie treats include Bombay Mix, Rice Chewdo, Tikha Gathia and selection of large biscuits. For non-sweet snack attacks there's samosa and kachori-dal.

Willesden

Olive Tree
Organic food, supplements and natural cosmetics

⊡ *152 Willesden Lane, NW6*
☎ *020 7328 9078*
🚃 *Kilburn LU*
🕙 *Mon-Tues, Thurs-Sat 10am-6pm, Wed 1pm-7pm*

Growing from strength to strength, formerly a small shop at 84 Willesden Lane, the Olive Tree has now moved to larger premises at 152. They now offer a much wider selection of whole and organic foods and other health products. It's still noted for their fresh fruit and veg together with their bread that is delivered three times a week. The organic wine selection has now expanded with several vegan wines as well as organic beer. The Olive Tree also offers vegetarian takeaway snacks, salads and sandwiches. The atmosphere here is friendly and the staff helpful making this a wonderful example of a local wholefood store.

North

New Southgate / Willesden

Kingsbury

Gayatri Sweet Mart
Indian sweets, takeaway snacks

⌨ *467 Kingsbury Road, NW9*

☎   *020 8206 1677*

✐ *www.gayatri.co.uk*

🚌 *Kingsbury LU 2min walk*

🕐 *Mon-Fri 10.30am-6.30pm, Sat 10am-6.30pm, Sun 9am-4pm*

This modern fronted store has been established for over 25years. Gayatri's top seller is the Mawa Penda – balls made from milk saffron and sugar – and very good it tastes too. The sweets are all made on the premises by the friendly and helpful staff who are more than willing to explain the different exotic sweets on display. If you don't have a sweet tooth, they also offer savoury Indian snacks such as Bombay Mix.

Hendon

Chandni Sweet Mart
Indian Fast Food Takeaway, Drink, Sweets

⌨ *141 The Broadway, West Hendon, NW9*

☎ *020 8202 9625*

✐ *www.chandnisweetmart.co.uk*

🚌 *Hendon BR, 7 min walk*

🕐 *Tues-Sat 9am-6pm, Sun 9am-4pm*

🥕 *Vegan options*

i *Takeaway Service 10am-7pm except Tuesdays.*

Bright fronted shop selling Gujarati snacks such as samosas, spring rolls and bharjias but with an emphasis on Indian sweets. With branches in Edware and Kenton and their own factory in Willesden, they are heavily geared up for catering for big parties and weddings.

Gupta Confectioners (London) Ltd

⌨ *262 Watford Way, NW4*

☎ *020 8203 4044*

🕐 *Tue-Sun 10am-6pm*

See Euston Branch (page 253).

Rajen's Thali Restaurant
Indian fast food, drink, sweets

⌨ *195-197 The Broadway,*
West Hendon, NW9

☎ *020 8203 8522*

🚌 *Hendon BR, 1 min walk*

☉ *Wed-Mon 10am-7pm, (closed Tues)*

🥕 *Vegan options*

i *Takeaway Service*
Free car park at back in evenings

Modern, Indian fast food takeaway. They offer good samosas, bhel puris, juices. Recommended is the Dabeli – a fabulous roll ooozing with spicy potato with Bombay mix in a tamarind chutney, onions and coriander, which is delicious for just £2.50. They have a small table area for those that want to eat-in and also offer catering for weddings and parties.

Finchley & Golders Green

Temple Health Food
Vitamins & minerals, beauty product & takeout eats

⌨ *17 Temple Fortune Parade, NW11*

☎ *020 8458 6087*

🚌 *Golders Green LU, 10min walk*

☉ *Mon-Fri 9am-6pm, Sat 9am-5.30pm, Sun 10am-2pm*

The product range here divides evenly between mineral and vitamin supplement and upmarket organic beauty products. They also stock the very affordable Green People organic beauty and grooming range. Temple Health Food does good lunchtime takeout trade in pre-packed vegetarian sandwiches, samosas, organic ice cream, and organic drinks. Of note is their range of organic dried fruits and they have a very good chilled and frozen vegetarian food selection.

West London

Knightbridge, Kensington, Chelsea & Pimlico

Bamford
Organic clothes, skincare.

- 169 Draycott Avenue, SW3
- ☎ 020 7589 8729
- bamford.co.uk
- South Kensington
- ⏰ Mon-Sat 12noon-6pm

This bright and well appointed store has three floors offering well cut ethical women's clothes with a purely organic section. Of note on a recent visit were the organic shirts made with undyed natural fabric.

Bamford and Sons
Organic clothes, skincare

- The Old Bank, 31, Sloane Square, SW1
- ☎ 020 7881 8010
- bamfordandsons.com
- Sloane Square LU,
- ⏰ Mon-Sat 9am-6pm, Sun 12noon-5pm

Classic men's country clothes with a modern twist. They offer excellent quality 100% organic cotton shirts, T-shirts and denim jeans, jackets and sweaters. They clothing is expensive but the quality and workmanship is very high.

Chelsea Health Store
General organic and wholefood provisions

- 400 Kings Road, SW10
- ☎ 020 7352 4663
- www.chelseahealthstore.com
- Sloane Square LU
- ⏰ Mon-Fri 9am-7pm, Sat 9am-6pm, Sun 11am-6pm

This popular neighbourhood health store has now moved to larger premises with a wider range of stock. The successful format remains much the same with a clean, modern store offering a bewildering array of food supplements, vitamins and packaged foods such as musli. Helpful staff are on hand should you need any help or advice.

Daylesford Organic – Pimlico
Fine food, beauty products

- 🏠 *44b Pimlico Road, SW1*
- ☎ *020 7881 8060*
- ✍ *www.daylesfordorganic.com*
- 🚌 *Sloane Square LU, 4 min walk*
- 🕐 *Mon-Sat 8am-7pm, Sun 10am-4pm*

Fine food and organic store that also sells meat. In the basement you can find Organic wines, vodka, organic beers and ciders.

The ground floor has an excellent selection of breads including a very popular rye bread and spelt breads. They also offer a good selection of vegetarian cheeses, preserves, juices, fresh deli salads and a great choice of fruit and veg from their own organic farm. The range and quality of the produce is difficult to beat with 13 different types of heritage tomatoes and potatoes to choose from. Daylesfords is a stylish and well organised organic store that seems to have a formula for success.

For Organic Daylesford Pimlico restaurant review see page 76.

New store at: 208-212 Westbourne Grove, W11, Tel: 020 7313 8050.

HERE Organic Warehouse
Organic Supermarket

- 🏠 *125 Sydney Street, Chelsea Farmer's Market, SW3*
- ☎ *020 7351 4321*
- 🚌 *Sloane Square LU*
- 🕐 *Mon-Sat 9.30-8pm, Sun 10am-6.30pm*

This modern well–designed organic store has been highly commended by the Soil Association Award. It offers a very good selection of fruit and veg, extensive skincare products selection and a great choice of dietary supplements. Surprisingly, there is a paucity of veggie eateries in this area but HERE fills the gap with a range of organic sandwiches. They also offer a range of biodynamic foods.

The Organic Pharmacy
Natural and organic medicines and beauty products

- 🏠 *169 Kensington High Street, W8*
- ☎ *020 7376 9200*
- ✍ *www.theorganicpharmacy.com*
- 🚌 *Kensington LU (5min walk)*
- 🕐 *Mon-Sat 9.30-6pm, Sun 12noon-6pm*
- ✉ *Mail order*

See next page for the review.

The Organic Pharmacy
Natural and organic medicines and beauty products

- 396 King's Road, SW10
- 020 7351 2232
- www.theorganicpharmacy.com
- Sloane Square LU (then bus 11)
- Mon-Sat 9.30-6pm, Sun 12noon-6pm
- Mail order

This place is modern and bright like a pharmacy but specialises in herbal and homeopathic remedies. They freshly make skin care and beauty products using certified organic cold pressed oils and essential oils and botanicals. The shelves are well stacked with quality organic beauty products and their own brand has expanded considerably and now includes sun protection, baby care and hair products. Downstairs is a clinic and beauty rooms.

Planet Organic
Organic Food, Drinks, Household items

- 25 Effie Road, SW6
- 020 7731 7222
- www.planetorganic.com
- Fulham Broadway LU
- Mon-Fri 8.30am-8.30pm, Sat 9am-7pm, Sun,11am-5pm
- i   Counter Service and takeaway
- Vegan options
- Child friendly
- Mail order

Opened in June 2004, this is the third store in this independent supermarket chain. It's smaller than the flagship store, but does a good job of punching above its weight with a great selection of fresh and packaged organic produce.
For more details see Planet Organic, Westbourne Grove (page 267).

Space NK
Environmentaly friendly skin, haircare and baby products

- 307 King's Road, SW3
- 020 7351 7209
- www.spacenk.co.uk
- Sloane Square LU
- Mon, Wed-Sat 10am-6pm, Tues 12noon-6pm, Sun 12noon-5pm
- Mail order: 020 8740 2085

West

Knightsbridge, Kensington, Chelsea & Pimlico

Apothecary store with outlets throughout London. Among the highly desirable products here are the Erbaviva range. The Ren brand, whilst not labelled organic, uses only 100% natural fragrances. Space NK also stocks Jurlique, a high quality product range that is environmentally friendly but not yet organic certified. There are over twenty stores in London – refer to their website to find your nearest branch.

Whole Foods Market Kensington
Organic food, drink, beauty products, clothes

⌨ *The Barkers Building, 63-97 Kensington High Street, W8*

☎ *020 7368 4500*

🖱 *www.wholefoodsmarket.com*

🚌 *Kensington LU, 3 min walk*

🕐 *Mon-Sat 8am-10pm (Store), Sun (Upstairs at Market) 10am-6pm*
   Sun (Market Hall) 12noon-6pm

Whole Foods Market Kensington is the biggest natural and organic food store in the world, so big there's a free map to help you get around. Start your trek on the ground floor with it's wide selection of organic breads, cakes and treats made by the Village Bakery Melmerby. Further inside there's an array of takeaway salad and hot food stations with plenty of choices for vegetarians. Not to be missed at the back, the Cheese Ageing Room has clearly marked vegetarian cheeses including Berkswell, Ticklemore, and Hawes Wensleydale.

The lower ground Market Hall has a plethora of organic soups and pastas and an impressive bulk food section of organic nuts as well as organic spices and all the Green & Black chocolate you could ever want. Also on this floor there's an extensive selection of frozen organic and vegetarian packaged foods. Not everything is organic at Whole Foods Market Kensington but where items are not organic the policy is to offer the highest quality alternative. Bargain seekers may find their own brand products less expensive, however, it's worth checking the labels as in some cases the level of organic may be only 70% to keep the prices down. There's also a very wide selection of health and beauty products including the John Masters Organic Shampoo range, Jason and Green People. The eco–clothing section offers Howies organic clothes and an attractive range of jeans. On the top floor is a very impressive sit down dining space, see page 174 for a detailed food review.

Whole Foods Market Kensington is more than the sum of its departments and eateries, offering a really stylish environment in which to shop and eat for the best organic and vegetarian food.

Notting Hill

Bamford and Sons
Organic clothes, skincare

▫ *The Old Workshop, 79 Ledbury Road, W11*

☎ *020 7881 8010*

✑ *www.bamfordandsons.com*

🚌 *Notting Hill Gate LU,*

🕐 *Mon-Sat 9am-6pm, Sun 12noon-5pm*

See Bamford & Sons Sloane Square for review (page 262).

Urban Bliss
Food, vitamins, herbal medicines, books, footware and health clinic

▫ *333 Portobello Road, W10*

☎ *020 8969 3331*

✑ *www.urban-bliss.com*

🚌 *Ladbroke Grove LU*

🕐 *Mon-Fri 9am-9pm, Sat 9am-6pm*

✉ *Mail order*

Bright stylish modern store with white walls and concealed lighting – a stark contrast to the idyllic homely appearance of most health shops. Bliss is largely a health clinic offering acupuncture, reflexology and massage and sells an extensive range of vitamins, aromatherapy oils and herbal remedies. Their dispensary makes up formulations using organic herbs.

Books for Cooks
Vegetarian and organic books and courses

▫ *4 Blenheim Crescent, W11*

☎ *020 7221 1992*

✑ *www.booksforcooks.com*

🚌 *Ladbroke Grove LU, Notting Hill Gate LU*

🕐 *Tues-Sat 9.30-6pm*

Salivate at this treasure trove of 300–400 vegetarian cook books with about another 8,000 cookbooks if you are hungry for more. Upstairs you can extend your cooking expertise further with one of their veggie cookery courses. The staff are friendly and knowledgeable and will help you find even the most obscure publication. They also have a wonderful café/restaurant at the back of the store (see page 179).

Green Baby
Baby clothes and products

⌨ *5 Elgin Crescent, W11*

☏ *020 7792 8140*

✎ *www.greenbaby.co.uk*

🚌 *Notting Hill Gate LU, 5 mins walk*

🕐 *Mon-Fri 10am-5pm, Sat 10am-6pm, Sun 11am-4pm*

✉ *Mail order: 0870 240 6894*

See review for the main Islington branch (page 251).

Natural Mat
Organic bedding for babies and kids

⌨ *99 Talbot Road, W11*

☏ *020 7985 0474*

✎ *www.naturalmat.co.uk*

🚌 *Notting Hill Gate LU*

🕐 *Mon-Fri 9am-6pm, Sat 10am-4pm*

✉ *Mail order*

Their organic certified bedding guarantees that no pesticides, insecticides, and heavy metals are used in their products and that no child labour is employed as they uphold a fair trade policy. They stock a great range for babies, children and adults. The natural fibres used allow mattresses to breathe and so prevent overheating and help keep them clean.

Planet Organic
Food, drinks, household items

⌨ *42 Westbourne Grove , W2*

☏ *020 7727 2227*

✎ *www.planetorganic.com*

🚌 *Bayswater or Queensway LU*

🕐 *Mon-Sat 9.30am-8pm, Sun 12noon-6pm*

✉ *Mail order*

This is one of the best known and smartest organic stores in London which continues to offer quality organic produce in a stylish contemporary environment. The range of organic fruit and veg and breads is very impressive, but the store is large enough to contain all you need for your weekly shop including organic home wares and an extensive choice of baby products from the likes of Green Baby, Baby Basic. A definite must for those visiting Portobello Market and a great place to relax and enjoy a shot of wheatgrass. See index on page 311 for other branches.

West

Notting Hill

Portobello Wholefoods
Vegetarian and organic foods

⊞ 266 Portobello Road, W10

☎ 020 8968 9133

🚇 Ladbroke Grove LU

🕐 Mon-Sat 9.30am-6pm, Sun 11am-5pm

A small, classic wholefood store with a pedigree going back to 1982. It is popular with Notting Hill locals for its healthy food selection and varied choice of breads. They have recently expanded the back of the store to accommodate two big fridges, substantially increasing their selection of chilled foods. Those looking for supplements and natural remedies will not be disappointed here and if you prefer your vitamins as nature provided them they have a great selection of organic fruit and veg. This store has succeeded by providing a great service and well chosen stock and continues to go from strength to strength.

The Tea and Coffee Plant
Specialist coffee retailer and wholesaler

⊞ 180 Portobello Road, W11

☎ 020 7221 8137

🖉 www.coffee.uk.com

🕐 Mon-Sat 7.45am-6.30pm, Sun 9am-4.30pm

🚇 Ladbroke Grove LU

✉ Mail order

A popular funky coffee bar offers some 30 blends of coffee including 12 that are Soil Association certified organic. With a sweeping bar this is a popular place to get a caffine fix whilst exploring Portobello Market. The company claims to have the largest range of organic and/or fair traded coffee in the UK and does a great deal of business selling packets of coffee to take home and has a well organised mail order service. Best sellers are the Organic Fair trade Italian Roast and Organic House Blend. The coffee is roasted twice a week at their premises in Spitalfields and delivered daily to their Notting Hill shop. Many London restaurants get their coffee here, which is a good indication of the quality.

Hammersmith & Shepherd's Bush

Buchanans Organic Deli
Wholefoods, organic produce, café

⌨ *22 Aldensley Road, W6*

☎ *020 8741 2138*

🕐 *Mon-Fri 7am-5pm, Sat 7am-4pm, Sun 8am-2pm*

A medium size traditional deli that manages to cram a good deal into its limited floor space with a well stocked organic deli as well as a café offering all kinds delicious organic snacks, vegetarian hot foods and coffee. The deli has a good selection of organic produce from fresh fruit and veg, to cheeses and frozen goods. Since it's opening in 1999, Buchanans has become a firm favourite with locals. It's a friendly place with a notice board awash with adverts for local events and services. A great shop.

Bushwacker Wholefoods
Wholefoods, natural remedies

⌨ *132 King Street, W6*

☎ *020 8748 2061*

🚌 *Hammersmith LU, 5 min walk*

🕐 *Mon-Sat 9am-6pm*

Set along a busy high street, the shop's noticeboard campaigns against GM products and highlights food and health issues. The store stocks vegetarian, vegan and organic produce including fresh fruit and veg, soya drinks, health remedies and books. It is located conveniently opposite Sagar Vegetarian Restaurant (see page 186).

Chiswick

Apotheke 20-20
Natural Health and Wellness Centre

⌨ *296-300 Chiswick High Road, W4*

☎ *020 8995 2293*

✎ *www.apotheke20-20.co.uk*

🚌 *Turnham Green LU, 5 minwalk*

🕐 *Mon-Tue 10am-6pm, Wed-Fri 10am-8pm*
Sat 9.30-6pm and Sun 11am-5pm

Just next to the Jurlique Day Spa, this flagship retail shop stocks the whole Jurlique range and offers natural health consultations. Of note is the new men's range that is 98% organic and biodynamic. 95% of the herbs are grown on Jurliques own farms in South Australia. The Jurlique Herbal Shaving Gel is good and the Face and Body Moisturising Lotion comes up light and suitable for oily skins and a real treat. All Jurliques product are suitable for vegetarians.

As Nature Intended
Remedies, organic produce, household provisions

🖎 *www.asnatureintended.uk.com*

▣ *201 Chiswick High Road, W4*

☎ *020 8742 8838*

🚇 *Turnham Green LU*

🕓 *Mon-Fri 9am-8pm, Sat 9am-7pm, Sun 10.30am-6.30pm*

This huge health store is similar to Planet Organic, stocking just about every conceivable type of wholefood and enough range for customers to to get their entire weeks' shop under one roof. Of note are the organic cereals, breads and pastries and a good choice of fresh fruit and veg as well. The store also has a large natural remedy section and lots of organic baby foods. A great store and well worth checking out.

Other stores at:
17-21, High Street, Ealing, W5
186-188 Balham High Road, Balham, SW12.

The Jurlique Day Spa and Sanctuary
Spa treatments using natural & organic products

▣ *Holly House, 300-302 Chiswick High Road, W4*

☎ *020 8995 2293*

🕓 *Mon-Fri 10am-8pm, Sat 9.30am-6pm, Sun 11am-5pm*

🚇 *Turnham Green LU, 5 minwalk*

An oasis to relax with organic de-stress and beauty treatments. It is popular with local, looks-conscious women with money to spend. The Jurlique treatment is not restricted to women, in recent years men have been admitted into its smart interior to be pampered with a range of treatments including organic facial treatments, revitalisers and even flotation therapy.

Ealing

FarmW5
Fine English and Mediterranean organic foods

⊞ 19 The Green, W5
☎ 020 8566 1965
✎ www.farmw5.com
🚇 Ealing Broadway LU, 5 min walk
🕐 Mon-Sat 8am-7pm, Sun 10-6pm

Followers of a healthy Mediterranean diet are spoilt for choices at this well stocked store which is notable for its fresh, organic fruit and veg. The deli counter has a choice of all-organic salads and the other fine foods on display include organic chutneys and jams from Devon and Somerset and vegan pesto, mayonnaise and chocolate cake. With a quality range of organic coffees, juices and wines and a few delicious vegetarian cheeses, FarmW5 really is a great place to source quality prepared foods and ingredients. Many of the shop's ingredients are used in the café's recipes, so having some refreshment is a great way to try before you buy.
For a detailed review of the café see page 191.

Maida Vale

The Organic Grocer
Organic provisions and delivery service

⊞ 17 Clifton Road, W9
☎ 020 7286 1400
🚇 Warwick Avenue LU (3min)
🕐 Mon-Sat 8.30am-8.30pm,
    Sun 10am-7pm

This small shop makes up for its lack of space with ingenious displays and a contemporary but simple style of décor. The store sells the full selection of organic products including fresh fruit and veg, bread, freezer foods, beers and wines, organic baby products. Despite the size of the place they even manage to fit in a reasonable deli counter. The shop also offers a local delivery service.

West

Ealing/ Maida Vale

South London

Brixton

Brixton Whole Foods
Food, drink, eats, herbs

⊞ *59 Atlantic Rd, Brixton, SW9*

☎ *020 77372210*

🚌 *Brixton LU*

🕐 *Mon 9.30am-7pm, Tue-Sat 9.30am-5.30pm, Fri 9.30am-5.30pm*

General organic fruit, veg and grocery provisions and some items for babies and children. It offers 'serve yourself' culinary organic herbs and spices with over 300 from which to choose. More decadent delights await in the freezer in the form of Green and Blacks organic ice cream whilst beauty in a bottle is available with a selection of cruelty-free cosmetics. Of particular interest to raw food enthusiasts are the raw chocolates. A great little store and now something of a Brixton institution.

Clapham & Wandsworth

Breads Etcetera
Organic bakery

⊞ *127 Clapham High Street, SW4*

🚌 *Clapham Common LU*

🕐 *Tue-Sat 10am-6pm, Sun 10am-4pm, Mon 2pm-7pm (bread sales only)*

The bread shop at the front of the café sells high quality organic Danish Rye, Light Rye, Six Seed, Fruit, Walnut and Ciabatta. With several awards under their belt, the actual bakery is in Stockwell. They also supply other retailers such as Planet Organic, As Nature Intended and the Apostrophe coffee shop chain. Takeaway sandwiches are available.

Breads Etcetera
Organic bakery

⊞ *64 Northcote Road, SW11*

🚌 *Clapham Junction Rail*

🕐 *Daily 8am-6pm*

The same high quality organic breads as the Clapham High Street branch. Takeaway vegetarian sandwiches and organic coffee are also available.

Dandelion
Vegetarian Take-away and Food Supplements

- 120 Northcote Rd, SW11
- 020 7350 0902
- Clapham Junction BR
- Mon-Sat 9am-6pm

With Northcote Road becoming a smart shopping area swamped with wholefood stores, Dandelion has downsized it's stock in response to fierce competition. Now it concentrates on high quality vegetarian and vegan takeaways, coupled with a comprehensive selection of supplements and natural remedies. It has a few tables outside for eating.

Esca
Mediterranean foods and drink

- 160 Clapham High Street, SW4
- 020 7622 2288
- www.escauk.com
- Clapham Common LU
- Mon-Fri 9am-8pm, Sat 9am-8pm

There's a great atmosphere in this bustling delicatessen and café. Shelves to the ceiling carry a great selection of high quality organic breads, pastas and pre-packed deli items such as honey, jam, chutney, dried fruit, coffee and beer. Esca also offer a good choice of freshly made salads and a magnificent array of vegetarian cakes. For a full review of the café see page 198.

Whole Foods Market
Organic Food, Drink & Eats

- 305–311 Lavender Hill, SW11
- 020 7585 1488
- www.wholefoodsmarket.com
- Clapham Junction BR
- Mon-Fri 8am-8.30pm, Sat 8.30am-7.30pm, Sun 11am-6pm

Bigger than the Camden branch, the amount of produce boldly labelled 'Organic' is striking and has proved popular with affluent customers from Wandsworth and Battersea. The store is well laid out and easy to navigate. Besides, the good grocery section, there's a good tofu selection, some Green Baby organic clothes and a large beauty, and health section. Whilst the wine section here is relatively small the on-site café is large with plenty of seating for a break after your shop. For the food review for this branch see page 174.

Vauxhall

Farm-a-round Ltd
Organic food home delivery service

⌨ *New Covent Garden Market, Elms Lane, SW8*

☏ *020 7627 8066*

✍ *www.farmaround.co.uk*

This wholesale business provides Londoners with home delivered organic fruit and veg as well as other staples like eggs, fruit juice, olive oil and pasta. Most customers order a weekly delivery which can be arranged over the phone or via their website.

Luscious Organic Deli
International, Organic,

⌨ *40-42 Kensington High St, SW8*

☏ *020 7371 6987*

✍ *www.lusciousorganic.co.uk*

🚌 *High Street Kensington LU*

🕐 *Mon-Fri 8.30am-8.30pm, Sat-Sun 9.30am-9pm,*

This Soil Association approved minimarket stocks a full range of organic products and foods. The store is well organised and laid out with some fine organic produce such as Italissima Jams. The wide selection of artisan breads, including some loaves catering for those with special nutritional needs, are worth checking out. At the serving counter there are also a selection of sweet treats such as flax muffins, small sugar-free muffins, vegetarian date & walnut and apricot and almond cake.

Luscious has an extensive range of Infinity organic grains, beans, nuts and seeds, as well as purveying fresh organic fruit and veg, pastas, supplements and organic beauty products. The selection of thirty organic wines is well chosen and for those with a sweet tooth there are some fine organic chocolates. Also of note is the excellent Truuuly Scrumptious baby food range and Dr Hauschka skin products – staff are trained by Dr Hauschka to give you the best advice. This is a great independent organic store that is doing its best to fend off competition from larger corporate rivals on the street.

For a review of the café see page 170.

Tooting

Ambala Foods
Specialist pickles and chutneys, Indian sweets

⌨ *48 Upper Tooting Road, SW17*

☎ *020 8767 1747*

✎ *www.ambalafoods.com*

🕐 *Daily 10am-8pm*

See Ambala Foods, Drummond Street for review (page 252).

Plumstead

Ambala Foods
Specialist pickles and chutneys, Indian sweets

⌨ *62a High Street, SE18*

☎ *020 8317 0202*

✎ *www.ambalafoods.com*

🕐 *Daily 11am-11pm*

See Ambala Foods, Drummond Street for review (page 252).

Blackheath

Provender Blackheath
Wholefood, drink, eats,

⌨ *50, Tranquil Vale, SE3.*

☎ *020 8318 1694*

✎ *www.provender.org.uk*

🚋 *Blackheath BR, 5min walk*

🕐 *Mon-Sat 8am-6.30pm, Sun 10.30am-4pm*

This wholefood store established a good reputation in Dulwich, and hopes to continue its success from its new location in Blackheath.

Provender sells a wide range of home-baked breads and pastries and organic fruit vegetable, which are used in the café's recipes (see page 207). They stock organic dairy products, fresh olives, herbal teas, spices, wholefoods, ecological body care and washing products. They also provide an organic fruit and veg box service.

Well Bean Health Foods
Organic foods, household items and supplements

⌗   *9 Old Dover Road, SE3*

☎   *020 8858 6854*

🚌   *Blackheath BR*

🕐   *Mon-Sat 9am-5.30pm, Sun 1pm-4pm*

Vegan speciality neighbourhood shop which is split between food and food supplements. Among the goods on offer are gluten-free breads, rice cakes, Green &Black organic chocolate, hazelnut and peanut butter, vegan ice-cream and quality soya vegetarian sausages.

Greenwich

Green Baby
Baby clothes & products

⌗   *52 Greenwich Church St, SE10*

☎   *020 8858 6690*

✍   *www.greenbaby.co.uk*

🚌   *Maritime Greenwich DLR LU*

🕐   *Mon-Sat 9.30am-5.30pm*

✉   *Mail order: 0870 240 6894*

The latest branch of the Green Baby, it's located right by the Cutty Sark. *For shop review see Green Baby, Islington branch (page 251).*

SO Organic
Organic beauty care, baby products & household goods

⌗   *Eagle House, 7 Turpin Lane, SE10*

☎   *0800 169 2579*

✍   *www. soorganic.com*

🚌   *Greenwich Mainline or Cutty Sark DLR (2min walk)*

🕐   *Mon-Tues 11am-6pm, Wed-Sun 10am-6pm*

This well known organic e-tailer has confidently moved into retailing in Greenwich offering a massive range of organic products. Besides stocking their own So Organic range of skin and hair care products, baby products and organic paint there are other big name organic brands too. At front of house is a dedicated beauty counter while at the back is their homes department with organic textiles and home gifts, green cleaning products and a range of natural paints.

Dulwich

Health Matters
Natural cosmetics, vitamins, supplements & remedies

🖵 *47 Lordship Lane, SE22*
☎ *020 8299 6040*
🚌 *East Dulwich Rail*
🕐 *Mon-Fri 9am-6.30pm, Sat 9am-6pm, Sun 10.30am-4.30pm*

Complementary health centre offering various alternative treatments, reference library and oodles of free leaflets. Whilst selling supplements and natural remeides amongst its natural cosmetic range is Dr Hauschka, Jason and Organic Pharmacy products.

Tooting

Abel and Cole Ltd
Organic foods & household goods delivery service

🖵 *16 Waterside Way, SW17*
☎ *0845 262 6364*
🖰 *www.abelandcole.co.uk*
✉ *Delivery only*

Excellent organic food delivery service that was awarded Observer Best Organic Delivery Service in 2008. The company offers free delivery to your door providing you exceed the minimum organic food order of £8. Based in Herne Hill, they cover the whole of London except the City's square mile – where delivery is very difficult. About 80% of their customers opt for the weekly organic mixed vegetable box scheme, consisting of a selection of fresh organic produce based on what is seasonally available and costing £14.80. Other boxes are available to suit individual needs and all the boxes are suitable for vegetarians. They have a notable exclusions service that enables customers to customise their own box. One Abel & Cole idea that is proving very popular is the Brain Food organic fruit delivery service aimed at helping people to stay healthy at work. Weekly boxes start at £19.50 (with free delivery), which enough for ten people. Also available are soya burgers and sausages and their own range of tomato sauces, jams and pickles. Recipes and food storage advice is available on their website.

Abel and Cole delivers organic wines which are suitable for vegetarians and Ecover cleaning products and various books. They are also involved in a not-for-profit scheme with schools advocating healthy eating.

Herne Hill

Four Way Pharmacy
Organic & natural products children & mothers

⌷   *12 Half Moon Lane, Herne Hill, SE24*

✎   *www.fourwaypharmacy.co.uk*

☎   *020 7924 9344*

🚌   *Herne Hill BR*

🕐   *Mon-Fri 9am-7pm, Sat 9am-6pm*

Small NHS pharmacy which is strong on organic baby foods, herbal teas and eco-friendly baby products. It has a large stock of bio-degradable, disposable nappies which attracts eco-aware shoppers from outside London.

Crystal Palace

The Spirited Place
Organic, vegan foods, drinks & health products

⌷   *105 Church Road, SE19*

☎   *020 8768 0609*

🚌   *Crystal Palace BR, 5 min walk,*
      Gypsy Hill BR, 10min walk

🕐   *Tue-Fri 11am-10pm, Sat-Sun 2pm-10pm*

This shop offers a good range of health food products and fresh homemade food and drink. In their café they specialise in Caribbean cuisine.
For food review see page 209

Wimbledon

Bamford and Sons
Organic clothes, skincare

⌷   *The Village Store,*
      32 The High Street, SW19

☎   *020 8944 7806*

🚌   *Wimbledon LU, (5 min walk)*

🕐   *Mon-Sat 10am-6pm, Sun 12noon-5pm*

See Bamford & Sons Sloane Square for review (page 262).

East London

Brick Lane & Bethnal Green

Ambala Foods
Specialist pickles and chutneys, Indian sweets

🖼 *55 Brick Lane*

☎ *020 7247 8569*

🚇 *Aldgate East, E1*

🕐 *Daily 9am-9pm*

See Ambala, Drummond St for review, page 252)

Friends Organic
Organic and vegetarian food and drink

🖼 *83 Roman Road, E2*

☎ *020 8980 1843*

🚇 *Bethnal Green LU, 5 min walk*

🕐 *Mon-Fri 10am-6.30pm, Sat 10am-6pm*

Friends Organic is a modern well designed shop offering an excellent range of organic fruit and veg, packaged wholefoods and natural remedies and food supplements. Globe Town might not seem the ideal location for such a venture, but business seems to be going well and their take-away sandwiches have proved very popular with the locals. One of the reasons for the stores success is the helpful and friendly service you get here with lots of free advice and staff willing to take time out to chat. Friends Organic is associated with London Buddhist Centre just up the road.

Spitalfields Organics
Organic, wholefoods, health and beauty

🖼 *92 Commercial Street, E1*

☎ *020 7377 8909*

🚇 *Liverpool St BR/LU*

🕐 *Daily 11am-7.30pm*

A committed organic store with groceries, health, beauty and nutrition products all under one roof. As well as organic it is also totally vegetarian with all the leading veggie brands on display. It offers a reasonable selection of dried foods, provisions, organic breads and freezer goods. It lacks some of the fresh produce to be found in other similar health stores, but much of this can be found in the market. It is Popular with city workers looking for a healthy lunch .

East

Brick Lane & Bethnal Green

Clapton

Organic and Natural
Organic food, produce and beauty products

🖃 *191 Lower Clapton Road, E5*

☎ *020 8986 1783*

✎ *www.villageorganics.info*

🚃 *Hackney Downs BR, 10 min walk*

🕓 *Mon-Sat, 9am-9pm, Sun 10am-6pm*

Popular local organic store with brown façade opposite Clapton Common with a notable selection of breads, fruits and nuts as well as household eco-cleaning products. Also has a garden at the back where you can enjoy organic coffee and vegetarian cakes, organic salads and snacks

Forest Gate

Ambala Foods
Specialist pickles and chutneys, Indian sweets

🖃 *284 Green Street, E7*

☎ *020 8472 6004*

🕓 *Daily 9am-9pm*

See Ambala, Drummond St for review (page 252).

Ambala Foods
Specialist pickles and chutneys, Indian sweets

🖃 *253 Green Street, E7*

☎ *020 8470 4946*

🕓 *Daily 9am-9pm*

See Ambala, Drummond St for review (page 252).

City Sweet Centre
Indian, classic

🖃 *510-512 Romford Road, E7*

☎ *020 8472 5459*

🚃 *Woodgrange Park LU*

🕓 *Wed-Mon 10am -8pm (closed Tues)*

Join the queue at this busy shop that offers classic Indian sweets. The sweets may seem strange but they are freshly made and delicious. The staff will help if you need help choosing.

East

Forest Gate

Eastern Foods
Indian vegetarian sweet shop

⌨ *165 Green Street, E7*
☎ *020 8472 0030*
🚌 *Upton Park LU, 5min walk*
🕐 *Daily 10am-7pm*

Indian sweets suitable for those allergic to cows milk. The sweets contain Buffalo milk that has 58% more calcium, 40% more protein and 43% less cholesterol than cows milk. The Burfi fudge here is quite good and is colourant-free. The shop also sells Indian savouries such as samosa, pakora, aloo tiki and julab jamun.

Mishtidesh
Indian vegetarian savoury and sweet shop

⌨ *278 Green Street, E7*
☎ *020 8472 9505*
🚌 *Upton Park LUe, 5min walk*
🕐 *Daily 10am-7pm*
i *Takeaway*

A wide selection of Punjabi, Gujarati and Bengali foods including Rosmalai yogurt and rasgulla (flour balls in syrup).

Broadway Market

Altun Broadway Organics
Organic fruit & veg and provisions

⌧ 25 Broadway Market, E8

🕐 Daily 8am-8pm

Opened in December 2007, this well stocked shop sells a good selection of groceries and including fresh fruit and veg. The store is well located in a street which has undergone considerable regeneration in recent years. It is at its busiest on Saturdays when the market is in full flow.

Dalston

Wholsum
Organic, wholefoods and natural care

⌧ 16 Dalston Lane, E8

☎ 020 7249 9601

🕐 Mon-Fri 8am-5pm

🌱 Vegan options

☀ Outside seating

Located on the corner Dalston and Beechwood Lanes, in January 2008 the place was completely gutted out and refurbished and will be fantastic for Crossrail travellers coming out of the new Dalston station. Well stocked shelves of a wide range of organic foods that include some not readily available rices, beans and coffees. In the cooler cabinet are organic ginger beers, fruit juices, smoothies, Rachel's Ice Cream. At the back is Ecover refills for washing up liquid, and household cleaning products and a good selection of organic beauty and skin care products. Relaxed, knowledgeable service from expert veggie Caribbean chef Fitzroy Thomas.

Leyton

Ambala Foods (Leyton)
Specialist pickles and chutneys, Indian sweets

⌧ 680 High Road, E10

☎ 020 8558 0385

🖉 www.ambalafoods.com

🕐 Daily 9am-9pm

See Ambala, Drummond St for review on page 252.

Wanstead

The Larder
Organic foods, provisions, pastries

⌨ *32 High Street, E11*

☎ *020 8989 7181*

🚌 *Wanstead LU, 2min walk*

🕐 *Mon-Fri 9am-7pm, Sat 9am-5pm, Sun 10am-4pm*

Feast your eyes on the central table of pastries and the well stocked shelves. Organic vegetable bolognaise sauce, tomato ketchup, mint sauce, sweet chestnut puree and assorted organic pastas are available as are organic eggs, organic sprouting seed and hummus.

The Larder has a good selection of organic bottled beers, including Whistable Organic Ale and Caledonian Golden Promise, but surprisingly only a small choice of organic wines although they recently had a very reasonable certified organic Domaine De La Vallongue.

Surprisingly, The Larder does not do fruit and veg or organic bread, but maybe that's due to the shortage of space. Instead there's a massive Truuly Scrumptious Baby Food chiller counter at the back and lots of the space is taken up by the café (see page 237).

Manor Park

Jalaram Sweetmart
Vegetarian sweet shop

⌨ *649 Romford Road, E12*

☎ *020 8553 0894*

🚌 *Woodgrange Park BR , 5min walk*

🕐 *Daily 9.30am-7pm*

i *Takeaway*

A small, modern Gujarati Indian sweet and fast food snack takeout. They specialise in curries and savouries such as Pata Gatia – a kind of crisp of gram flour with black pepper. The display of sweets is very impressive and the staff are usually pretty good at explaining any unusual varieties.

Upton Park

Annapurna Sweetmart
Vegetarian sweet shop

- 199 Plashet Road, E13
- ☎ 020 8471 6249
- 🚌 Woodgrange Park BR
- 🕐 Tues-Sun 9.30am-7pm
- *i* Takeaway

Fresh kachoris, samosas and spring roll. The coconut pista looks delicious as does the pinapple hawa and green coloured banana burfi. A great Indian snack selection and friendly service.

Walthamstow

Ambala Foods
Specialist pickles and chutneys, Indian sweets

- 480 Hoe Street, E17
- ☎ 020 8539 6695
- 🕐 Daily 10am-8.30pm
- 🚌 Walthamstow LU

See Ambala, Drummond St for review (page 252).

Second Nature Wholefoods
Organic wholefoods and provisions

- 78 Wood St, E17
- ☎ 020 8520 7995
- 🕐 Mon-Sat 9am-5pm
- 🚌 St James St BR, 8min walk
- 🥕 Vegan options

Set along a very long shopping street and some distance from Walthamstow Market, everything on sale at this well-established neighbourhood wholefood shop is vegetarian. Organic fruit and veg can be bought throughout the week and their policy is to only buy from organic suppliers that don't handle conventionally grown produce.

Second Nature is hot on avoiding GM ingredients, foods with additives and products tested on animals. It sells a wide range of food and drink including organic chocolates, skincare products, sunblocks and biodynamic wine. They deliver all over East London with no minimum order and to the rest of London with an additional carriage charge.

Alcoholic Drink for Vegetarians

There are lots of pitfalls for vegetarians wanting to enjoy alcoholic drink without consuming animal products. Below are details about vegetarian alcoholic drink. The choice for those seeking organic drink is far wider and easy to identify – just look out for the Soil Association symbol.

Wine

It is during the fining process that animal products are added to wine. Among the ingredients that may be used are isinglass, gelatin, egg albumen, modified casein, chitin or on rare occasions ox blood. The use of such animal derived products is not necessary with plenty of vegetarian alternatives. Most organic wines avoid using animal products, but some do. Thorsons Organic Wine Guide is a good reference to check the veggie credentials of most wines. For a list of organic wine merchants visit www.infolondon.ukf.net/organic/

Beer

Cask-conditioned ales use isinglass to clear the remnants of fermentation. Bottled, naturally conditioned beers will not always use isinglass. Lagers and Keg Beers are pasteurised and usually passed through Chill Filters. This also applies to canned beers and some bottled beers.

Cider

The main brands of cider have been fined using gelatine. Scrumpy ciders are usually not fined using animal products, but always check to be sure.

Spirits

Vegetarians have less worries when choosing a spirit, most of which are made without using animal products. There are exceptions such as some Malt Whiskies and blended whiskies and Spanish Brandies which may have animal contaminants from the cask. Another pitfall are certain Vodkas which may have been passed through a bone charcoal filter

Fortified Wines

With the exception of crusted port, all ports use gelatin in the fining process. There are brands of sherry which do not use animal products, but the majority use animal products for fining.

Colourants

The main animal based colourant is E120 which is derived from insects and is used in a limited number of red wines, some soft drinks and Campari.

For goods approved by the Vegetarian Society visit their website www.vegsoc.org

FARMERS' MARKETS

London Farmers' Markets

☎ 020 7704 9659

✍ www.lfm.org.uk

Farmers' markets are very a much apart of life in London with the idea proving a great success and providing a vital lifeline for struggling English Farmers. The markets are for farmers selling their own produce direct to the public. No produce is bought in and all food sold at the markets is from within 100 miles of the M25.

For vegetarians and those interested in quality organic produce, these markets are a great place to find quality naturally grown seasonal produce. It also affords visitors the opportunity to talk with the farmers that grow the food and share some of the passion they clearly have for their work. One farmer at Pimlico Farmers' Market proudly showed off his diabetic jam which he developed to cater for a regular customer. You don't find that kind of enthusiasm at your local supermarket!

Below is a list of all the current markets run by the organisation know as London Farmers' Markets, as well contact details for the organisation.

Acton W3

Public Square on Acton High
Street/King Street
Open: Sat 9am-1pm

Blackheath SE3

Blackheath Rail Station Car Park,
2 Blackheath Village
Open: Sun 10am-2pm

Clapham SW4

Bonneville Primary School,
Bonneville Gardens
Open: Sun 10am-2pm

Ealing W13

Leeland Road, West Ealing
Open: Sat 9am-1pm

Islington N1

William Tyndale School,
Upper Street
Open: Sun 10am-2pm

Marylebone W1

Cramer Street Car Park,
Corner Moxon Street
(off Marylebone High Street)
Open: Sun 10am-2pm

Notting Hill W8

Car Park behind Waterstones
(access via Kensington Place)
Open: Sat 9am-1pm

Pimlico Road SW1

Orange Square, Corner of
Pimlico Road & Ebury Street
Open: Sat 9am-1pm

Queen's Park NW6

Salusbury Primary School,
Salusbury Road
Open: Sun 10am-2pm

South Kensington SW7

Bute Street
(just off Brompton Road)
Open: Sat 9am-1pm

Swiss Cottage NW3

Eton Avenue
(opposite Hampstead Theatre)
Open: Wed 10am-4pm

Twickenham TW1

Holly Road Car Park
(off King Street)
Open: Sat 9am-1pm

Walthamstow E17

Town Square by
Selbourne Walk Shopping Centre
(off King Street)
Open: Sun 10am-2pm

Wimbledon SW19

Wimbledon Park High School,
Havana Road
Open: Sat 9am-1pm

Growing Communities

www.growingcommunities.org
Stoke Newington Farmers' Market,
N16
William Patten School,
Stoke Newington Church Street
Open: Sat 10am-2.30pm
One of London's only independent farmers' market which is run
by a local food initiative called
Growing Communities.
The market is small, but the
quality of the food very high and
a great deal of effort is made to
ensure that the food sold at the
market is both 100% organic and
produced within 150 miles of
the market. With fresh bread,
organic fruit and veg and lots of
homemade delicious cakes, this is
a great place to do your shopping
and enjoy the atmosphere of a
genuine community market.

Peckham Farmers' Market, SE15

Peckham Square, Peckham High St
Open: Sun 9am-1pm
Tel: 07951 464 732
This farmers' market was initially
managed by London Farmers'
Markets, but is now run independently. The quality of the food is
still very high with all the bread,
eggs, meat, fruit and veg you
would expect from a good farmers' market.

Caterers

Central

Carnevale
Mediterranean, modern

⌧ *Whitecross Street, EC1*

☎ *020 7250 3452*

✍ *www.carnevalerestaurant.co.uk*

The staff of this well established vegetarian kitchen provide high quality vegetarian catering for all kinds of events from business meetings to family weddings. A very friendly company.

The Clerkenwell Kitchen
English, modern

⌧ *The Clerkenwell Workshops 27-31 Clerkenwell Close, EC1*

☎ *020 7101 9959*

✍ *www.theclerkenwellkitchen.co.uk*

Adept at private events, corporates and weddings. Emma, who runs Clerkenwell Kitchen, is a former chef at Mildreds and has lots of great ideas on veggie catering to make your party a success.

Futures!
International, classic

⌧ *8 Botolph Alley, Eastcheap, EC3*

☎ *020 7623 4529*

This company runs an excellent little café in the City, but also offers a first rate vegetarian catering service.

Noura Restaurants
Lebanese, classic

⌧ *Noura Belgravia, 16 Hobart Place, SW1*

☎ *020 7235 9444*

✍ *www.noura.co.uk*

This highly proficient restaurant group provides excellent vegetarian Lebanese food for all kinds of events and can also organise live entertainment.

Passion Organic
Organic food and drink, International

⌧ *177 Ferndale Road, SW9*

☎ *020 7501 9933*

✍ *www.passionorganic.com*

Passion Organic is a dedicated organic catering company offering everything from highly attractive canapés and finger buffets to inspiring full sit down formal dinners for twenty-five to five hundred people. Passion Organic has proved popular with the corporate market. They are well versed in catering for vegetarians with choices including Spanish Tortilla and parsley frittatas. The food is prepared to a very high standard using seasonal produce. A wide range of organic wines and cocktails are also available. Passion Organic covers all of London and is at the upper end of the price scale.

The Place Below
International, classic

⌂ St. Mary-le-Bow Church,
Cheapside, London, EC2.

☎ 020 7329 0789

✎ www.theplacebelow.co.uk

Vegetarian catering service
available. The crypt is popular
for weddings, confirmations and
private parties.

SAF
Organic vegan, modern

⌂ 152-154 Curtain Road
Shoreditch, EC2

☎ 020 7613 0007

✎ www.safrestaurant.co.uk

This renowned raw food
restaurant has a separate catering
company geared up for superb
vegan weddings. Corporate
parties and events are also catered
for. They have a fanatastic organic
wine and cocktail list.

North

Anupam Caterers
Vegetarian Indian, classic

⌂ 129 Bowes Road, N13

☎ 020 8889 9112

✎ www.anupamcaterer.com

This family business does 100%
vegetarian catering from 50 to
2,000 people with hundreds of
dishes from which to choose.
The repertoire extends to veggie
burgers and sausages too! Of
note is their Vegetarian Meals

on Wheels service from £5
per person. It does a free home
delivery service in a 5 mile radius
and has group discounts.

Greens & Beans
International, classic

⌂ 1131 Drummond Street, NW1

☎ 020 7380 0857

Attractive looking catering from
this popular vegetarian café.

Jaaneman Sweet Centre
Vegetarian Indian, Classic

⌂ 170 Bowes Road, N11

☎ 020 8888 1226

Pure vegetarian catering for
parties and function from this
sweet and snack specialist that also
has it's own restaurant (see page
153) and shop (see page 259).

Manna
Mediterranean, interna-
tional, modern and organic
choices

⌂ 4 Erskine Road, NW3

☎ 020 7609 3560

✎ www.mannav.com

This expert inventive vegetarian
and organic food specialist offer
a catering service that will dazzle
your guests.

West London

Raw Fairies

⌨ *Grand Union Centre*
   Unit 21 West Row, W10
☎ *07879 246 501 (8am-5pm)*
✍ *www.rawfairies.com*

Raw Fairies is run by Anja Ladra who also cooks at The Bonnington Café in Vauxhall (see page 201) for food review. Based in the Ladbroke Grove area, Raw Fairies is the UK's first raw food delivery service covering all of Central London. The dishes are made from scratch using organic vegetables, fruits, seeds and nuts – breakfasts and special birthday cakes are also available. Raw Fairies' clientele vary from raw food faddist individuals and those with special dietary needs to forward health thinking companies.

FarmW5
Mediterranean, classic

⌨ *19, The Green, W5*
☎ *020 8566 1965*
✍ *www.farmw5.com*

Cypriot and Lebanese organic veggie platters are the speciality here. Contact Bilal who will be glad to help make your party a great success.

South London

The Spirited Palace
Caribbean, organic vegan

⌨ *105 Church Road, SE19*
☎ *020 8768 0609*

Raw salads, small vegan pizzas and savoury pasties are just a few of the many choices. The caterers also have a restaurant in Crystal Palace.

East London

City Sweet Centre
Indian, classic

⌨ *510-512 Romford Road, E7*
☎ *020 8472 5459*
✍ *www. citysweetcentre.com*

As well as being speciality confectioners, The City Sweet Centre also cater for weddings, parties and all other functions. See restaurant and shop reviews (page 236 and 280).

Eastern Foods
Indian, classic

⌨ *165 Green Street, E7*
☎ *020 8472 0030*

Specialises in foods that use buffalo milk instead of cows milk.

Jalaram Sweetmart
Indian, classic

⌨ *649 Romford Road, E12*
☎ *020 8553 0894*

Tends to do small functions such as birthday parties and religious occasions in people's homes.

Contact Groups

Vegetarian Contact Groups

Curvenetics

☐ 020 8550 0916

✎ www.curvenetics.com

Vegetarian nutrition and dietary advice with gentle non-impact exercise technique giving excellent shape up results in just ten hours. Established 28 years ago, class courses are held at the Curvenetics Centre, 2 minutes from Oxford Circus tube. Nutritional advice is given by yours truly, Veggie and Organic London's author, Russell Rose, whilst the exercises are taught by ballet-trained Tracy Rose. Personal nutritional and exercise sessions can be tailored to individual requirements.

Gay Vegetarians and Vegans

☐ BM Box 5700, WC1N 3XX

☎ 020 8470 1873

Established in 1979, this is now a small group of mainly lesbians in their 60's-70's that meet and eat informally every Sunday lunch in East London. The group produces a magazine twice yearly named 'Green Queen' for which they are delighted to accept contributions in the form of letters, articles, news on vegetariansm, animal rights as well as fiction and poetry.

International Jewish Vegetarian Society

☐ Bet Teva
853/855 Finchley Road, NW11

☎ 020 8455 0692

🕐 Office hours 10-4, Mon-Thurs

www.jewishvegetarian@onetel.com

They advocate vegetarian ideals based on Genesis and Torah teachings. Meetings and functions are held at their Golders Green HQ. Set up in 1966, there are nearly 3,000 members throughout the country. The group is very social but also campaigns on serious matters. The Society gives lucid advice in the form of a quarterly magazine, 'The Jewish Vegetarian', which has detailed articles on vegetarian issues, recipes, nutritional health information, animal welfare, gardening tips and is a useful source of vegetarian and vegan contacts.

Lesbian Vegans

Contact Julie Pope,

✎ japope_1982@hotmail.co.uk

Affiliated to the Vegan Society, it's also open to vegetarian and bisexual women. They meet monthly for a chow down at a restaurant or enjoy picnics when the weather is fine.

London Vegans

⌨ *7 Deansbrook Road, Edgware Middlesex HA8 9BE*

☎ *020 8446 3480*

✐ *www.londonvegans.org.uk*

Meetings are on the last Wednesday of every month (apart from December) at Millman Street Community Rooms, Millman Street, WC1 – near Russell Square. They also arrange walks in and around the London area, restaurant visits and outings. For more information log onto their website which also features a useful accommodation listing.

Muslim Vegetarian Society

Contact Rafeeque Ahmed

⌨ *59 Brey Towers 136 Adelaide Road, NW3 3JU*

☎ *020 7483 1742*

Meets occasionally at vegetarian and vegan restaurants in Camden. It is a campaigning organisation which publishes a booklet – 'Islam and Vegetarianism'.

VEG-London

✐ *www.veglondon.org*

Affiliated to the Vegetarian Society, this group has been running since 2004. It organises social events for vegetarians in the London area. Restaurant visits have included the Inspiral Lounge in Camden and VitaOrganic in Soho and takes place on the second Sunday of the month

Vegetarian Society

⌨ *Parkdale, Dunham Road Altrincham WA14 4QG*

☎ *0161 925 2000*

✐ *www.vegsoc.org*

A wonderful registered charity dedicated to extolling the virtues of vegetarianism and disseminating veggie dietary information. The Vegetarian Society defines a vegetarian as a person that eats no meat, poultry, game, fish, shellfish or crustacea. Vegetarians also avoid the by-products of slaughter such as gelatine or rennet in cheese.

According to their surveys Londoners are highly switched on about the benefits of vegetarianism and have the highest awareness of the impact of meat consumption on global warming in the UK. A recent study indicated that thirty-five percent of people in London would consider having meat-free days in each week to reduce their carbon footprint, while a further twenty-two percent would be willing to try adopting a vegetarian or vegan diet.

The Vegetarian Society has a tremendously informative website with plenty of dietary advice and is the key driving force behind National Vegetarian Week which takes place every May.

Vegan Society

▢ *Donald Watson House*
   21, Hylton Street, Hockley
   Birmingham B18 6HJ
☎ *0845 458 8244*
✐ *www.vegansociety.com*

This campaigning organisation for vegans produces a magazine, books and pamphlets on veganism, animal rights and animal-free lifestyles.

Young Indian Vegetarians

   Contact: Nitin Mehta
▢ *226 London Road*
   West Croydon, Surrey CR0 2TF
☎ *020 8681 8884*
✐ *www.youngindianvegetarians. co.uk*

A campaigning group, founded in 1978 to promote animal rights and 'Ahisma' (respect for all living creatures). There's no formal membership and you don't have to be Indian. Events include an annual Hyde Park Vegetarian picnic and an annual newsletter. They visit some great Indian restaurants including Kastoori in Tooting and Rani in Finchley. The Young Indian Vegetarians also give talks at schools and colleges. The group also is involved in the Mahavir Medal Award for people who have done great work to end animal cruelty, promote animal rights and further vegetarianism.

Organic Contacts

Biodynamic Agricultural Association (BDAA)

▢ *Painswick Inn Project*
   Gloucester Street, Stroud,
   Gloucester, GL5 1QG
☎ *01453 759 501*
✐ *www.biodynamic.org.uk*

An organisation that aims to promote biodynamic farming and arranges conferences, meetings, produces literature and even helps enthusiasts find a job on biodynamic farms.

Biodynamic food, drinks and products are pesticide and chemical-free. Produce is grown according to the principles of Rudolf Steiner – at specific cycles of the moon and times of the day. Adherents to the Steiner approach envisage the farm as a self-contained organism, a carer of health, synergising soil, crops, stock and farmer in a cycle of virtuosity. Conceived in the 1920's, biodynamic farming is the forerunner of organic farming today.

Certified biodynamic and organic produce can be found at Fern Verrow Vegetables in Borough Market (see page 69) while biodynamic beauty brands include Dr Hauschka, Weleda, Just Pure and Talya.

Friends of the Earth

26-28 Underwood Street, N1

☎ 020 7 490 1555

🖉 www.foe.co.uk

The prominent environmental pressure group that is represented in 69 countries.

Green Events

48 Clifton Gardens
Herne Bay Kent CT6 8DE

☎ 01227 749 991

🖉 www.greenevents.co.uk

An alternative magazine with details of forthcoming events and festivals of an environmental nature. It is given away free at a number of vegetarian cafés and restaurants. The website also includes features.

Greenpeace

Canonbury Villas, N1

☎ 020 7865 8100

🖉 www.greenpeace.org.uk

A campaigning organisation that among other things actively opposes the release of GM food into environment. The website is useful and informative.

Local Food Works

🖉 www.localfoodworks.org

A useful site providing information for schools, hospitals and other groups who wish to source organic food and from local farmers. The organisation involves the Soil Association and the Countryside Agency.

Organic research

🖉 www.organic-research.com

Providing organic research and news with a database of 160,000 abstracted research article accessed by subscription only. There are free resources that include events, jobs, courses, farm lists and legal information.

Soil Association

Certification Ltd, Bristol House
40-56 Victoria Street
Bristol BS1 6BY

☎ 0117 914 2411

🖉 www.soilassociation.org

The largest UK organic certification body. Their excellent website gives clear information as organic food, recipes, news, issues and events. It is also one of the key bodies involved in organic certification.

Sustain

94 White Lion Street, N1

☎ 020 7837 1228

🖉 www.sustainweb.org

Based in Islington, Sustain is an alliance of organisations for better food and farming. It is an advocate for agriculture and food policies and practices that improve the health and welfare of people, animals and the living environment.

Their laudable 'Grab 5!' campaign aimed at actively promoting the eating of five portions of fruit or veg per day has now ended, but Sustain continues to encourage people to use the materials and approaches it has developed. Check out their website that has information packs on growing schemes and ideas to encourage children to eat more fruit and veg in schools and its importance to their health.

Also there's London Food Link, a project to help producers, consumers and retailers make positive choices about sustainable and local foods.

Courses

Vegetarian Cookery Courses

Books for Cooks

⌨ *4 Blenheim Crescent,, W11*
☎ *020 7221 1992*
✎ *www.booksforcooks.com*

This great shop runs several vegetarian cookery courses during the year at their tuition kitchen situated above the shop. The cookery courses combined with the excellent bookshop and café, make this one of the best culinary experiences in the capital – a must for veggie foodies.

Organic Gardening and Farming Courses

Garden Organic

⌨ *Ryton Organic Gardens Coventry CV8 3LG*
☎ *0247 630 3517*
✎ *www.gardenorganic.org.uk*

Garden Organic is the working name of HDRA, the Henry Doubleday Research Association that researches, demonstrates and campaigns for environmentally safer gardening. It runs one day courses to encourage environmentally friendly gardening and small scale edible gardens. Garden Organic has gardens in Kent and Essex which can be visited – see their website.

London South Bank University

⌨ *Department of Applied Science, FESBE*
    103 Borough Road, SE1 0AA
☎ *020 7815 7815*
✎ *www.lsbu.ac.uk*

LSBU offers a BSc (Hons) degree course in Organic Food Studies. The course is a mixture of Food Technology and Organic Food Production. In the final year students carry out the design and practical development of an organic food product. The innovative course has generated interest amongst retailers and manufacturers.

Organic Gardening Projects

Brockwell Community Greenhouses
Organic gardening

▱ Brockwell Park, SE24

☎ 020 7622 4913

🕑 Sunday 1pm-5.30pm

🕑 Members and inducted volunteers
Wed & Thurs 1pm-5.30pm

🚃 Herne Hill BR

An organic run garden with an orchard, vegetable garden, medicinal herbs and a pond. It's open to the public and a good place to while away a couple of hours. Produce such as runner beans, kale, spinach and garlic are availble to buy. School parties visit on educational trips. The place is run by enthusiastic volunteers, who are a mix of unemployed, retired and those seeking a break from the stresses of Brixton life.

Centre For Wildlife Gardening
Organic gardening

▱ Marsden Road, Peckham SE15

☎ 020 7252 9186

🖉 www.wildlondon.org.uk

This centre does gardening demonstrations among its herb garden, vegetable plots and nursery of wild flowers. Volunteers learn organic techniques and the trust also does good work for people with special needs and school groups. Those working in the gardens get to to take home their produce so there is a real sense of achievement.

Those just wanting to relax and do nothing can come along and spend a pleasant couple of hours in the gardens and visitor centre.

Culpeper Community Garden
Organic garden with allotments and community projects activities

▱ 1 Cloudsley Road, N1

☎ 020 7833 3951

🚃 Angel LU

🖉 www.culpeper.org.uk

Culpeper applies completely organic gardening principles to the development and upkeep of this community garden. It has monthly workdays for volunteers and provides 50 plots for people without gardens. Those getting the allotment live within a half mile of the garden and in return help out in community activities. Culpeper supports many community projects such as playgroups and a mental health gardening group.

Culpeper is tucked away behind Sainsbury car park and by the children's playground. It has a good atmosphere with plots of organic flowers, herbs and vegetables. Visitors can bring their own sarnies and drinks and eat at their tea hut. A swell place to visit for organic gardening enthusiasts. Their new community resource building is also available for hire.

East London Organic Gardeners

43 Arbour House, E1

☏ 020 7265 8257

✑ www.elog.org.uk

Affiliated to Garden Organic, East London Organic Gardeners (ELOG) is a voluntary group with monthly meetings most of the year. During the Summer they attend fairs and shows in East London. Their aims are to promote and advise on organic gardening and to promote the recycling of waste via composting. ELOG's secretary, Francis Schwartz, is a mine of useful information about the local organic allotment scene.

Meeting topics have included an 'apple day in the Autumn', organic food, and a 'year in the life of a seed merchant'. It's a good opportunity to meet organic gardeners and to network. All their activities are free and very useful to anyone new to the organic gardening scene and they also publish a quarterly newsletter.

Forest Farm Community Gardens

Organic food growing with allotments and garden projects

Hazelbrouck Gardens Hainault, Essex

☏ 07963 762 667

🚎 Hainault LU

Forest Farm is a collection of projects and individual allotments, committed to growing local, organic food as well as keeping alive traditional skills and crafts. Their increasing number of allotment holders practice a wide range of gardening styles but all producing excellent organic food. Amongst the community projects, Forest Farm Peace Garden works with refugees and asylum seekers, people recovering from mental illness, the probation service as well as the wider public. The Oasis Project works with young people with learning disabilities, teaching accredited horticulture courses and helping people into the job market. The Redbridge Conservation Team have created and maintained a wildflower meadow and orchard and other conservation projects. With an abundance of wildlife and many rare birds nesting and even a flock of white doves, Forest Farm is a place of unique character.

Growing Communities
Organic fruit and vegetable box scheme, organic market

🖥 *The Old Fire Station*
   61 Leswin Road, N16 7NY
☎ *020 7502 7588*
🖰 *www.growingcommunities.org*

Social enterprise promoting organic sustainable agriculture. They run a local organic box scheme for about 180 households in Hackney and also run an organic market of about 15 organic food stalls on a Saturday 10am-2.30pm.

Founded in 1994, all the produce is certified organic and some is locally grown with three farms near Stoke Newington certified by the Soil Association. Whilst also a commercial proposition, it enables people to meet and co-operate together - linked by the food they enjoy and an interest in sustainable food.

Produce is packed in bags and collected by customers from one of five locations. Various fruit and vegetable bags are ordered and picked up weekly. All the food comes from no further than 70 mile from the centre of London.

Collection points:
please check times on their website.

The Fire Station, *Leswin Road N16*
Chats Palace
42/44 Brooksbys Walk, E9
Pogo Café
Clarence Road, E5
Hackney City Farm
Hackney Road, E2
The Pavilion Café
by the lake in Victoria Park, E3

Organiclea
Organic Allotments

⊡ *c/o Hornbeam Environment
Centre, 458 Hoe Street, E17*

☏ *07786 657 713 for details*

⊘ *www.organiclea.org.uk*

A workers' co-operative on a formerly abandoned allotment in Chingford. It attracts volunteers from Hackney, Haringay, Redbridge and Walthamstow with a core group in their 20's-30's who want to get their hands dirty. Whilst not Soil Association approved, organic methods are used and 'chemical-free' fruit, veg and herbs are grown here.

It has some conventional beds, a polytunnel and forest garden that recreates a forest ecosystem producing edible and useful plants. There are pear and fig trees and some unusual plant varieties as well as herbs rhubarb, jerusalem artichokes and garlic.

Organiclea's open days for volunteers and visitors are on the 2nd and 4th Sundays of the month. Those who want to get stuck in with a bit of spade work will gets some great hands-on training. Participation is free and any food harvested is divided up with surplus food given to the community. An organic box scheme (collection-only) is also available at the Hornbeam Centre on Wednesdays 3.30pm-7.30pm. A weekly organic market is held on Saturdays from 10am-3pm.

Spa Hill Allotment Society Limited
Community run organic allotment and gardening club

⊡ *180 Spa Hill, SE19 3TU*

☏ *020 8653 5636*

⊕ *Sat-Sun 10am-12noon*

⊘ *www.spahill.org.uk*

On the south west side of Crystal Palace Hill there are 300 allotments, many of them organic. The place has been established for years with some plots in the same family for three generations. Novices to organic gardening get practical advice from experienced members and five times a year they run one day basic courses that attract up to 45 people .

The Spa Hill Organic Gardening Group (SHOGG) meets at Spa Hill on the third wednesday of each month at 8pm (except January and August). They run seed exchanges and put on demonstrations at local shows. The society also publishes a magazine, newsletters, organic gardening booklets, recipes and provides educational visits to schools.

Spitalfields City Farm
Organic farm, community projects

⌨ *Weaver Street, E1*
☎ *020 7247 8762*
🕐 *Tue-Sun 10am-4.30pm*
🚇 *Shoreditch LU, Liverpool St LU/BR*
🖱 *www.spitalfieldscityfarm.org*

This popular city farm runs the women only Coriander Club project for 20-25 Bangladeshi women to cultivate plants. At Spitalfields City Farm there are polytunnels where kodu gourds are grown. There is also a young offenders project. Community volunteers are welcome to pitch in and can get to know more about organic gardening and farming. The farm sells a selection of seasonal vegetables and herbs as well stocking home garden composters.

On Sundays, it's a place to chillout for an hour or so and enjoy the flora and fauna and a great opportunity for city kids to have contact with farm animals. Spitalfields City Farm is situated at the end of Pedley Street, E1.

Stepping Stones

⌨ *Stepney Way, E1 3DG*
☎ *020 7790 8204*
🕐 *Tue-Sun 10am-4pm*
🖱 *www.steppingstonesfarm.org.uk*

Stepping Stones is an urban farm with eight allotments. They provide 84 growing boxes to financially hard-up people without gardens. Most recipients are from the local community and they grow Bengali vegetables in an organic way.

Located at the junction of Stepney Way and Stepney High Street, there's a garden centre, shop and cafe serving tea, coffee and biscuits. Whilst not organically certified because of the certification costs, they do employ organic techniques. The garden centre is the source of income and sells runner beans, pumpkins, tomatoes, bedding plants, shrubs and in future organic fruits such as strawberry, grape and apples. The farm began about 30 years ago and now has some livestock including piglets, sheep and even cows – not bad for an organisation run on a voluntary basis.

Willing Workers on Organic Farms

PO Box 2154
Winslow
Buckingham MK18 3WS
www.wwoof.org.uk

WWOOF is a non-profit making organsation that produces a bi-monthly UK newsletter. The publication contains member's letters, calls for volunteers, campaign support updates, job vacancies in green and organic lines of work, funding, contacts, international news and classified ads with an annual subscription of £20.

Formerly called 'Working Workers on Organic Farms', the nearest farm is in Lewes, where there's a lot of hard graft involved in growing your own food and mucking in. The payback for volunteers is that they learn stacks about organic farming and plant growing in the beautiful Sussex countryside, get to eat own grown food and hopefully make a few like-minded friends. All the work is voluntary and you have to bring your own sleeping bag, wellington boots etc.

Hotels and Apartments

Central

City Inn Westminster
Hotel

🏠 *30 John Islip Street, SW1*
☎ *020 7932 4600*
✎ *www.cityinn.com*
🚌 *Pimlico or Westminster LU*
   Vegetarian breakfast, lunch
   and dinner
   Children-friendly
   Four Star Hotel

The place for the discerning vegetarian traveller to stay, the City Inn serves superb vegetarian cruising from breakfast through to lunch and dinner (see page 303) and boasts chic state-of-the-art bedrooms with all the computer connectivity you could wish for including complementary wi-fi access. There 's an abundance of conference rooms and the hotel does seem more geared for the business traveller than those in search of holiday luxury. At £265 (excluding breakfast) it's not cheap, but they do offer some good deals from £99 per night.

The modern snazzy bar on the first floor stays open as long as hotel guest want and was busy at 11pm when I visited. They also run their own art shows – well, it is near Tate Britain.

The Halkin Hotel
Hotel

🏠 *Halkin Street, SW1*
☎ *020 7333 1234*
🚌 *Hyde Park Corner*
   Four star deluxe
   Vegan choices

Fabulous, sophisticated, modern, ultra-chic boutique hotel that caters for the highly affluent with vegetarian requirements. Through the opulent lobby is a fine lounge bar and the excellent Nahm restaurant serving exquisite vegetarian Thai (see page 78 for review). Upstairs each floor is colour themed according to a different element – water, air, fire and sky. Each room is superbly furnished and has lots of technical wizardry for those that want to use it. The Halkin is a fave amongst discerning film stars and celebrities. Whilst a double room begins at £390 a night, service is highly personalised here and together with a meal at Nahm, is an unforgettably luxurious experience.

The Lanesborough
Hotel

- 🏠 *1 Lanesborough Place*
  Hyde Park Corner, SW1
- ☎ *020 7259 5599*
- ✎ *www.lanesborough.com*
- 🚌 *Hyde Park Corner LU*
  Five star
- *i* *Vegetarian food 24/7*

On Hyde Park Corner this is an ideal place to stay for well-heeled vegetarians who want top class accommodation, service and ambience. High quality vegetarian food is available 24 hours a day with individual nutritional requirements willingly catered for.

The hotel is in a grand style where guests are graciously received. 'The Library' is one of the best bars in London and regularly gets a high celeb quotient. Apsley's is a marvellous restaurant for breakfast, lunch, tea and dinner (see restaurant review page 73).

Inside the rooms there's lots of wooden panelling, swathes of luxurious curtaining not only for the windows but also the bed and the bath. All the rooms have an imposing classic writing desk and book selection for those in pensive literary mood or who just want to send a postcard to the folks back home.

North

Liz Heavenstone's Guest House
Self-catering organic accommodation

- 🏠 *Regent's Park Road, NW1*
- ☎ *020 7722 7139*
- ✎ *lizheavenstone@onetel.com*
- 🚌 *Chalk Farm LU*
- *i* *Early booking advisable*

The first organic bed and breakfast in London, it now consists of three pleasant apartments set on two top floors of Regency Terrace close to Primrose Hill. Operating now on a self catering basis, each room has a generous complimentary organic bowl of fruit, nuts and chocolate and bottled water. There's a nice kitchen with light self-catering cooking facilities.

Coffee and herbal drinks are available at all times. Most of the beds have organic mattresses and the bedlinen is natural fibre. A minute away is vegetarian restaurant, Manna and also very nearby, Cafe 79 for eats and Sesame the local wholefood shop.

A room is £75 per night (up to two people sharing, £100 for three). The Luxury one bed self-contained flat is £130 per night and will accommodate up to four people. The big plus with this place is that it becomes a completely self-contained apartment accommodation if all three rooms are taken.

The Hot List

Outstanding Veggie Cafés

Café Seventy Nine 119
Gossip, Broadway Market. 230
Inspiral Lounge, Camden 126
The Gallery Café 227
Wheatley Vegetarian Café,
Whole Meal Café 102

Traditional Veggie Cuisine

Mildreds 57
Noura, Piccadilly 59
Kastoori 205
Woodlands p.190

Modern Veggie Cuisine

222, West Kensington 192
The Gate, Hammersmith 184
Manna, Primrose Hill 128
Morgan M, Islington 114
Nahm, Hyde Park Corner 78
Rootmaster, Brick Lane 216
Roussillon, Sloane Sqaure 80
Saf, Shoreditch 94
Sketch, Mayfai 46r
Vanilla Black, Holborn 89

Low Budget Veggie Cuisine

Amitas, Forest Gate 234
Beatroot, Soho 51
Food for Thought, 24
Inspiral, Camden 126
Tibits, Piccadilly 64
IndianVeg Bhel Poori 111

Medium Budget Veggie Cuisine

The Gate, Hammersmith 184
Kastoori, Tooting 205
Manna, Primrose Hill 128
Mildreds, Soho 57
Peking Place, Archway 139
Rasa, Stoke Newington 148
Rootmaster, Brick Lane 216

Luxury Veggie Cuisine

Lanesborough Hotel 304
Roussillon, Sloane Square 80
Morgan M, Islington 114
Saf, Shoreditch 94
Sketch, Mayfair 46
Vanilla Black, Holborn 89

The Hip List

Domali, Crystal Palace 207
Eat and Two Veg, Marylebone 36
E&O, Notting Hill 180
Le Caprice, 75
Fifteen, Hoxton 92
Living Room, Heddon Street 56
Nahm, Hyde Park Corner 78
Rootmaster, Brick Lane 216
Saf, Shoreditch 94
Sketch, Mayfair 46
Zuma, Knightsbridge 177

Romantic Restaurants

Apsley's at the Lanesborough 73
Getti, Marylebone High Street 39
Nahm, Hyde Park Corner 78
Sarastro, Covent Garden 28
Zuma, Knightsbridge 177

Partying on a low Budget

Domali Café, Crystal Palace 207
Gallipoli, Islington 110
Indian Veg Bhel-Poori House,
Islington 111

Partying on a Big Budget

Apsley's at the Lanesborough 73
City Inn Westminster 303
Saf, Shoreditch 94
Vanilla Black, Holborn 89

Restaurants with a View

Carluccio's (Canary Wharf) 238
Inspiral Lounge, Camden 126
Pavilion Café, Highgate 141
Queen's Wood Café 142
Thai Square (Putney Bridge) 212
Water House, Shoreditch 97

Restaurants for Al Fresco Dining

Carluccio's (Marylebone and
Canary Wharf) 238 , 35
Domali Café, Crystal Palace 207
Hugo's, Kensington 167
The Living Room (Islington) 112
Neal's Yard Salad Bar, Covent
Garden 27
Pavilion Café, Highgate 231
Pepperton, Selhurst 211

Restaurants for Mock Carnivore Vegetarian Food

Eat and Two Veg 36
The Good Earth, Knightsbridge
165
Peking Palace, Archway 139
Saf, Shoreditch 94

Best Buffets

Inspiral, (low budget) 126
Rani (medium budget 134)
Tibits, (low budget), Piccadilly 64
VitaOrganic, (low budget) 65
Wai, 67

Recommended Pubs serving Vegetarian Choices

The Bull's Head (Chiswick) 189
The Living Room (Piccadilly) 56
The Living Room (Islington) 112
The Queen's Head 186

Vegetarian Fast Food

Amitas, Forest Gate 234
Beatroot, Soho 51
Futures! City of London 84
Just Falafs 54
Maoz, Soho 57
Red Veg, Soho 60

Raw/Live Foods

Whole Foods Market, Stoke
Newington 150
Inspiral Lounge 126
Raw Fairies at Bonnington Café,
Vauxhall 290
Saf, Shoreditch 94
VitaOrganic, Soho 65

Organic

Organic Restaurants
Acorn House, Bloomsbury 12
Daylesford, Pimlico 263
Duke Of Cambridge, Islington 109
Eat and Two Veg, Marylebone 36
Hugo's, Kensington 167
Manna, , Primrose Hill 128
Rootmaster, Brick Lane 216
Saf, Shoreditch 94
Water House, Shoreditch 97

Organic Pubs & Bars
Duke Of Cambridge, Islington 109
Inspiral Lounge, Camden 126
Saf, Shoreditch 94
Tibits, Piccadilly 64
The FleaPit, Bethnal Green 226

Outstanding Organic Juice Bars
Inspiral Lounge, Camden 126
Jumpin Juices,Spitalfield Market, Sundays only 224
Luscious Organic Café, Kensington 170
Natural Kitchen, Marylebone 42
Planet Organic,Westbourne Grove 267
VitaOrganic, Soho 65

Outstanding Organic Cafés
Inspiral Lounge, Camden 126
Luscious Organic Café, Kensington 170
Le Pain Quotidien, Marylebone (branches throughout London) 41
Provender Wholefoods and Bakery, Forest Hill 207, 275
Rose Bakery, Mayfair 45
Tiki Organic Coffee Shop, Hampstead 137

Organic Fast Food
Eat and Two Veg, Marylebone 36
Organic Pizza House 192
Story Deli, Brick Lane 219
Tibits, Piccadilly 64

Best Restaurants by Nationality

African/Caribbean
The Spirited Palace 209

American/Californian
Eat and Two Veg 36

Brazilian
Neal's Yard Salad Bar 27

British
Living Room (Heddon Street) 56
Living Room (Islington) 112
Vanilla Black 89

Central America
Cafe Pacifico 21

Chinese
Good Earth (Knightsbridge) 165
Peking Palace 139

Eastern European and Jewish
Milk 'n' Honey 133
Isola Bella 154

French
Roussillon 80
Morgan M 114

Indian
Amitas 234
Zaika 175
Kastoori 205
Mela 26
Woodlands (Chiswick) 190
Woodlands (Marylebone) 49
Sagar 62, 186

Italian
Apsley's 73
Esca 198
Fifteen and Trattoria 92
Carluccio's 35
Getti 38, 39
Pizza on the Park 80
Pizza Express 60

Japanese
Zuma (expensive 177)
Wagamama (inexpensive) 18, 48, 225, 238

Middle Eastern
Isola Bella 154
Özer 44
Noura 43, 59, 79,
Ottolenghi

Spanish/Portugese
El Pirata 38

Thai
Nahm 78
Thai Garden 228
Thai Square (Trafalgar Square) 31

Polish
Daquise 164

General Index

General Index

Subject Index

Gallipoli